The Real Mrs. Brown

Brian Beacom

Brendon O'Carroll was born in Dublin in 1955, the youngest of eleven children. He left school aged twelve and over the years worked in a variety of jobs before turning to stand-up comedy in his forties.

Since then the father-of-three has become a bestselling novelist and is now one of the world's most successful comedians.

Brian Beacom is an award-winning entertainment writer at the *Herald* and *Times* group of newspapers based in Glasgow. He has written four books and two plays.

THE REAL MRS. BROWN

The Brendan O'Carroll Story

Brian Beacom

HODDER

First published in Great Britain in 2013 by
Hodder & Stoughton
An Hachette UK company

First published in paperback in 2014

4

Copyright © Brian Beacom 2013

The right of Brian Beacom to be identified as the Author
of the Work has been asserted by him in accordance with the Copyright,
Designs and Patents Act 1988.

A CIP catalogue record for this title is available from the British Library

Paperback ISBN 978 1 444 75451 3
Ebook ISBN 978 1 444 75452 0

Printed and bound by Clays Ltd, St Ives plc

Hodder & Stoughton policy is to use papers that are natural,
renewable and recyclable products and made from wood grown in
sustainable forests. The logging and manufacturing processes are
expected to conform to the environmental regulations of the
country of origin.

Hodder & Stoughton Ltd
338 Euston Road
London NW1 3BH

www.hodder.co.uk

This book is dedicated to all the mammies out there who make sure their kids are okay. Especially my own, Florence, who although she still can't operate a DVD player manages to perform miracles every single day.

Contents

Preface	1
Prologue	7
Automatic Womb	9
The Growth	21
Jail Time	37
The Frog Chorus	45
The Leprechaun	52
Teenage Kicks	61
Cleaning Up	68
He's a Lucky God	79
The Mammy's Final Bow	85
Between Beirut and Baghdad	97
Pub Bombs	106
Standing Up	110
Outrageous Comedy	114
Radio Days	124
The Mammy Book	138
The Course	148
The Secret Millionaire	158
Going West	166

Deal Or No Deal   171
Hot Milk And Pepper   176
Mammy Mia!   180
Who's Agnes?   189
Rosie   197
Could the Sparrow Fly?   202
Mammy Films   212
The Last Wedding   220
Agnes Belongs to Glasgow   232
The Special One in Bethlehem   239
Moving On   250
Bigger Brown   259
The Dying Cow   270
Agnes Brown's World   280

Acknowledgements   294
Picture Acknowledgements   295

PREFACE

I NEVER wanted a date with Agnes Brown, the Dublin granny with the arthritic knee, baggy cardigan, mouth like a blocked sewer and more than a hint of facial hair.

Neither did I relish the idea of meeting up with the creator of the mighty matriarch, Brendan O'Carroll.

Yes, the Mrs Brown theatre shows were now established in a clutch of theatres in the UK, including my home town of Glasgow. But, despite it being part of the job to interview the stars of touring shows, the arrival of Mrs Brown and co. didn't set my keyboard fingers twitching.

Why? I'd had enough of drag acts. I felt dressing up as a woman was a device best left back in the 1960s. I'd seen the best of the men who'd provided huge laughs as a woman, from Stanley Baxter to Alastair Sim, from Les Dawson to Dick Emery. They'd all done great jobs in dragging up, mimicking female traits, but without being feminine.

Now, here was a little Irishman doing the same thing. What did he have to offer that was new?

There was another factor. The Mrs Brown shows were playing at Glasgow's Pavilion Theatre, about which I'd come to feel slightly snooty. Not in a full-on Hyacinth Bouquet way, but I'd seen too many 'earthy', home-grown comedy plays containing clunking stink-bombers of lines. I'd feared Agnes Brown was a close relative of this level of nonsense.

Yet, how could I ignore this Irish intruder? The Mrs Brown shows weren't simply successful; they were a phenomenon in this corner of the city, playing to sell-out crowds for two-week stints. And the success was down to word of mouth. The show wasn't hugely advertised and the star had done very few interviews.

So I researched Brendan O'Carroll. Friends in Ireland said he was essentially a (very) risqué stand-up comedian who wrote funny plays. He certainly divided opinion. Newspaper critics reckoned he was either a genius, reworking the old comic styles into something cutting edge and contemporary, or he was a crude little bollix (to use local terminology), rehashing ancient gags and reliant upon double entendres and innuendo.

I learned he liked to work mostly with family and friends, and could throw out one-liners faster than a north Dublin barmaid could eject late-night drunks. But 'funny' is subjective, isn't it? What makes one audience in Dublin or Glasgow laugh doesn't work for everyone.

Regardless, I agreed to interview Brendan on the phone, just before the show was due to arrive in Glasgow. And there was real friendliness in his voice. And a half-hour chat ran to a couple of hours. And he told me little stories about his childhood, about growing up in a large Dublin family, and about his life before breaking into showbiz.

I think we had only reached the teenage years by the time the chat came to an end. And that was only because he had to head off to get ready for his show that night.

But as well as sounding likeable and clever, and very warm, what came across was that here was a man with a fascinating story to tell. And I asked him, 'Why haven't you written your autobiography?'

'I guess I have had a bit of a life, Brian. You don't see it yourself, though. It's only when it's pointed out to you that you realise it is something out of the ordinary. You think everyone's been through the sort of adventures I've had. But that apart, I'm too busy with the plays.'

'Hasn't any Irish journalist ever suggested writing your story?'

'No. I guess they always figured I'd write it meself.'

'Here's a thought, Brendan. Would you be interested in me writing it?'

'Well, I would. But look, let's talk about it. Let's meet up next week when I'm in Glasgow.'

Before that, I went to see his show. The result? I've never laughed so hard and so often in one single sitting. I vowed to spread the word that this man was indeed a comedy messiah.

This certainly made the prospect of meeting the writer/ performer so much more interesting. And the following Saturday we did meet up, in a theme bar.

My first reaction? I smiled. Brendan looked as though he'd tied a blindfold round his head, covered his body in glue and run through someone else's wardrobe. Someone with little taste – or a huge sense of humour.

He was wearing a red T-shirt under a yellow jumper, pale blue trousers, green socks and white trainers. He looked like Robin Williams in *Mork and Mindy*. (It was a relief to discover later that he is in fact colour blind.)

Then Brendan O'Carroll revealed himself to be an Olympian-level hugger. Now, Scottish people, traditionally brought up on a diet of repression and porridge, don't hug anything other than babies and heavy winter blankets, and this display of huge affection came as a great surprise.

I later learned the southern Irish are incredibly European in this way, but this little Irishman particularly so. Yet, his accompanying 'Howareye, Brian!' and huge welcoming smile made the hug seem natural even for me.

'It's grand to meet ya. You sound like an interesting fella, so let's talk about a book.'

We didn't start by talking about the book, as it happened. We chatted. About anything and everything. And it was hard not to like the man. He talked a little about life on the road with a touring company, and even when he was complaining, he was hilarious. Even when he spoke about the huge difficulties in taking 20-plus people around the country, his description was funny. He spoke about working with difficult theatre managers, and the way he shaped his criticism was pure Agnes Brown.

And underpinning everything he said was a warmth in his voice. When he explained his troupe was made up of family and friends, you could see his eyes light up. He spoke of his home in Florida and how much he loved Disneyland and you could see the child in him. This was a man who really didn't want to grow up. Brendan's world seemed a very happy one indeed.

But my new pal didn't simply sit and sip cappuccino and talk about himself.

He enquired about me. He wanted to know about my politics, about what I'd studied at university (Politics); he asked about my family. He asked my thoughts on everything from New Labour to Scottish Presbyterianism to Nationalism. He asked what I knew of Irish history, about the Irish connection in my family, and smiled when he discovered my grandfather was a freedom fighter who'd fled to Scotland in the 1930s.

Brendan's curiosity didn't stop there. He asked about my partner, he asked about my job as a showbiz journalist, he asked about my literary heroes, and we spoke at length about playwright Neil Simon and Oscar Wilde and comedy. He asked about favourite TV shows, and we both revealed a love for Bilko and Lucille Ball. He asked about spirituality, about how all our lives connect, and he asked a great deal about my mother; he wanted to know about the woman who'd brought up three kids on her own, and I guess he was making comparisons with his own mother.

He wanted to know about the experiences that had formed and informed me. We talked about schooldays, about awful teachers, about hopes and dreams for the future. But none of it came in the form of a grilling. It was gentle. It was born out of curiosity. You sense he cared. And he listened intently. I realised quickly that Brendan O'Carroll has the ability to make you feel you're the most important person in the world. I honestly don't think I've ever met an individual with such a power.

At the same time, he wasn't about to bare his soul to a new acquaintance. Yet, he seemed really happy we'd met up.

'I feel we'll be friends,' he said over the last cappuccino several hours later. 'But if you're going to write this book, you'll have to come to Dublin. Come to Finglas, where I grew up. Come on the road with me. Meet the family, come to the house in Florida and see how we live. We've got a great crowd with us.'

And he laughed. 'You'll have a great time, and it will all be worth it because one day, Brian, I'll be a huge feckin' star.'

And he was right.

But then he added something at the end of the conversation that made me think either he had some incredible foresight, a sixth sense, or that perhaps this genial Irishman was a couple of Guinnesses short of a party box.

'I get a really good feeling about you,' he said. 'I don't know exactly what it is, but I know us coming together will produce something special.'

I left the bar slightly baffled. But delighted. Not only was I going to write a book on a complex, fascinating character, I'd met someone I felt would be a major new presence in my life.

Prologue

THE CURTAIN had just come down on *Mrs Brown's Last Wedding* at Hull's New Theatre that wet and windy Saturday night on 25 November 2009, when Brendan called together the cast for a meeting.

Those who'd watched the show, a reprise of the very first Mrs Brown stage adventure featuring Agnes and her dysfunctional family, had laughed till they cried and applauded till their hands ached.

But only 150 people had turned out that night, in a theatre that held 1,159. And this wasn't the first box-office disaster of the tour. Every theatre reported a major drop in ticket sales.

Brendan O'Carroll, aka Agnes Brown, knew the writing wasn't only on the wall; it was on the invoices and final demands from sound crews, advertising agencies, car companies, and hotels – and all in red ink.

So he'd come to a decision. As the doors of the theatre were clattering shut and the slowest members of the audience shuffling home, Brendan asked the whole troupe to sit down on the stage. Tearfully he told them that it was all over, the end of Mrs Brown on tour – he simply couldn't afford to keep the show on the road.

Struggling to hold his voice steady, he informed the cast, including his wife, his son, his daughter, his sister, his son-in-law, his daughter-in-law and friends he'd known for 20 years, that tonight was the last hurrah. The cast were stunned, if not entirely surprised. They offered each other consolatory hugs and sniffled against Mrs Brown's beige cardie.

And at the end of the night, each shuffled off into the darkness, facing a future with little hope. The Mrs Brown dream, their lives together, the fun of touring, the very comfortable living they'd made, was over. How would bills be paid? These weren't career actors; most had only ever worked on stage alongside Agnes Brown. The air hung heavy with the dark, unspoken reality. The fat lady was finally singing.

Or was she?

Brendan's lucky leprechaun was waiting in the wings. Ready to find a way to silence her.

Automatic Womb

FROM that day we first met, ten years ago, Brendan and I established a pattern in our relationship. When Brendan arrived in Glasgow we'd meet up in his favourite café and talk right through the afternoon hours.

The chats would seldom pass uninterrupted, however. Aside from the waiters and waitresses coming over to say hello (he knew not only their first names, but little details of their lives), the members of the Mrs Brown circus would pop in: wife Jenny, son Danny or friend Bugsy. They'd all say hi and offer a quick hug. I was drawn into this close world. (I could see Brendan didn't need to seek out the new. Everything and everybody he needed travelled with him.)

We were close, and it was all very relaxed when we got down to the matter of his life story.

'I suppose I'd better start with my grandmother's story,' he says, taking a sip of cappuccino, as if to fuel the tale that was about to unfold.

'Flashback to 17 September 1911, in Dublin City, Ireland. And seventeen-year-old Lizzie was set to marry Michael

McHugh. The pair were madly in love and ready to head to America together to start a new life – but without telling Lizzie's parents.

'Why did they need to elope? Well, Ireland was a desperate place at the time; life was tough and young people were emigrating across the globe. But for them there was more than that. Lizzie's father, you see, was deeply against them marrying. Michael was a Republican associated with Michael Collins' "Brotherhood", which Lizzie's father detested, and Michael, in his mid-thirties, was almost the same age as Lizzie's father himself.

'So, when Lizzie's father heard of the romance, he pummelled Michael with the poker, breaking his forearm and collarbone. Michael and Lizzie knew there and then that they had to escape Ireland. That's why they had saved for a year to buy the tickets for the long sea voyage.

'But Lizzie's mother found out about the plan and convinced her husband he had to accept Michael, or he'd lose his daughter for ever.

'And he did. Michael and Lizzie's father shook hands and everyone hugged and, the next day, Michael McHugh put an advertisement in the Classified Section of the newspaper offering his boat tickets for sale.

'He sold the tickets for the journey to America to a young policeman and his newly married wife. There were four tickets. Two of them would take the couple by train down to Queenstown in Cork, and the other two were for their sea voyage across the Atlantic Ocean to America.

'And the ship they would sail on? The SS *Titanic*. The policeman survived, but not his new wife.

'Meanwhile, Lizzie and Michael became Mr and Mrs McHugh and, ten months later, a child was born, just skipping scandal by a week. A baby girl. She was christened Maureen. And she was my mammy.'

And she was the woman who provided most of the inspiration for Brendan's sitcom heroine, Agnes Brown.

'Agnes Brown is Che Guevara in a dress,' he says, grinning.

Guevara was of course a bearded, cigar-puffing, sweat-stained Argentinian who died in a Bolivian ambush. But he fought unfairness in his world, to protect the unprotected. And so too did Maureen O'Carroll.

'People used to ask me if Agnes Brown was based on my mother, and I'd say no. But in recent times, I've come to realise just how close they are.'

Indeed. Indeed. Both are battlers. Both could find a colourful adjective when roused, although Maureen was smarter, and way more ambitious than the havoc-creating, uneducated fruit-market worker. Maureen O'Carroll could definitely deliver a cutting one-liner, just as Agnes Brown does. Maureen could also take a simple tea towel and turn it into a weapon, as Agnes frequently does. Both Maureen and Agnes would lay down their lives for their kids, but loved to make fun of them.

Brendan's mammy also had that ability to get what she wanted out of people, just as Agnes can, using the cleverest of psychology, becoming a little bit pathetic when required. And if that didn't work, like Agnes, she would tell the world exactly where it was going wrong.

Maureen's healthy disrespect for authority – life is to be challenged; rules are there to be broken – is evident in Agnes. As Agnes does, Maureen lived in crowded houses, and managed to create her own safe little world.

There are more similarities. Maureen wasn't entirely comfortable with modern devices either. She had little time for small-minded people.

And Agnes Brown now, and Maureen O'Carroll then, would be ready and willing to smack the face of injustice with the back of their hands.

Maureen McHugh, as she was before marriage, certainly didn't have to search far to find inequity in early 20th-century Ireland.

Born on 29 March 1913, her father Michael was an academic, a schoolteacher from Galway who was also a freedom fighter; not in the sense of taking to the streets of Dublin with a gun to fight the Black and Tans during the 1916 uprising, but working behind the scenes. And he was arrested and spent time in a British prison.

But Michael McHugh, who only ever spoke Gaelic, believed Irish Catholic equality could only come about through education. And he instilled in his four children – including his eldest, his daughter Maureen, to whom he was especially close – that they could be anything they wanted to be in life. Just so long as they learned.

When Michael McHugh died however, aged 48 (he'd contracted TB from his time in prison), his slim, dark-haired 12-year-old daughter's future looked bleak. At the time, secondary education in Ireland had to be paid for, and Maureen could, at best, expect to become a seamstress or a waitress. But money was filtered down to the family from an organisation called The White Cross, a fund raised by the IRA to educate children of the men who'd given their lives to the cause.

As a result, young Maureen was sent to County Mayo, 250 kilometres away on the other side of the country (traditionally, Irish girls were sent away, to England, or abroad, in the hope of a better life), to a boarding school, to be taught by the nuns who would become her surrogate family.

Maureen was, at first, broken-hearted to be parted from her mammy Lizzie and her siblings, but the young girl was very clever, very religious, and realised the way ahead was to please the nuns. And so why not become one?

Maureen had incredible energy and studied hard, and her reward was to be sent on to University College Galway, a rare achievement for women at the time, as a novice nun.

It's not clear what made Maureen McHugh rethink her life plan and decide to renounce her vows. Perhaps university opened a window on another world? Perhaps the huge personality and determination she would later reveal meant her life was not best suited to subservience and being married to Jesus. Or perhaps she realised she'd one day prefer to be married to an actual, living man.

Whatever, Maureen, like her father, believed Ireland's future was dependent upon educating people out of poverty. And so she became a teacher of languages, and loved her career. But perhaps what she taught best were human values.

Once, she invited an artistically gifted pupil to camouflage a crack in the classroom window by painting a version of *The Last Supper* on it. The result was so impressive that she invited the child's parents to the school to see their daughter's work. However, paying no attention to the painting, they presumed that the youngster had broken the window. In later years, Mrs O'Carroll would remind Brendan to always look at the picture, not the crack.

Meantime, the earthly man she did fall in love with had appeared on the scene, Gerard O'Carroll. The O'Carrolls were said to descend from one of the kings of Ireland, who fought with the 11th-century Irish king, Brian Boru. Gerry, however, wasn't a fighter. He was a soft-spoken, gentle cabinet-maker (the basis for Mr Wiseman, the cabinet-maker in

Brendan's early books), with an easy-going personality. But, like most Dubliners, he hadn't managed to avoid the collateral damage of the freedom-fighting movement.

'Aged nine, he was almost killed by Black and Tan gunmen who came to the house looking for his IRA-serving older brothers,' says Brendan. 'The Black and Tans didn't find them, but they left my grandfather bleeding and my dad's grandfather lying dead beside him.'

Gerry O'Carroll didn't hold onto his anger. He didn't preach politics to his kids, although he would argue party politics with his future wife, Maureen. Gerry supported Fianna Fáil (the party opposed to the treaty with England), while Maureen backed the Irish Labour movement.

Yet, the pair were soulmates. They were opposites in terms of personality (which had to be the case, given Maureen's was so large), but there was a connection that made them inseparable.

The couple planned their life together in an area called Cowstown, which once formed Dublin's city centre before the city swelled. Comprising several streets of tiny little red-brick terraced houses, it was so called because cattle were once herded through the streets on their way to market.

'The walls of the little houses around Cowper Street and Stoneybatter still have the foot-scrapers near the front doors, used for cleaning off the cow dung,' says Brendan, taking me on a tour of the neighbourhood.

'This is the very same street in which I drive a hearse when I play the undertaker in *Angela's Ashes*. Moore Street is not far away from here, where Agnes Brown has a market stall.

'And the women who work there *are* Mrs Brown. As you go along the street, past the flower and fruit stalls, the women get madder and madder, but they're absolute sweethearts. I love them. When I was at school, I would run down to Moore Street after the bell rang, stash my schoolbag and run errands for the old wans.

'You know, they still give me a bunch of flowers and say, "That's for your mammy." Now, my mother has been dead for thirty years, but it still reveals their innate kindness.'

We strolled over to look closely at his two-bedroomed house, which once had an outside toilet.

'It's been done up now. In fact, this area is now gentrified, home to starter families and young professionals who work close by in the city.'

North Dublin was, and is, the poorer part of the city. The river Liffey separates north from south, rich from the poorer. The largest cathedral is on the south side, while the largest dole office is on the north. The Houses of Parliament are on the south, the Sanitary Department on the north. Even the Liffey segregates, dumping the litter and effluent on its northern bank.

The O'Carrolls lived on the north side. And so too did struggle and adversity. It's ironic that fruit-market trader Agnes Browne (as her surname was spelt originally), of Brendan's novels, works in Moore Street from daybreak; this was a place surrounded by food – yet food was often unaffordable.

But as well as facing the endemic poverty that Ireland suffered in the 1940s, newly-weds Maureen and Gerry faced an immediate crisis. On the day she was married in 1936, Maureen O'Carroll was fired from her job. It was illegal for female teachers in Ireland (indeed all female civil servants) to be married.

Did Maureen O'Carroll take this lying down? In a scene from Brendan's first book, *The Mammy*, Agnes, hearing her daughter Cathy has had her hair cut forcibly by nuns, approaches the convent sister 'and somehow finds herself skelping the head nun in the face with a cucumber.'

Maureen O'Carroll took the cucumber approach when dealing with the Irish establishment and fighting for women's rights.

'My mother was a force of nature,' Brendan recalls. 'She said, "I'm not having that!" and joined the union and battled to get that law changed. She shares that feisty, fighting spirit with Agnes Brown.

'But there was more to anger my mother,' he remembers. 'Ireland at this time was in the Middle Ages. For example, it was legal in the Fifties to beat your wife with a stick, provided the stick wasn't longer than your forearm.'

Maureen O'Carroll would fight to have that law changed. She became a local activist and helped set up the Lower Prices Council, which campaigned against high prices and black marketeering in the aftermath of the Second World War. It's an angry, argumentative approach to life that Mrs Brown also manifests.

It wasn't such a huge surprise when the Irish Labour Party asked her to run for parliament, the Dáil Éireann. But it was a surprise when she won in the General Election of 1954 for Dublin North Central. There had been other female Teachta Dála's (TDs, the Irish equivalent of an MP) elected to Parliament, but only as part of the tradition of widows automatically taking their husbands' places.

Maureen O'Carroll won on her own ticket, becoming not only the first female Chief Whip in any political parliament, but also Labour's Shadow Minster for Foreign Affairs.

It was remarkable for a working-class female to achieve that level of success. But what made her achievement even more extraordinary was that she had given birth to nine children.

'The woman had a womb like a machine gun,' says Brendan.

And, in what offers an insight into the character of Maureen O'Carroll, one of her kids, Phil, was adopted.

Why would a lady who'd had Leonard (who died as an infant), Maureen, Martha, Pat, Gerard, Finbar, Fiona, Michael and Eilish even contemplate taking in someone else's child?

'My mother's brother's wife's sister had a baby, Phil, who was brought up by the grandmother,' Brendan recalls. 'And the mother was always going to rear her son, when she got work and married.

'But the grandmother died when Phil was seven. And his mother's boyfriend didn't want to take him on. Phil went into reform school, because there were no care homes in Ireland at the time. And he would have stayed there for the rest of his young life.'

When Phil came to visit the O'Carrolls, he became besotted with Maureen. And she adored him. He was one of the lucky ones, taken to the Dáil for a visit. And when Phil returned to the reform school, he started writing to her. Maureen would then invite Phil to spend the summer holidays and Christmas with her family. One summer he fell off the garden wall and broke his arm. It was a blessing in disguise. That night, Maureen gathered the family around.

'Why don't we keep him?'

'Oh, for Christ's sake, Maureen,' said her husband. 'Sure, we've enough mouths to feed.'

'So we wouldn't even notice another one.'

That night, Martha O'Carroll went up to the boys' room and said to Phil, 'How would you like to live with us forever?'

Phil threw his arms around her, in silence, scarcely believing it could be possible. But officialdom reared its frightening head. The reform school headmaster told Maureen O'Carroll she couldn't go around adopting stray kids. There were rules.

Maureen O'Carroll was indignant. She kicked up such a fuss you could see the dust clouds in Cork. Somehow, the story was leaked to the press (most likely by Maureen), and her willingness to right this particular wrong would certainly have inspired Che Guevara had he heard about it in Cuba. She tackled the Minister for Education and phoned the head of government, Éamon de Valera himself.

'How's the form with the Big Fella?' she said to his secretary, in a tone that Mrs Brown would have been proud of.

And her boldness and reputation saw her put through to de Valera. Strings were pulled. And, shortly afterwards, Phil came to live with the family.

Somehow, the O'Carrolls got by in their little two-bedroomed house.

'The girls were in one room, the boys in the other, and my father slept in the boys' room,' Brendan recalls. 'He built bunk beds up the sides of the wall. It was like living in a feckin' submarine.'

Eilish, the baby of the family, didn't even have a bunk. For the first few years of her life she slept in a top drawer. But the kids were happy in this congested world. There was a safety in numbers, a security. And they didn't know any better. Most of the families in their street were also huge, and everyone struggled. So what if you had to sleep in a drawer, or share a bed with a few sisters? What was important was a sense of being loved.

Yet, it would be wrong to suggest Maureen O'Carroll's priority in life was scooping up underprivileged children, or indeed spending every waking hour looking after her own. There's no doubt she loved kids. She would make soup and homemade bread. But she was no Ma Walton. Maureen had her work to focus on. The kids had her attention until a political crisis took her off on a mission. It was Gerry O'Carroll who'd bathe the kids, wash the clothes, feed hungry faces porridge before he left for work. Maureen O'Carroll was a woman ahead of her time, but when it came to battling causes, her time was her own.

And sometimes she would use it to indulge her duchess-like habit of taking to her bed when things got a little demanding. And it would often be Martha or Patricia who would tend to the needs of her siblings when Gerry O'Carroll was at work.

But when Maureen was at home, she made her presence felt. If the kids incurred her displeasure, they wouldn't have to open the door to leave the room, they could slither out underneath it. Yet, she also had the talent of making people feel they were the most special in the world, a skill her youngest certainly inherited.

When Maureen felt happy, in control and fulfilled, everyone was happy.

Being a TD made Maureen O'Carroll very happy. And there was enough money for the family to buy a house in Ballymun, with three bedrooms (Maureen had a room to herself while Gerry shared a room with the boys), but with a separate kitchen and a large dining room.

However, in February 1955, Maureen O'Carroll had real reason to take to her bed. The 41-year-old mother-of-nine felt sick. She had serious stomach problems. And she worried there was something badly wrong. Or perhaps she was going through the change?

Her doctor examined her. That night she went home and wrote in her diary: 'Went to see Dr Carney today. I'm either pregnant or I have a growth. (Please, God it's a growth.)'

Seven months later, on 15 September, the growth arrived weighing nine pounds three ounces.

She called it Brendan.

THE GROWTH

FORTUNATELY, the growth wasn't malignant, although it did make a bit of a noise at first and demand regular attention. Yet the O'Carrolls took to this blond-haired, blue-eyed little boy immediately. Seven-year-old Fiona was certainly in raptures from the moment she first clapped eyes on him.

And there was a sense in which Brendan was indeed special. After all, the other kids had been born at home but Maureen O'Carroll deemed her final child would be born in a private nursing home.

Three-year-old Eilish, however, no longer the baby of the family, didn't think her baby brother to be *that* special. She wasn't quite so happy at the spotlight being shunted away. (A few years later during her weekly confession, after she'd admitted to 'a few fecks', she'd confess to beating her little brother about the head on a regular basis.)

And it's fair to say Brendan was an attention grabber. Incredibly quick to learn, he almost bypassed the walking stage by running, a little boy who already seemed to have pressed the fast-forward button on life. (And his state of perpetual motion hasn't stopped since.)

Brendan was talking by the age of two and even a great imitator. He'd be in his high chair while the family were having dinner and the little Woody Woodpecker-like high voice (which would later become Agnes Brown's) would yell out, 'You're all fecked now!' And Maureen O'Carroll would yell, 'Who taught him to say that?'

The clever little foul-mouth (start as you mean to go on) could manipulate his sisters. Lying in bed, he'd say to Fiona, 'Draw a map on my back'. And when she stopped, he'd say, 'No, you've only drawn Ireland! It's too small. Draw Russia!'

Patricia was the sister most often left in charge of the baby brother while Mammy was off saving the world. And he was a handful. When doing the housework, she wanted the fast-moving infant out of the way, so she'd lift him up by his little dungarees and hang him up on a hook on the door. He'd just smile and say 'Oh, oh!'

'I loved it up on that hook,' he recalls, grinning.

Brendan had arrived into an already noisy world with nine siblings, and the older O'Carroll kids reaching their hormone-fuelled teens (Maureen, the oldest, was 18).

And it was a constant competition for everything, from space to food to attention. Whoever could shout the loudest was heard. Whoever could eat fastest got seconds. Whoever could sing best was applauded. And the talent competition's sole judge and jury? Maureen O'Carroll.

When Brendan was three and a half months old, however, the overcrowding problem might have been eased by illness. Brendan developed serious pneumonia. Maureen was bereft. She sobbed to the family that there was a real chance the baby might not come home from hospital. The doctors feared the worst and Maureen asked the kids to pray to God he would be saved. (Three-year-old Eilish prayed he wouldn't;

she'd be the baby again and get all the attention that came with the job. Then she realised she'd committed the biggest sin she'd ever make – and wanted to go straight to the confessional.) But Brendan, clearly with a toughness the family were yet to realise, made it back home to Ballymun.

Those safe four walls were soon to disappear, however. In 1957, Maureen lost her seat in the Dáil. She'd been involved in a campaign to prevent canned food company Batchelors from operating a national monopoly, and it's claimed big business interests conspired to have her ousted.

Maureen would never stop lobbying for the working classes of Dublin, particularly women's groups, but the loss of the job and decent salary meant the O'Carrolls could no longer afford to live in the 'big' house. All they could do was to throw themselves on the mercy of the Corporation and accept the keys to a new home at 11 Casemont Grove, in Finglas.

Finglas is a housing estate, ten miles from Brendan's first home and built around a tiny medieval hamlet that dates back to Cromwell's time in Ireland.

It was reinvented in the 1950s to house the Dubliners decanted from crumbling homes in the city centre. The idea, as was the case with many such schemes in the UK, was sound in theory. The small red-brick semis had gardens and were surrounded by green fields; perfect for playing football and producing stars of the future such as Liverpool's Ronnie Whelan.

Brendan invited me over to Ireland, to see the area where he grew up. What caught the eye in driving into Finglas, some 50 yards from Brendan's home in Casemont Grove, was a horse standing alone on a grass verge. What was it doing there?

'Sure, we all had horses as kids,' he tells me, grinning. 'They almost roamed wild and we'd all ride them and leave them to feed in the fields.'

But that was the problem with Finglas. There was little around *but* green fields.

'There was nothing,' says Brendan, his despondent voice reflecting the hard times. 'You could play football in those fields, and that was about it.'

The town planners, in their haste to build a brave new world, had ignored the fact that people needed more, such as shops, schools, swimming pools and community centres. There was at least an old cinema, The Casino, built in the 1940s in the old village, which hosted John Wayne and Audie Murphy movies, and Brendan would see films there until it closed in the early 1970s.

'Mammy and I spent any night out we had at the pictures. If we really liked a film we would go see it again, but if it were an afternoon showing we'd sit through it two or three times, as you could in those days. We saw *Mary Poppins* twenty-eight times, which is still one of my favourites, *Kelly's Heroes* twenty times, *The Wrong Box* fifteen times, and when I became a teenager I watched *The Producers* fifteen times.

'I loved the fact you could go to the pictures and imagine you were the boy up there on the screen. I never thought that one day I'd ever be in a movie, that would have been crazy, but the films allowed you the chance to dream, to use your imagination. And I suppose what I also got from the movies was the sense of storytelling. I loved a good story. And *Mary Poppins* was a great story.

'What I also realised at the time was I loved a story with a happy ending.' Fundamentally, Finglas had next-to-nothing. But what it did have in abundance was kids. It was 99 per cent Catholic and most families had at least eight children. If a family unit had three or four kids they were regarded as a rarity; people often presumed the parents didn't get on.

Most of the kids who roamed happily in their hordes around Finglas wore regulation plastic shoes, and when the plastic wore out, the shoes were filled with linoleum inserts. Most young people, especially girls, stayed only until they were old enough to move abroad to find employment.

The O'Carroll household in the early 1960s was a little different from every other in Finglas, however, in that it had a telephone; Maureen O'Carroll insisted on that.

And it was a happy household – thanks, to a great extent, to the laughing, energetic youngest child. But it's often the saddest memories that stick in the mind.

'My earliest memory of Daddy was not a nice one. It's of him half dragging, half trying to carry me as I screamed and cried, the tears streaming from my eyes like a waterfall. I had scarlet fever and he was taking me into hospital. I now know that I was just three years old.

'We were driven to hospital in a friend's – Ina's – car. When I came out of hospital my dad had bought me a little puppy, which I called Tip. What I do know is I never got into Ina's car again.

'Other than that traumatic memory, I don't remember much about my dad. I remember how he would balance his right heel on his left knee when sitting, and how he would lie me with my arse in the triangle it made and my head on his knee. He would then puff away, watching the Saturday afternoon wrestling, cheering on Mick McManus or Billy Two Rivers, all the while tapping his left foot to make a rocking motion, putting me asleep. That triangle felt like a very safe place to be.'

Michael, Eilish and Brendan were the youngsters in the family, and the rest began to fly the coop, with the females all moving to England or Canada. Phil joined the RAF, aged 14.

'I recall once coming upon my father and my mother embracing as she cried. It was the night before my sister Fiona, Finbar's twin, then eighteen, was to emigrate to Canada. I entered the dim hallway from the toilet. Daddy was holding Mammy in a big hug and Mammy was sobbing.

'"I don't want her to go, Gerry," she was pleading as he held her tightly and rubbed his hand on her back.

'"I know, love, but you have to let them fly, you must."

'Then the weirdest thing happened. Daddy noticed me standing watching and he pushed Mammy away, as if I had caught him in some compromising position.

'"Up to bed, you young man!" he bellowed. So I did. Young man? I had to have been maybe five.'

Brendan continued to be Maureen's Special One throughout her life. He possessed the ability to make his mammy laugh loudest. She'd take him to see films and Brendan would cry with infectious laughter, and she was delighted.

Maureen adored this funny little boy with the amazing imagination, and she was the first to recognise his talent. He spent ages drawing, but he'd also attach a story to his drawings. 'That man with the rifle, well, he's got a friend who was shot . . .'

And, being a teacher, she loved his ability to learn.

'I can remember back when I was five, she would sit me on the dinner table, look me in the face, pinch my cheek and say, "You can be anything you want to be." I grew up believing, "Oh yes, I can. I can fly."' As Michael McHugh had once said to his daughter.

Yet, Maureen hadn't morphed into an Earth Mother after his arrival. Even though she had lost her seat in the Dáil (and suffered reduced status and income), she still had great fights to win, battling for women's rights such as having the word 'illegitimate' removed from birth certificates.

Fiona O'Carroll recalls being at school, listening to other girls talk about their mammies doing regular household chores on certain days of the week, and she'd be wishing hers was the type who did the usual things, like the laundry on a Monday.

Not Maureen O'Carroll.

'Her attitude was, the only thing you can give your children is individuality and the confidence to accept the responsibility that goes with that,' says Brendan.

Sound advice, or a convenient truth? Perhaps both. And while Maureen taught her kids that anything was possible, she wasn't averse to sharing what she believed to be home truths.

When Eilish made her First Holy Communion, aged seven, Maureen displayed an Agnes Brown-like insensitivity.

'Ah, darling!' she said to her little girl. 'God didn't make you very beautiful, but he made you ever so lovable.'

More than likely, Agnes would have then smiled and added, 'Sure, I was just joking with yer.'

Whatever the other kids might have endured, Brendan's confidence was continually boosted.

And so it was, believing everything was possible, that Brendan set off for the run-down St. Gabriel's School in O'Devaney Gardens in Stoneybatter.

'I had to go to school ten miles away. Stoneybatter had been my mother's constituency and I had been born there. But to get to school required two bus journeys: the number forty bus from our home in Casement Grove to Heart's Corner, and then I would then walk a mile or so to Doyle's Corner and catch either a ten, nine, or a four up to Oxmantown Road.

'The journey took about an hour, but when you are just five years old it felt like crossing Africa, every day. The cost was threepence.

'But at the time I didn't realise the school was a dump. Teachers did not apply to work there, they ended up there.

'I recall so much of that first day in school. There were two teachers of the same name, Heydon. One was a big stout woman and the other a tiny, wiry thing. I have no idea if they were related. They introduced themselves as Big Miss Heydon and Little Miss Heydon. They both looked scary, and they were. I prayed that I would not be with one of them. My prayers were answered. I got a lovely woman, Miss Nealon. The place seemed huge and the boys from senior school upstairs looked like giants. There was a gigantic picture of Jesus in the hallway, His heart exposed and a red light burning in front of Him. The weird thing about this picture was that not only did His eyes follow you wherever you went, but if you came into the hallway late for school, His face seemed to frown at you.'

He adds, grinning, 'You know I thought I'd left a lot of this religious stuff behind, but I've realised when I'm speaking I'm capitalising "Him" and "His". I guess you never lose the habit.

'But overall, I hated school. What I know now that I didn't know then is that I am dyslexic. The teachers didn't know it either.'

Brendan wasn't diagnosed until many years later, when his son, Eric, revealed symptoms.

'I realised very early that I couldn't learn the way the others learned, so I developed my own way of absorbing information, "perspective thinking". It worked, and I was able to keep up without anybody noticing. Little did I know that what I was doing would many years later be described as "thinking outside the box".'

But he believes such problems can often come with a silver lining.

'Eighty per cent of the prison population are dyslexic. And we don't realise the potential of these people. When you get twelve-year-olds who can open a car with a coat hanger in ten seconds flat and drive it off, we don't recognise that talent and utilise it, we make him a prisoner. Now, just think. There's a lot to be said for using a thief to catch a thief. Look how the insurance company used the thief in the true-life movie, *Catch Me If You Can*. We need to consider how people think.'

The classrooms of St Gabriel's School, packed tight with 40-odd kids, were the scene of many painful memories. Literally. 'I came to detest the place. The teachers were dreadful. Alcoholics and child-beaters. I can remember being beaten by one Christian Brother who had a belt with "The Wrath of God" written across it. It was terrifying to be in a classroom with him.

'I can recall being caned by a teacher with a bamboo stick, and when he gave me the three on each hand I wasn't crying. So he went again and again until my hands bled. I won. I still didn't cry, but believe me it was a pyrrhic victory, long before I knew what a pyrrhic victory was.'

School might not have been Brendan's favourite place, but he wasn't unintelligent. (He's now a member of Mensa, with an IQ of 156, which takes him into the top 2 per cent of the population.) And his dyslexia has never been a barrier to achieving anything he set out to do, nor did it hamper his thirst for knowledge – or his popularity. He became an altar boy, soon allowed to serve Mass, which was a great honour. He played football, and became a star player. In fact, mistaken as he might have been, he believed there wasn't anything he couldn't do.

'I'd be out with my best pals John Breen and Jimmy Matthews, and they'd dare each other to jump across ditches, or drop from trees. Some of them would sometimes have a go but I'd *always* have a go, even if I didn't make it across the ditch and I ended up on my arse covered in muck. They called me the Can-Do Kid.'

There wasn't a lot of organised activity for young boys.

'Me and my pals would go and camp out at the power station in our little two-man tent, and we'd spend the night listening to the electricity generator crackle and hum and marvel at the blue light all around. It was magical to us little boys, a wonderland.' (Of course, the connection with exposure to power lines and cancer hadn't yet been made in the early 1960s.)

Brendan has always believed he has a sixth sense. 'As a youngster I was known as St Anthony, because of my knack of finding anything that was lost. I would imagine the lost item in my mind's eye and simply walk over and find it. It's a fantastic ability. I can still do it today.

'The first time I remember it happening was when I was six. I was at the beach in County Cork with Mammy, an aunt and a load of my cousins. My aunt was paddling with a couple of her kids and she was grabbing big wet handfuls of sand, but when she came back to our rug where the rest of us were, she noticed she had lost her wedding ring.

'It was one of the only bits of jewellery she had and she was devastated at losing it. But Mammy told her not to worry because I would find it. It seemed a daft idea that I could find a ring that was lost on a huge beach, but Mammy was convinced. So we walked to where my aunt thought she had been. I put my hands into the wet sand and as I pulled them up, her wedding ring was dangling off my little finger.

'She couldn't believe it, but I didn't think it was any big deal.'

Special powers or not, Brendan's imagination was, it seems, unlimited. For his First Holy Communion he was bought new grey trousers, a red sash, a First Holy Communion book and a shirt as white as the stairway to heaven. Two days later, Brendan wore the shirt outside when playing cowboys with his friend John Breen. Later, when he went indoors, half of one shirtsleeve was missing.

'Johnny Breen cut himself,' he explained to his mammy. 'I had to stop the bleeding.'

Clearly, he'd been watching too many episodes of *Laramie* or *Rawhide*. (And clearly he wasn't overly concerned about the cost of a replacement shirt.)

And he could certainly tell a good tale.

'Once, I set fire to a hedgerow at the back of the house and blamed it on my brother, Michael. My dad was very proud of that hedgerow and he went mad when he saw it go up in flames. My brother was trying to put the fire out with a blanket and I ran away. Michael got the hiding of his life and then my mammy battered him for using a good blanket to put out the fire. I didn't own up until my twenty-first birthday.' He was a rogue, but always a lovable rogue.

His imagination, or perhaps his dyslexia, made Brendan look at the world differently from other children. Once, he took the time to write Fiona a two-page letter. But he wrote it backwards. Not back to front, but every word a mirror image. Fiona had to hold it up to a mirror to read it.

Outside of the family, Brendan's fun time was spent with John Breen and Jimmy Matthews. The trio were inseparable.

'We all went to different schools, and mine was the worst of the three. Jimmy went to St Vincent's, a semi-private school, and John went to St Peter's, near to his dad's garage, and his father took him there on the back of a Honda Fifty every day.'

Back in Problem Primary, Brendan's thinking outside the box could only take him so far. He needed help, particularly with his reading. And encouragement. Strange as it may seem, former teacher Maureen O'Carroll didn't coach her son; instead she was content to let him forge his own destiny, while she attacked soup-making multinationals and corrupt council officials.

'My older brothers and sisters would later complain that they heard their mother on the radio railing about how many kids in Ireland were illiterate, yet they couldn't get her to help with their homework.'

Brendan spent lots of one-on-one time with his mum, though.

'I remember bus journeys with Mammy into the City. Finglas was a very working-class area, and yet to go to town my mother would dress up. I sat there beside her upstairs on the bus, her wearing an emerald green mohair coat, her mink stole – there were three full minks stitched together arse-to-nose – around her neck, a peacock-feather hat, diamanté glasses and her cigarette holder. This was about eight inches long, and her Consulate menthol cigarette was firmly held in place.

'I didn't realise how well known she was, but I do recall that no bus conductor ever asked for her fare, and there was always someone ready to light her Consulate once it had been inserted into the holder.

'I wasn't dressed up. I sat there with the arse out of my trousers, but just loving being in her company. And it was on one of these journeys I had my first piece of what I would call "Little Mo's Wisdoms". As the bus trundled along towards town, we were chatting and Mammy was trying to make the point to me, a six-year-old, that how you feel about yourself is more important than how others feel about you. She believed that the correct state of mind could move mountains.

'"Let me tell you, Brendan, if you have only enough money for two cups of coffee in a café, go into the best hotel and spend it on *one*. From the first you will leave full of coffee, from the second you will leave like a king."'

Gerry O'Carroll helped with the kids as much as he could. But he seemed to be cursed by continual illness.

'When I was still seven, but only just, I remember standing in a corridor of the Richmond Hospital in Dublin with Mammy. We were waiting to be joined by my father. The hospital was a creepy old place. I expected to see Florence Nightingale scamper across the corridor, lamp held in front of her.

'There were moans and groans coming from somewhere and I was very, very scared. I squeezed a little tighter on my mammy's kid-gloved hand. Not for the first time in my life, nor the last, Mammy calmly said to me, "Relax Brendan. There is nothing to fear here."

'So I did. Then a figure arrived from a doorway. A skeleton of a man. It was my daddy. He was wearing his tartan dressing gown, but it was wrapped around him in such a way that the side pocket was at the front. I looked at Mammy and she smiled at me, her loosening grip signalling to me to go to him. So I did. He stooped, and instead of picking me up as he would usually do, he hugged me as I stood on tiptoe.

'"My God, you are getting so big," he said, smiling.

'He had no teeth. Daddy never had teeth. He had had them all taken out, as was the fashion in those days, and had replaced them with a set of dentures. He wore the dentures for a few days but abandoned them. He was also lying. I was not getting big. I was the smallest boy in my class, in the school; probably the smallest seven-year-old in the world.

'I don't remember too much more about my dad. I think it's because the memories I have of him are of seeing him looking ill. And it's not hard to see why I would have blocked them out.'

The smallest seven-year-old still needed space to grow.

'Mum and Dad slept in separate rooms. How they had ten kids is beyond me. They must have had an extension cord.'

Brendan recalls his dad used to sleep with the door of the coal shed under his mattress. Gerry O'Carroll reckoned his bad back needed support. But the back pain was the result of something more sinister, which would be discovered two years down the line.

What's confusing about Maureen O'Carroll is why a woman who had so much political ambition would burden herself with so many children.

Yes, Irish Catholics traditionally bred like rabbits. But why choose to have so many? Was Maureen out to create Walton's Mountain in Stoneybatter?

Some years later, Maureen answered that question when put delicately to her by youngest daughter, Eilish.

'What woman in her right mind chooses to have ten kids, Eilish?'

'So why have them?'

'Well, for all my education, I was very ignorant. I wanted my first child, the rest of you were mistakes. Not that I would send any of you back. No! Every child brings its own welcome. You see, I just didn't know I had a choice. We didn't have access to contraception other than rubber johnnies, and whilst we tried them occasionally, we felt so guilty. Besides, it wasn't worth the bollocking we got from the priest at confession. The only form of contraception open to us was the rhythm method, or practise self-denial.

'Well, the rhythm method failed me nine times and, as for self-denial, what a load of bollix that was. And your father and I enjoyed our sex. We had little else. We had little money. We couldn't even afford a babysitter. Our only pleasure was ten Woodbines at the weekend, the odd bottle of stout – and sex.'

It was a speech so bold and honest it could have been made by Agnes Brown herself.

Brendan had certainly been born in a crowd. Now, he was determined to stand out, succeed. Whatever it took. It might have come from being the youngest in the family, the need to have a voice. But then the other younger kids such as Eilish and Michael didn't have the same need to be heard. It seemed Brendan's DNA was different from the rest of the O'Carroll kids'. He was enigmatic, challenging and imaginative right from the moment he was born.

He had an energy and a smile that his family warmed to. He did everything at double speed.

He wanted to achieve everything, to make people laugh, to be the centre of attention, to be the very best at anything he turned his hand to.

'I always had an earner. I sold sticks door-to-door, little bundles of kindling. I would spend the week gathering wood from factories around Finglas, then chop them up and bind them in bundles of six. By Saturday my barrow, which I made myself, was full, and I sold them at two bunches for a penny. I also washed windows, I'd clean shops. I always earned, and of course every penny went to Mammy.'

And his mammy was delighted at Brendan's efforts to improve their lot. But not at all cost.

JAIL TIME

BRENDAN'S school was full of tough kids. But he didn't become the class clown in order to survive. He might have been the smallest boy in the class, but only in terms of height.

'I wasn't one of those stereotypical kids that did all the funny stuff to keep the bullies away. I was well able to take care of myself, the bullies stayed away anyway.'

Meanwhile, Maureen O'Carroll might not have spent endless hours teaching her youngest spelling and arithmetic. But she taught him to think.

'When I was only nine years of age, my mother would ask my opinion. And I didn't know the answer, so I'd start to read the newspapers, watch documentaries, anything so's I could have one. While other kids were watching *Tom and Jerry*, I'd be watching the *Seven Days* news show. "Dear Santa, Please bring me an Almanac this year."

'I'd listen to her talk about political demographics. And she'd say things to me like, "There's more than one way to skin a cat", and I'd ask her to explain what this meant.

'My brother Finbar was a magnificent footballer. And I remember going to see him play once with my mother and heard her say, "Sure, your brother has natural talent." And I said, "What do you mean by natural talent?" And she went on to say it was something you can't learn, you can't analyse it, you just dance to it.

'Ever since then I've realised if something is funny, don't analyse it. Just go with it. But these words of wisdom that passed my way were like nuggets. I hung on her every word.'

As did many people. Maureen now worked for Dublin Corporation, helping to establish a shelter for homeless women. But it was Gerry O'Carroll's support that enabled her to do this. He was the glue that kept the family together. And theirs was a true love story. When Maureen arrived off the bus at 8.20 in the morning having worked during the night at the refuge, her husband would have her porridge on the steamer. She'd have his dinner ready when he came in at 6 p.m.

And, with the older offspring gone, the couple had more of a chance to enjoy their relationship. They'd go into the kitchen, smoke and talk. And if the kids wandered in for a cup of tea, they'd get frowning looks, exactly like those that Agnes often gives to her kids now. But Gerry showed increasing signs of ill-health. Visits to the doctors became more frequent. He had been hospitalised several times with respiratory problems. Maureen worried, and hoped for the best.

Brendan, thankfully, didn't see much of this angst. Or at least he chooses to remember the happier times in Finglas.

'I remember my brother Phil on his visits home from the RAF. He played trombone in the RAF band.

'I remember my sister Martha's wedding and the reception after it in a marquee in our back garden. She forced me to wear short trousers she had made herself. Royal blue, they were. And she cut my hair into a Mohican. I was mortified.'

There wasn't a lot of money around, but Maureen O'Carroll was to the manner born. When her older sons moved out of the house, the young footballers would return to Finglas to play football, and afterwards enjoy a beer in the Cappagh House pub, near to the O'Carroll home. For the sake of convenience, they'd park their cars outside their mother's house and go and have a drink.

Maureen would be seething that her sons hadn't invited her along. It wasn't because they didn't want their mammy around. It was because she would only drink cognac.

'If you only drink cognac, you can still keep your wits about you,' she argued in her defence. The reality was, she was not a Guinness type of lady. She liked the expensive. And her youngest son didn't grow up hankering after bottles of stout either. He liked to spend time at nights with 'Mr Smirnoff'. Brendan's dad had to pay the Electricity Supply Board every month. And, given the expense, he'd go round turning off the lights on a regular basis. But Maureen would argue the kids would go blind from not having the light to do their homework. Go into Brendan's home today and the lights burn bright constantly. He never wants dark days to befall him again.

It's fair to say that the O'Carroll house was constantly chaotic. Football boots were dumped in doorways to the point that the girls were reluctant to bring friends home. But they did, anyway. Maureen loved having people around. The more the merrier. Maureen's boys were always her priority, though. Sunday dinner would go on hold if the boys were playing football. Maureen would often quote Shakespeare, paraphrasing it with lines such as 'My sons, my sons, my kingdom for my sons.' And she wasn't joking. But her youngest son, the Special One, was the centre of her world.

While Brendan joined his older brothers in playing football, he was the only one writing poetry, some so clever that Eilish, who left school at 12 to attend commercial college, would type it up and show it to her friends.

'Look,' she'd yell out, 'this kid is nine! He's a genius.'

He was also well-mannered.

'Manners are very important to me. That comes from my own upbringing, from my mother. I could murder six nuns in my own home, but if I said "Please" and "Thank you" and opened the gate for them when they were coming in, my mother would forgive me anything.'

Perhaps Maureen O'Carroll was a little too forgiving of her youngest son. He had been an altar boy since the age of eight, but outside of the chapel, and the home, he was becoming a little feral.

'I was attracting some interest from the Garda Siochána, the police. I became a bit of a tearaway. Growing up in Finglas was tough so, in order to "fit in", one had to accept the responsibility of a little petty crime from time to time.

'I could drive by the time I was eight, and ours was the first call neighbours made if they happened to be locked out of their car or house. But I never stole a car or burgled a home in my life. However, like all children then, I was partial to a little shoplifting.'

But there would be a price to pay. When he was almost nine, a new supermarket finally opened in Finglas and Brendan, with a couple of pals, decided to check it out. Or rather they decided to attempt their very own version of *Supermarket Sweep*.

'That 17 September 1964 was a beautiful sunny day. The day held much promise, for my treat every birthday was that Mammy would take me to Bewley's Oriental Café, where I was allowed a cappuccino and two chocolate éclairs. It was exciting and today Mammy had me dress in my best clothes.

'But not for the birthday treat. You see, before we could paint the town red, there was the little matter of a court case.

'Let me explain. I had been caught – you always are – and I had on me a roll of Sellotape and a bicycle lock. I had nothing to stick, nor did I have a bike, so don't ask me why I lifted them, I have no idea. They were there.' (Maureen O'Carroll couldn't afford to buy Brendan a bike, but the following Christmas his brother Michael, now working, saved all his money and bought his little brother the bike he craved. 'And it wasn't even stolen,' Brendan would boast to his friends.)

'Yet, the court case could have been avoided. My mammy had enough pull to get it overlooked and for the store to accept an apology. But she had a different thought. She knew that the crime was so petty that I would only be scolded by the judge and given the benefit of the Probation Act.

'And she truly believed the day in court would frighten the daylights out of me and deter any future crimes. It was a good plan.

'But what she had not figured into the equation was a judge whose appointment she had objected to. I was sent down. Three months in a reform school in County Laois.

'It was a strange day. We left the courtroom that morning, Mammy smiling. Outside I asked her what had happened. She brushed the question off with a "Don't worry about it." So we headed for the bus into town to celebrate my birthday.

'What an amazing day we had. We laughed and laughed that day. I was always able to make Mammy laugh heartily and nothing ever gave me more pleasure. In Bewley's, they would normally bring to the table a three-tiered plate that had on it two cream slices, two cream buns, two cream puffs, and two chocolate éclairs. But not today. I saw Mammy whisper something to the waitress, the woman smiled and the plate arrived with eight chocolate éclairs on it. I can still see the picture in my mind, the waitresses in their black uniforms with white lace headdress and aprons, standing in a circle singing "Happy Birthday, dear Brendan" and before me *just* éclairs.

'Mammy prompted me on until I had eaten every one of the eight. No problem. We then went to Barney's, a slot machine and game palace. We played every game and in the photo booth we got our strip of shots done while Mammy howled with laughter. Today, these are the only remaining photos I have of the two of us together while in my childhood.

'We arrived home that evening exhausted. Mammy dropped into her armchair and I ran a basin full of hot water and added some Epsom salts to it. I carried it in and lay it in front of her. Then I pulled off her suede boots and placed her feet into the footbath. She rolled her eyes and giggled with pleasure. I sat on the footstool just smiling at her.

'"Thanks Mammy. That was the best day of my life," I said, and meant it. She sat up and leaned over to stroke my cheek.

'"I'm afraid it goes downhill from here Brendan," and I could hear the seriousness in her voice.

'At nine o'clock the next morning, I stood outside Pearse Street Police Station. My brother Finbar had accompanied me to the door but he wouldn't come in. I had a pair of trousers, three pairs of jockeys, three T-shirts and three pairs of socks packed into the only bag that was available in the house. A pink weekend case.

'I was taken by police car to the place of incarceration and shown into a dormitory full of beds. I cannot begin to tell you how frightened I was. After putting my clothes away and hiding the weekend case, I was taken to the office where I was allowed to call my mother and let her know I had arrived safely. Actually, this was seen as a novelty by the Christian Brothers who ran this place. They had never had a boy in there whose family had a phone.

'"Are you okay?" Mammy asked. She sounded sadder than I was.

'"I'm frightened Mammy."

'There was a pause. "You have nothing to fear there, Brendan. Nothing!"

'She was so positive this was the case that I believed her and, I swear it, there and then my fear just dissipated.

'When the call was done, the Brother began to question me. "Do you attend Mass, son?"

'"Yes, Brother."

'"Regularly?"

'"Yes, Brother."

'"Were you at Mass last Sunday?"

'"Yes, Brother. Three Masses last Sunday."

'He stared at me. "Don't lie to me boy!" he growled.

'"I'm not, Brother. I serve Mass and I served three last Sunday." I tried to convince him I was not lying.

'"Why three?" he asked, now a little more gently once he discovered I was an altar boy.

'"Well Brother, three of the priests will not celebrate the Mass in English, and there are only two of us that can serve it in Latin."

'I had answered truthfully. His eyes widened and a huge smile crossed his face.

'"You serve in Latin?" He gave me a huge pat on the back.

'"Are you frightened, son? About being here?"

'"No Brother, not now." Then I explained. "Me mammy said there was nothing for me to fear here."

'"Your mammy is wrong, boy," he said dismissively.

'"No, Brother. She's not. Mammy is never wrong."

'He just smiled.

'I received a letter from Mammy every day I was there. But I wasn't there for the three months demanded. I was out in three weeks. Mammy pulled every string she could and got me out. I never found out how. But I remember the morning I got out. We were in the mess hall having breakfast and the Brother in charge of the mess called out my name. The hall went silent and I stood.

'"Where are you working today, Brendan?"

'"In the sheds, Brother," I answered at the top of my voice, for we were at either ends of the hall.

'"Well, let the Brother in charge know you will not be there today. When you finish breakfast, go to your dorm and pack. You are going home today."

'There was an almighty cheer in the room. Tears streamed from my face as I ran across the football pitch to the dorm to pack. I was going home. I had learned my lesson. I vowed there and then never ever again to get caught. I'd never put myself in that sort of position again.

'And the lesson according to my mother? "If you do something and it turns out good, you stand on the rooftops, and you tell the world. But you've got to do the same if it goes pear-shaped."'

He adds, looking uncomfortable, 'Me mammy used to boast that she had eleven children but had never stood in a courtroom with any of them. And then I let her down.'

Brendan didn't suffer too much in reform school. And he didn't dwell on the bicycle locks and Sellotape experience. As always, he was set to move onto the next challenge.

But what?

THE FROG CHORUS

ST GAYBO'S was full of dead-end kids and no-hope teachers desperate just to get through the day. Brendan was taught by many uninterested supply teachers.

'We had a teacher once called Mr Muldoon. He made a point of telling me I would always be a loser.'

Regular teachers simply didn't last too long in an old, worn-out school filled with unruly kids that sucked the energy out of their very being. Brendan, at the time, saw it as the normal way of things. He got on with his life, which at this time involved being a part-time pigeon-fancier.

But the sky suddenly darkened the day Brendan was taken to see his dad in hospital. Gerry O'Carroll's breathing had worsened.

'Just as it was time to go my daddy held before me two florins. Four shillings. "Happy Birthday, young man," he smiled, and I took the shiny coins with the leaping salmon on them.

'"Thanks, Daddy," and I meant it. This was big money.

'"So what will you do with all this money, Brendan?"

'"I'm going to buy two more pigeons. Tumblers," I said gleefully. I already had three birds, and I loved keeping pigeons.

'"Yes, Mammy tells me you have pigeons. Where do you keep them?"

'"I made a kinda box from two pop-soda wooden crates. I keep them there," I was proud to say.

'Daddy leaned down, picked me up in his arms and whispered into my ear, "When I get out of here son, I will make you the best pigeon loft in Finglas."

'I was thrilled. My daddy, it was well known to all, was probably the finest cabinet-maker in Dublin. I knew he could make the best loft. I knew it. I floated from the hospital that day.'

Gerard O'Carroll never got the chance. Eight days after he gave Brendan his two shiny coins, he died from asbestos poisoning, contracted on one of the many jobs he'd taken on that had involved working with asbestos sheeting.

'He died in the same hospital where they took him when he had been shot as a kid.

'Mammy told me in the best way she could. "Brendan, Daddy is gone to heaven son." Then, holding me close, she wept. I looked at her with widened eyes.

'"But, what about my pigeon loft?" I asked.

'I guess I was sort of used to seeing my father go into hospital. So I didn't miss him as much as I would have. And I somehow knew life would be all about me and my mammy. I hadn't had the chance to really get to know my dad. I guess I felt like I was the man of the house now. I was the one responsible for my mammy.

'And, as strange and as sad a time as it should have been, my abiding memory of the week of the funeral was one of excitement. You see, a lot of my brothers and sisters had emigrated. Now, suddenly, they were all coming home, from Canada, America and England. And I spent the days at the arrivals gate at Dublin Airport. To this day, my favourite place to be is at arrivals in any airport meeting someone. Sometimes, I still pop into arrivals around Christmas time to witness the joy of people reuniting as they emerge from those sliding doors, arms outstretched and engulfing family or friends they have missed and who have missed them. And yes, I cry as I watch.'

It's not hard to see how Brendan would later come up with a Mrs Brown plot line, set at Christmas time, when Agnes would be beside herself at the thought of her son Trevor arriving home from America.

Meantime, the death of Gerry O'Carroll resulted in a new dynamic in the house. Brendan had always been his mammy's favourite, the chosen one. But with her husband gone, the focus on her tiny son sharpened.

'The event changed everything. The day my daddy died, I released the birds. And my mammy spent a bit less time in local politics. I'd get much more of her attention. The attention of a genius.'

Back at school, however, in the summer of 1965, Brendan was in for an entirely unexpected surprise.

'In my absence, the class had got a new teacher. Not a stand-in, I was told by the lads, but a real, full-time teacher. His name was Billy Flood. As a young man, Billy Flood believed he had a vocation to the Church. He began his journey to train as a Christian Brother but changed his mind. However, he still wanted to teach. I now know that Billy Flood was born to teach. He couldn't have been more than 21 years old – and looked about 16. I took one look at this baby-faced, horn-rimmed eejit and thought, "He won't last long" because we were quite an intimidating bunch and had scared off more than a few hopefuls in our time.

'But here's the first thing I noticed about him that was different: he wasn't afraid of us. The second, which puzzled me even more, was that he actually seemed to like us.

'Now, to the modern-day school kid, the change Billy Flood brought to our classroom will seem petty, but not to us, who had spent our previous school years being beaten senseless, having the Three Rs rammed into us, and in general being despised by the men who were charged with preparing us for life as good citizens.

'This was not Mr Flood's way. He taught us to sing. At first we thought he was a queer, the word we used back then for gay. Sing? Us? When he announced this, we laughed. Boy, how we laughed. Then we sang. And he moved from desk to desk, tapping a tuning fork and getting each of us to sing the note. Using this guide, he divided the class into three groups and had us perform first, second and third harmonies.

'This took an age, for there were some of the lads that wouldn't do it at first and some who sounded like frogs masturbating. But by one o'clock that afternoon we were singing "Three Blind Mice" in virtually perfect harmony. I didn't know it then, but at that moment, on that September afternoon, thanks to the enthusiasm of a baby-faced young teacher, my life was about to change.'

Brendan hadn't had a singing epiphany, or decided to launch himself as a pop star of the future (although he can certainly sing, as those who've witnessed his stand-up show will testify).

'I knew that I could do something different. I didn't know what it was, nor did I have the words to explain it, but I could feel that I was expressing myself. I knew a group of people together, singing, or whatever, could have a great time. Even in a school classroom.

'One of the first things Mr Flood did was set up a library, in a Tayto Crisps box. I presume he used his own books from home. Then he put two of the hardest kids in the class in charge of it, so that protected it from miscreants but also gave it kudos. The very first book I took out was *Treasure Island*. I know today that I'm dyslexic, which explains why it took an age to read it, but I read it – and I loved it. I loved being transported to tiny islands on the high seas. I could feel the ship ploughing through the ocean, taste the salt of the sea water. It was magical. When I was finished, I returned it – well, you had to. It wasn't like a real library. If you didn't return it, you didn't get fined, you got the shit kicked out of you by one of our "librarians" who had three ears between them.

'I took another book out, but only read a bit of it. I put that one back and got *Treasure Island* out and read it again and again and again. Over the next three years, I must have taken it out fifteen times, and read it from cover to cover each time.'

Mr Flood had shown Brendan other worlds could exist in the imagination. He introduced him to Tolkien's *Lord of the Rings* and Brendan was mesmerised. The youngster realised now the power of invention, of creating wonderful characters and weaving life stories around them.

Brendan discovered this new-found power of storytelling could be utilised in other ways, too. 'I'd now reached the age where I was doing things I should have been confessing to the priest, so I made things up.'

But of course he never imagined one day he'd make a career out of making up stories.

Mr Flood also instilled the absolute importance of education, ironically something Brendan hadn't really experienced at home.

'There was no such thing as free secondary school education back then. If you couldn't afford to go onto the next level, you stayed in the primary school until you were fourteen and then let out to face the world. But Mr Flood told us one afternoon that Des O'Malley TD was about to change all that, and the only thing we needed to do in three years' time was to pass an entrance exam. And he added he was determined that as many of us as possible would. And you know, we believed him.'

Meantime, Brendan had to undergo another test. His first kiss.

'It was with Mardi Deegan, and I adored her. I was still ten, and I remember it was in the middle of winter. I remember it well because I had what used to be called a Number Eleven – two lines of snot running down my nose. Anyway, I took Mardi to The Casino cinema and all the other boys in the village were waiting to see if she would kiss me. Well, she did. And it was a big smack. I remember thinking, "I hope my nose is clean." But when she pulled away there were two silver spots on her upper lip. I had made my mark. Everyone saw it, but no one told her. Surprisingly enough, she still speaks to me today.'

In the summer of 1966, Brendan visited his sister Maureen in London, and had a great time. But he didn't realise he'd become too caught up in the occasion.

'My brother-in-law took me to my first soccer match. It was at Wembley to see Mexico playing England in the World Cup. I nearly got lynched when I came back home to Ireland because everything I was wearing had a Union Jack on it.'

Aged 12 and a half, Brendan took his entrance exam and came second top, all ready to progress to secondary school after his birthday in September. But it seems the combined weight of Robert Louis Stevenson and Billy Flood couldn't persuade him to carry on with his education.

He was too intent on getting to the next chapter. But he did take the time to write to sister Fiona in Toronto. Fiona had asked Brendan to write to her, but not to write too much because heavy letters were expensive to mail. He took her at her word. She would laugh when she opened the airmail envelope to read just two words, *Dear Fiona . . .*

Brendan played football now for local club Home Farm, and he remembers a club tour, but not so much for the playing.

'We were on a trip to Blackpool, and we all went along to see *The Sound Of Music*. I came out singing all the songs. I'd seen a lot of Western films at The Casino, but for some reason Julie Andrews stuck in my mind.'

Perhaps he was already in close touch with his theatrical side. Not long after, Brendan went to the theatre for the first time, to see a children's play *It's A Two Foot Six Inches Above The Ground World*, at the Gate Theatre as part of the Dublin Theatre Festival.

The play depicted life from a kid's perspective, with all the children played by adults. Brendan sat with his mouth open as wide as the River Liffey, captivated by the entertainers.

'It was utter magic. When the curtain went down I told my mother that's what I wanted to do with my life. I had found myself transported into another world. But it wasn't just a place where my imagination could fly off to. I realised that the performers up there on stage had this amazing power over someone like me. This was incredible. I wanted some day to have that sort of power over an audience.'

But for the time being, he pushed that dream to the back of his head. Brendan had real life to be getting on with.

THE LEPRECHAUN

FINGLAS made moves towards modernity in the late 1960s when a bingo hall was built in the west side of the town, which also served as the football dressing rooms, the boxing club and the tenants' association HQ. And a new cabaret house, the 600-seater Drake Inn, was built, where international stars such as Gene Pitney and Frank Ifield would appear and locals could relax and enjoy the talent.

However, Ireland's education system was still locked in the Dark Ages. It's almost unimaginable these days to consider a little boy could leave school aged just 12 and go to work full time.

But that's exactly what Brendan did in the summer of 1967.

Legislation hadn't quite yet been passed to make secondary education free to all, but more than likely, even if it had been, Brendan would not have taken up the opportunity. Why? He was always older than his years. And cocky. He believed he could make it in the world without a leaving certificate. And, of course, none of his family had made it through secondary, so a precedent had been set.

He also wanted money. He'd had a taste of it, with a news-paper round and selling kindling from a barrow. And it's not hard to appreciate why he wanted to contribute to the family purse. Since his dad had passed away, money had been tight. Sometimes Brendan would be sent to bed at 5 p.m. because there was no dinner.

'The Dublin mothers didn't want the kids to be feeling hunger pains all night,' he says with a wry smile.

'I used to think I had two uncles called Vincent and Paul. It was only a few years later that I realised that the blokes who came round on a Tuesday to give us some money were from the charity, St Vincent de Paul.'

And there was the letter from America. It wasn't just correspondence. It was money. It was a lifeline. It was the cheque or postal order that the relatives living abroad would send back home, from the likes of big sister Fiona who had emigrated to Canada.

One year, Maureen Junior came back to Dublin from England and bought her mother a fridge, telling her it would be fantastic, and she'd now be able to store the food, the milk etc. Her mammy thought it wonderful. But when the generous daughter returned the following year, she realised it wasn't plugged in. Not as part of a drive to save energy, no. Brendan's mammy might have been a genius, but she'd reck-oned the fridge was a cupboard. And of course none of her friends had a fridge. How would she have known?

It seems that Billy Flood had already sensed his star pupil might not come back to school after the holidays, although Brendan himself didn't know at this time. When the moment came for the summer break, Mr Flood chose to commemo-rate the passing, to say a thanks to the three-part harmony singers he'd been so in tune with.

Some would, of course, return to wait out the remaining two years, and one or two would make it into secondary school. But many would leave for good.

And he revealed his emotions to these angels with dirty faces in a scene that could have been written for the classic film, *Goodbye Mr Chips*.

'Billy Flood gave all the kids a goody bag containing sweets and crisps. But my old brown paper bag was a little heavier. And inside it was a copy of *Treasure Island*. I gasped when I saw it. Inside the cover the teacher had written, "*I stood and looked and my wonder grew, that such a small head could hold all that he knew.*"

'As I read this, he just looked me in the eye and said, "O'Carroll, I don't know for sure what, but I tell you now, son, you will be something, something special."

'I was almost in tears. He was a wonderful bloke.'

Billy Flood would later go on to teach Marty Devany, Brendan's future son-in-law, and enjoy a long career in education.

Meantime, Brendan knew what his mammy really needed wasn't a fridge, but another income. And, although he was still 12, Brendan reckoned he was man enough to make it out there on his own. After all, his brothers had all left school at the same age. Why shouldn't he get out there and act like a grown-up? On top of all that, Brendan's natural precociousness, his determination to race forward into life, couldn't be contained.

'I asked me mammy to get me a job that summer. And because of her work as a trade unionist, she had lots of connections with the Hotel and Catering branch of the Transport and General Workers' Union. And a new hotel had opened up in the centre of Dublin called The Scullion

Hotel. So she made a phone call and I was sent along for an interview.

'The head waiter was called Teddy Gough, and he took one look at me, and then called for the rest of the staff to appear. I was a bit taken aback at this because he then lined me up in front of everyone and announced, "Look at this one! I asked the union to send me a waiter and they've sent me a leprechaun!"'

Yet, Teddy took the leprechaun on. And the commis waiter instantly loved this new world, the American accents of the hotel guests, his new colleagues, and the wage was good at £1 18s 6d a week.

'I was soon making four or five quid a week on tips. It was fantastic. So came the end of the summer and there was no way I was going back to school. I'd made my mind up. Meantime, my mother was away in Canada, doing work with the Teamsters Union. She'd be in touch every day making sure my uniform was ironed, all that stuff, but when school restarted, I didn't.'

When Maureen O'Carroll returned from Canada, she had no idea her youngest son had dumped class to join the ranks of the full-time working classes.

'Every morning I'd go down to the hotel, take off my school uniform, put it in a locker and put on my waiter's uniform. Then, at three o'clock, which was when we had a break, I'd meet me mam, and go home and pretend to do my homework. At six, I'd go back to the hotel and my mother reckoned this was me working part-time.

'And I got away with this for some time. The school didn't even send out letters to truants like me. I guess they thought I just wasn't going back and accepted the notion.

'It was only one day at Christmas when me mammy was in a department store, she bumped into my Latin teacher,

Mr Fidelius. He said, "Mrs O'Carroll, so nice to see you. How's Brendan getting on?"

'"Mr Fidelius, I was about to ask you the same thing!"

'So I came home from "school" that day and my mother said to me: "Hi, Brendan. What homework have you got? How's your Latin coming on?"

'And I read out a few declensions, but that didn't fool her. My mother had been a Latin teacher and she was still pretty good and she said, "No, no, Brendan. That's first-year stuff." She had me sussed, me mammy. And then she went feckin' bananas. She yelled at me and I became so upset that she was upset.'

And Maureen O'Carroll was right to become upset. Brendan hadn't been honest with her. And she felt conflicting emotions. Despite the fact she'd once been a teacher and had gone on to become an Irish MP, none of her children had made it through secondary school. And Maureen desperately wanted Brendan to do well. She knew he was highly intelligent.

Yet, she had let the rest of her kids go to work at the age of 12. And perhaps part of her acceptance of Brendan's decision not to return to school was influenced by the fact that she couldn't afford to send him on to secondary, that he'd simply be festering for the next two years in Gaybo's.

Regardless, Brendan wasn't prepared to go back to learning Latin verbs.

'I protested I was doing what I wanted to do. And I argued my brothers were chefs, and if working in a hotel was good enough for them . . . And I so desperately didn't want to go back to school.

'So, reluctantly, she agreed. But she said that if I were going to be a waiter, it would be in the very best hotel where I could get training.'

That was how Brendan came to work for the Intercontinental Hotel, now called Jurys, and he was in his element.

'I just loved the life. Who knew there were so many wondrous things about becoming a waiter, about the history of food, about culture, about artistry, about how phrases like Romanoff Sauce came about. It was creative; it was fantastic.

'How could I not be captivated by this whole new world that had opened up to me?'

Brendan has always believed that if you take a job on you should do it to the best of your ability. Later, when he cleaned windows, he'd be an excellent window-cleaner. And if he goes into politics, as he has intimated he might, he may well go right to the top and become President of Ireland. (And who would bet against it?) Back in 1967, however, he vowed to become the very best waiter imaginable.

'I created an original coffee, Café Diablo, which was amazing,' he says, the pride in his voice audible.

But there were important things he hadn't yet learned.

'There were about twenty kids there at the time, like me, training to become waiters. Yet, after six months, I went home one night and realised that I hadn't made a single friend. I'd look at myself in the mirror and think, "What is wrong with you?" I thought I was a nice enough guy, and I was a lot of fun. But then it dawned on me. I realised that I had too much to say for myself.

'I just seemed to know too much. I was this little boy who, if someone had said to me the moon was made of green cheese, I'd have to rebuke them and say, "No, actually that's a myth, it's made of an iron core with a collection of cosmic particles . . ." and then I'd find myself sitting in the canteen on my own.

'But once I realised why this was happening, I changed. If someone said to me, "Didn't the moon look like a big piece of cheese last night?" I'd say something equally daft like "Cheese? No I thought it was made of ice cream."'

Brendan was learning to downplay his intelligence. And, in coming up with gags, he'd win over even more people. Thanks to his new-found pragmatism, he made some new friends.

But no one could have mistaken Brendan for a shrinking violet. One holiday, Brendan took off up to the woods of Finglas, on the other side of town, to make his mark. Literally. He was carving his initials BOC on a tree when a gang of likely lads from the McKelvey area appeared (Brendan would later cheekily describe the area in Finglas East as an estate for 'problem families'). The lads read him the riot act for his encroachment, telling this 'little scud' he should get back to his own area.

One member of this junior territorial army was called Gerry Browne, a boy who would later play a massive part in Brendan's life.

'My nickname as a kid was BOC,' says Brendan. 'Kids just called me by my initials. You can imagine what Finbar and Fiona had to go through.'

Meantime, he worked hard. He learned waiting skills. He learned that people eat with their eyes, that 80 per cent of eating pleasure is in the aesthetics, in the presentation. It's a lesson he's taken forward into comedy.

'If you're going to be a waiter, look like a waiter. If you work in a circus, look like a clown. If you're playing an effete character, then give the audience a hint with a walk or whatever. Let them in on that, so's they can work it out and feel clever.'

The young Brendan understood you had to play the part of the waiter completely and put yourself to one side.

'When I'd get a complaint I'd always agree.

'"Waiter, this piece of steak isn't quite right . . ."

'"Quite right? You're right, sir. It looks like shite. Let me take it back for you."

'"Well, it's edible, I suppose."

'"Edible? No way. It's fit for the bin! Let me sort it."

'What I learned was that the customer wasn't always right. But he was always the customer. And your job is to make sure his experience is the best you can make it.'

And so he learned how to please people. Brendan would never forget this when it came to creating the Mrs Brown stage show. Early on, when he wrote gags, there were times when the audience didn't laugh. But he'd try to stick with them because he believed they would work. And they wouldn't, no matter how they were presented. Brendan came to realise the audience is always right. The job is to please them, not your own ego. But at times it was hard. Indeed, one experience could have resulted in less robust people spending fortunes on a treatment couch.

'The German hotel manager lived in a suite with his wife. And Mrs Herr would have room service every day. But the waiters hated to serve her because she was a horror.

'One day, I placed this lady's order on her table, all perfectly prepared, and she was about to dismiss me. But before doing so she dipped her finger in the French dressing, which every waiter prepared, including me.'

'"And vast ees dis?"

'"It's French dressing."

'"Dees is not. It ees deesgusting."

'And she walked away, got a piece of paper and a pen and wrote out a recipe for French dressing, which she then pinned to my jacket. She told me I was not to enter her apartment for the next six months unless I had the recipe pinned to my lapel. And so it remained there. I worked at cocktail parties with this recipe still attached. People looked at it and laughed. And it was humiliating. But I knew that if I reacted she would win. I wasn't going to let her win.'

Brendan had a way of dealing with the ignominy.

'I decided that the recipe wasn't pinned to me, it was pinned to my jacket. You can always take off the jacket.'

At the end of the six-month sentence, Brendan unpinned the recipe. And that afternoon as he carried a tray across the restaurant, he was apprehended by an angry Mrs Herr.

'"Where is dat recipe?"

'"Mrs Herr, the six months is over. And unless you can think of a very good reason why I should pin it back on, I won't."'

Brendan had learned a great deal in his first year as a waiter. But life was soon to serve him up problems that he'd really struggle to cope with.

TEENAGE KICKS

BRENDAN and his two Finglas friends John and Jimmy were always on the lookout for new ways to have fun. One night Brendan 'sourced' a vehicle. That didn't mean he stole it; he just borrowed it for a night.

'It was a Mini,' he recalled, as he chatted to me in a Glasgow bar late one night, having just appeared as Mrs Brown on stage.

'And I drove the three of us all the way over to Cavan – 65 miles from Dublin – with me driving, in second gear all the way.'

The getaway driver could barely see over the steering wheel.

'We went to Cavan because there was a fairground there and so we all got onto the helter-skelter, and slid down the mats. But at the bottom John got up, and then collapsed. And he was white as a ghost. So we said, "Are you okay?" And he wasn't, so we headed home. And on the way back, I said, "John, that was so scary. We were worried for you," and he said, "Yes, but don't tell me mammy. She won't let me go to school tomorrow."

'Now, can you imagine a kid saying that? But he was so bright and so eager, and the best footballer I'd ever seen. And he was a really good-looking bastard. If there were three good-looking girls around, he'd get the three of them.'

John Breen managed to go to school the next day but the collapse had been a warning of things to come. He died just two years later of leukaemia.

'John knew he was dying, although his parents never told him what was wrong with him. But he worked it out, checked the symptoms in an encyclopedia. And he never told his parents he knew.'

Brendan had lost his dad. Now he'd lost his best friend. It made him all the more determined to get the very most out of life. But the death of John broke up the trio. Things were never the same again. Jimmy spent more time with another pal.

Brendan never considered turning to God for help in getting over his grief. By this time, his relationship with the Catholic Church had taken a turn for the worst. He was becoming a little tearaway. And with a skinhead haircut and the cheek of the devil, he didn't exactly endear himself to youth club managers and the owners of local teen discos. So, just going on fourteen, and still working at the Intercontinental, he decided to open his own nightclub.

'Me and my pals couldn't get in anywhere, so I had the idea of opening my own disco. And I discovered the man who owned the building I wanted was called Bill Fuller.

'I went in one day and asked his secretary if I could see the owner. She looked at me curiously and then showed me into his office.

'"What can I do for you, son?"

'"Well, Mr Fuller, I want to rent your basement out, at Number Thirteen Gardiner Road."

'"*You* want to rent the basement?"

'"Yes, yes, I do."

'"For what?"

'"For a disco."

'"A disco?"

'"Yes."

'And amazingly, he agreed. And it was ten bob a week rent.'

'It does sound a bit precocious, but I also remember a bloke called Jeff Serratt, now the managing director of Pepsi-Cola in Ireland, who was a rep at the time. And one day he knocked at the door of the nightclub.

'Jeff said, "Is your father in?"

'"My father's dead."

'"Well, I'm looking for the person who owns the nightclub."

'"That'll be me."

'And he said, incredulously, "You?" But after this initial shock I got on great with him. And not only did he supply me with Pepsi, he built us a sign for the nightclub.'

Brendan's story was almost a movie script, Dublin's own *Expresso Bongo*.

'I thought I was the dog's bollocks at the time. The taxi men in Finglas in fact used to call me Little Lord Fauntleroy, because I wouldn't take a bus anywhere.'

Brendan had picked up on Maureen O'Carroll's preference for living a little of the high life.

'Oh, sure,' he goes on. 'If I were buying a pair of boots in the city, I'd take a taxi, go into the shop and try them on, and have the taxi wait to bring me back.'

The club was open on a Thursday, Friday and Saturday. But how would a 14-year-old club boss cope with facing trouble from irate punters, or local gangs?

'There was no problem with the local gangs because, well, I was in the local gangs,' he says, smiling.

'And I had three bouncers who were the McCourt brothers, and they all boxed for Ireland. So, you see, there were simply no problems.

'And you have to remember that the skinheads didn't want to get barred out of the only place they could get into.'

The little basement club, run by Dublin's Bugsy Malone, 'made a small fortune', charging two shillings and sixpence entrance money.

'It was like running a party every night.'

One night, a young Finglas lady called Doreen Dowdall came to the party.

A stunning, dark-haired girl with brown, twinkly eyes, Brendan liked her immediately.

'She was the most beautiful thing I'd ever seen in my life. She had pierced ears, her head shaved back, a black Crombie coat with a velvet collar, black polo neck, black three-quarter-length skirt, black knee-length stockings and black loafers.

'I thought she looked incredible. I knew then I wanted her to be my girlfriend. She was just so special.'

Brendan clearly liked black. But he knew a relationship would be highly problematic.

Doreen, who worked for a clothing manufacturers, came from the other side of the tracks. Not in a Montague-Capulet sense – there was little economic divide in Finglas; everyone was skint. But Doreen lived in an area into which Brendan's gang, the boys from the Hardy Street area, dared not walk.

Yet, the little skinhead pushed his concerns aside.

'I let her – and her mates – in for free,' he says, offering irrefutable evidence of his interest in the young lady.

'Then I asked her to dance and she said, "I wouldn't have anything to do with ya, ya sap." So I pursued her for six months, but she was always with her mates.

'She told me years later that she took terrible advantage of me. She would ring me up and say, "I saw a pair of Wranglers in a shop window in town."

'"What size are you?"

'"Ten."

'"Right, I'll sort it."

'And I would get her the jeans. And the following day she'd call and say, "I'd love another pair of those Wranglers." And I'd say, "A ten?" And she'd say, "No, get me an eight."

'The next week it would be a twelve. She was getting jeans for all her pals. And I knew this, of course. But it didn't matter. What mattered was she was interested in me. And I was captivated. Eventually, she agreed I could go to the pictures with her – but she'd bring her friends along as well.

'Meanwhile, my own mates were slagging me, telling me I was wasting my time. But it was a challenge for me. And I told my pals that once she had agreed to go out with me, I'd tell her to forget it.

'Anyway, I think what happened was I stopped ringing her. I didn't see her for maybe a week. And she rang me, saying, "I miss you." I said, "Tough, that's the way it goes." But we agreed to meet that night and she said she would go out with me.'

A first love always finds a way. But the way ahead was rocky.

'I told all my mates. And they said, "Right, when are you dumping her?" And I hummed a bit and said, "I never said I would definitely do that . . ."'

He didn't. And Brendan and Doreen became a couple. They conquered the gangland divide, and the relationship developed. The disco didn't, however. Brendan spent the profits on Wranglers and taxis, and the punters gradually fell away.

But now there were two women in Brendan's life. Since his father had died, his mother had been reliant upon the Special One more than ever, for company, conversation and laughter. The pair sparked off each other. But they argued with an intensity that only people who care for each other can do. And they loved to push each other to the limits.

Yet, although Brendan was precocious, determined to grow up as quickly as possible, he was in no rush to leave his mammy behind.

'When I was fifteen, Dublin Corporation decided that people should be able to buy their Corporation houses. And I remember the letter coming through the door at the time and I thought, "Jesus, I'll buy this!" But they wouldn't sell the house to me. They would only sell it to my mother and me, just in case I was the type to throw my mother out and they'd have to find another house for her.

'So we bought it in joint names, and I just gave her the money every week for it. It was seventeen hundred quid, thanks to the allowance we got for all the rent that had been paid previously. And that's what we did.'

The plan would later come back to haunt him. And there were other signs he was rushing in the direction of adulthood way too fast.

'I was mad into the dogs,' he recalls of visits to the racetrack. 'The thirty-second climax they used to call it, because that's all it takes for the fastest dog to run a race. What happened was that the first three times I went to the dogs, I won big. On the third occasion, I was only fourteen years of age, I had five shillings. And I won eight hundred and fifteen pounds, eighteen shillings and sixpence on that night. I thought, "This is easy." Big mistake.

'I was hooked, and it got worse as I got older. I used to get off the bus at Shelbourne Park on a Saturday night after getting my wages. I'd walk across the road to the bus stop where you got a bus back into town. But I'd lift the sod at the bus stop and put a 50p piece under the sod and leave it there so that I'd at least have my bus fare when I came out. I knew I was going in to lose my bollocks.

'Doreen used to bring me to the pictures on a Sunday night because I'd have no money left. She'd go out to the jacks – the toilet – and I'd be into her bag, snaring a fiver. Monday night, I'd go out to Harold's Cross with that fiver. She told me years later that she left a fiver in her purse, right there for me to get it every Sunday night. She knew me so well.

'The stupidity only slowly became apparent to me. One night, after winning on the sixth and seventh race, I came out with twenty-three quid. I got onto the bus. On the way home, I was so delighted. But I had gone in with thirty-five. Here I was, celebrating losing twelve pounds. I thought to myself, "This is sick!" I stopped that night. My life as a gambler was over.'

A racetrack gambler, perhaps. He'd gamble later in life, for far bigger stakes than a few weeks' wages.

CLEANING UP

BRENDAN was still playing the part of the perfect waiter. But in the meantime he took everything he could from the experience.

'I didn't see the job as simply serving people. For me it was a history lesson, it was about how the Ottomans introduced coffee to the West and the colour of the Capuchin monks' robes gave cappuccino its name. It was about developing people skills.'

Brendan drank in the knowledge. And he loved looking after people.

'After I served my apprenticeship, I began working at weddings, at the likes of Ashbourne House (in the wealthy North Dublin suburb where he would later live).

'I loved it when a young couple came to me in January, with the wedding planned for September, to play a part in making sure this was the happiest day of their lives.

'And I don't think anything has changed. You go on stage now and you present an experience, make it the very best it can be. You want the audience to remember who made the night that bit special.

'At sixteen I had qualified as a waiter and I was getting a full adult wage. And I was happy enough. But at seventeen, I remember one night in the hotel serving a bunch of guys who were at school with me who had come out to dinner to celebrate having passed their leaving exam. I remember thinking that night, "These guys might become doctors or lawyers or bank managers. I might have made a mistake." But it was a mistake I could live with.

'And, from seventeen on, I was always in and out of jobs. Sometimes I'd leave a job, sometimes I'd be headhunted, getting a bit more money each time. Always doing the best I could. I had a good work ethic. But, just as importantly, I had a belief all would be fine.

'My mother was always getting one of my brothers – who shall remain nameless – jobs. And I remember one time saying to her, "Jaysus, Ma, why don't you get *me* a job?" And she smiled and said, "You'll be all right, Brendan."

'She never, ever, said to me, "What are you going to do for the rest of your life?" And I suppose I wondered, "Did she not give a damn – or did she know something?" So one day I asked her about what I'd end up doing and she said, "Stop worrying, Brendan. Your future's assured."'

Brendan was happy to be seen as the best waiter in Dublin, but there were signs his eye was on something else.

'In 1972, I was a fresh-faced waiter in the Green Isle Hotel in Clondalkin. And every Saturday night we had a cabaret in the restaurant, with Norman Metcalf playing the organ and various artists plying their trade. I was lucky enough to have seen Cecil Sheridan there.'

Cecil Sheridan was a parody master, a panto king, a variety star at the likes of Dublin's Queen's Theatre and later the Olympia.

One of his stage characters was a larger-than-life Dublin woman, who was incredibly funny.

'I'd seen him perform as a kid and he was fantastic. This woman he'd played – I can't remember her name – stuck with me. I was so pleased to meet Cecil. And surprised to discover he had a terrible stutter, particularly as on stage there was no sign of one. "Doctor Theatre cures everything," he said to me.'

Sheridan gave the young waiter an insight into what makes an audience laugh. (And perhaps partly inspired Agnes Brown.) He got to see how Sheridan could take the nuances of a woman and create a character, but without playing her as outwardly feminine. And Brendan understood that a man playing a woman can get away with so much more than a female actress: there's a licence to be cheeky that comes with drag – if done right. Cecil Sheridan had managed to get the line just right, offering a heightened, but believable woman. And Sheridan had a lovely, whimsical sense of humour.

'He told me he was at the Metropole Ballroom in Dublin and went to the toilets where you had to put a penny in the slot. A guy coming out of a cubicle held it open for him so he got in for nothing. When he came out, the janitor said to Cecil, "I see you got a freebie there!" Cecil insisted on giving him the penny, telling him he would not like to get him into trouble if he were stocktaking for each motion. He told that story on stage and the place fell apart. And he explained the joke didn't work just because it was risqué. He said it worked because people recognised the truth in it. I think Mrs Brown works because people recognise the essential truth in her.'

Yet, while Brendan was a Sheridan fan, the Saturday night star that shone brightest for him was Hal Roach, the Irish comedy legend whose catchphrase was, 'Write it down.'

'He was a genius. He stood, his left heel tucked into the arch of his right foot, his hand pulling on an invisible beard as if he were searching for the next story. He'd come out with surreal gags like: "Murphy found himself very late one night in London in the Underground subway station. He walked along to the escalator. And on the escalator it was written, 'Dogs must be carried on the escalator.' And he thought, 'God, where am I going to find a dog at this hour of the night?'"

'I watched and learnt and laughed and laughed. I would serve him a cup of coffee after his act and then I'd go home and do his whole stand-up routine for my mother, who would be in stitches.

'One night, I worked up the courage and said to him, "Mr Roach, I want to be a comedian."

'"Son, there is no such thing as a comedian under thirty years of age."

'"Mr Roach, I think I am going to be the biggest comedian in Ireland before I'm twenty-five."

'"My God. I think I'm going to have one of my turns!"'

Brendan learned a great deal from Hal Roach, about comic timing, about movement and expression.

'Look closely at Mrs Brown. Even Agnes Brown's voice has a little bit of Hal in there, if you listen closely.'

While talking to Hal Roach, Brendan had articulated what had always been inside his head. He already knew he was funny. Other waiters constantly told him he was funny. But for the first time he had admitted he wanted to be a comedian. Brendan had had the thought in his head for some time. But he had never had the confidence to release it. He would have been laughed at, he felt. Now, though, here he was working with a man who'd had a career in the business.

But how to achieve his stated ambition? Brendan took his first step into the entertainment world a year later with a stint on ARD, Alternative Radio Dublin, where he appeared on a kids' show, as Uncle Brendy – The Kiddies' Friend. Brendan had read in the *Dublin Herald* how the radio station was looking for volunteers and had offered his services. Yet he was drawn to comedy, and was helped by a chance encounter with bearded Irish entertainer Brendan Grace.

Grace was hugely popular across the country, famous for his 'Bottler' act, where he'd dress up as a scampish schoolboy (echoes of Jimmy Krankie) and appear regularly at venues like the Drake Inn.

One night, the two Brendans got talking and the youngster agreed to go to work for the legend as his assistant, driving him around and making sure he was looked after. The young O'Carroll hoped greatness would rub off on him and he watched and learned and helped his comedy master with his scripts.

After a couple of years, the Sorcerer and his Apprentice parted, but not before Brendan reckoned he had learned enough to try his hand as a solo performer.

'What I learned from Brendan Grace was if you tell the audience you're a star, they'll believe you. But you can't go out half-hearted.'

This was Brendan playing the part. And when a Dublin-wide talent competition was held in the Drake Inn, Brendan entered as a stand-up comedian. Incredibly, he won the £100 prize. Just as importantly, he was now recognised in the community as a funny guy.

'Brendan became a star that night,' says Gerry Browne, who would later become Brendan's partner, and who was working that night as a glass collector.

'He went up there on stage and blew the audience away, telling them little stories about his life in Finglas, stuff everyone could identify with. It was like watching a young Billy Connolly. Brendan had that hall in stitches.'

Yet, although his mammy had told him he could fly, waiters don't drop trays and become entertainers. Not when they're from Finglas and financially bereft. Do they? And Maureen O'Carroll didn't ever say, 'Brendan, you really should be on the stage.' Hers was a quiet encouragement, and he knew his mammy would always support whichever path he took.

But she wasn't so quiet in other areas. Every so often arguments would break out, the fierceness of which could have necessitated negotiation by UN peacekeeping forces.

Once, Brendan took his mother to Quinn's supermarket and he was in a hurry, ready to get off to a football match. Maureen went to get some shopping, saying she'd be five minutes at most. Twenty minutes later, no Mammy. So Brendan approached the security guards at the front of the store and told them his mother was inside, but she had no money in her purse. He added she had a mental condition and would most likely steal everything she could get her hands on. Could they just remove her safely? Maureen was thrown out, effin' and blindin' as she was bundled into the car.

Later that night, she was still irate, and still keeping up the argument until Brendan said, 'I'm tellin' you now, Ma. If you keep this up I'm going to steal your teeth.'

And she did. And he did. Before you could say 'Steradent', he had her false teeth in his hand. And he put them in his pocket and went out for the night.

But while Maureen O'Carroll and her son would often go at it hammer and tongs and niggle each other constantly, they laughed just as much. She loved the laughter he created. And she knew he adored her. Even if he stole the teeth from her mouth.

But what he also took from his mother was her mantra: never compromise. And grab life with both hands while you can. As a teenager, that already made sense to him. He'd lost his dad, one of his best friends in John Breen. And now the other . . .

'Jimmy Matthews was killed in a car accident, aged eighteen, on the night of his engagement.'

Brendan adds, reflectively: 'Never did the death of Jimmy or John scare me. I was never afraid of death. I always thought I was invincible.'

But in real life Brendan was less Superman and more Clark Kent, still a freelance waiter and hoping that work such as Aer Lingus Catering would take him on to bigger things. Such as the Irish Open Golf Championship.

'I'd work at the golf for four days, for example, and get a month's wages. One time I picked up a thousand-pound tip. And at the end of the stint I bought a car on the money I made.'

He had the car, and the girlfriend. And with the girlfriend came the girlfriend's mother. Dolly Dowdall was another larger-than-life Dublin woman to whom Brendan became close. (He would later dedicate his novel, *The Chisellers*, to Dolly). Dolly Dowdall worked in the street markets, just like Agnes. Her husband was ill with a bad back, just like Agnes. And Dolly had to become the breadwinner. Dolly also lived for her family; she battled to make sure her five girls grew up to be fine young ladies. And Dolly would later be absorbed into the character of Agnes Brown, both funny and wicked.

But she had money problems. Or rather, she had a problem paying money back.

'Dolly borrowed nine quid from a money-lender, to pay it back at a pound a week. But she got into difficulties. And after a couple of months, the debt, with compound interest, was over five hundred.

'So I went along to see this loan shark, who was based in a Dublin pub. In an office off the side of the bar, the "secretary" said the guy I was looking for wasn't in.

'"I'll wait."

'"But he could be out all day," said the barmaid.

'"Well, I'll still wait."'

And he did. He sat down and waited. And as he looked around he could see the office from the bar. And he waited. And he saw the secretary pick up the phone and speak very quietly.

Brendan realised there was an adjacent office.

'I thought to myself, "He's here!"

'So I walked right through the office door, and up to the guy's desk. And I slammed the debt books right on top of it. And I said to him, "You will charge no more money on this account. That's the end of it."'

And he slammed the books down again, just for added dramatic effect. And made his grand exit.

'Except that I didn't,' he says, with a look of mock horror on his face.

'I had worked up to this big moment and was so focused on being angry instead of walking out the door, I charged straight into a walk-in cupboard. And I slammed it behind me.

'And now, here I was, standing in the dark in a cupboard. And then I had to walk back out again, and walk out the real office door.'

Brendan might have had to suffer a little ignominy, but Dolly Dowdall never again heard from the money-lender.

Yet, while he solved Dolly's immediate problem, he was doing his best to pay the mortgage at home in Finglas, to make ends meet, working all the hours he could. He would finish waiting tables at seven o'clock and then start a cleaning job at nine.

'I took a job working for Jeyes, the company that makes toilet products.'

He adds, grinning, 'And here's the thing: I love cleaning away. It's quite weird. If I go into a supermarket in America and find myself in the detergent aisle, I'm salivating. But I loved the job. I made sure I was a great cleaner. In fact, I introduced a new cleaning system in that place and the bosses agreed to introduce it. It saved them a fortune.'

He has an explanation for the hard work, other than the satisfaction you can achieve from doing a job well.

'Somewhere in my mind, I'm convinced that I'm lazy, that I'd rather be on the couch watching television. And because I know that, I work doubly hard to prove I'm not lazy.

'So when I was in Jeyes I wanted to run the factory. If I see something, in any business, I try and sort out a problem.'

Meanwhile his relationship with Doreen was moving forward. Brendan says it had its own momentum. 'We grew to be great friends. And when I joined a football club, Doreen got on with the other players' girlfriends. It was all cosy, and everyone we knew seemed to be getting married all of a sudden. And before we knew what was happening, we were getting married too.'

Brendan, heavily prompted by his mother, went to see a priest to make his confession, with the idea that his soul would be scrubbed clean for the start of his new married life.

'But instead I ended up getting into an argument with the priest. He'd asked me to confess how much I drank, and I told him I didn't really drink much at all, which was true. But he insisted I was lying and I should confess all. I was fuming. And that was me done with confessing.'

The wedding itself wasn't the wondrous day he'd have hoped for.

'I remember thinking it didn't feel like magic. But then, I couldn't picture life without Doreen either. And it wasn't that there was someone else in my life. She was the business.

'I also remember panicking a bit, thinking, "What if this isn't real love, it's more a brother/sister love? And what if someone bumps into me in the street in five years' time, and I suddenly fall in love . . .?"

'But I reconciled myself and reminded myself that I had made a promise.'

Brendan and Doreen, both aged 19, announced their wedding and, on 18 July 1975, they walked down the aisle of St Canice's Church in Finglas.

Brendan had told his mother that the Archbishop of Dublin would be joining the couple in Holy Matrimony. She laughed. This was of course another of Brendan's wind-ups. Except that it wasn't. The Archbishop did indeed perform the ceremony.

Maureen O'Carroll was delighted. And she would drop it into every conversation for months to come. However, his mammy wasn't convinced the relationship would work out.

'She felt it could go either way. My mother wasn't sure if we were going through life at the same speed. She'd say, "Opportunity is a train that goes in a circle. And it keeps coming round. But it never stops. And the only way you can get on that train is to jump on it. But you can't jump with a weight on your back. Whoever is with you will have to jump by themselves. And someday, whoever is with you will have to jump on that train.

"'That's the way it will happen, Brendan. I hope that Doreen will jump with you.'"

Would Doreen jump?

HE'S A LUCKY GOD

THERE was no doubt that if Brendan could see a train going past headed towards opportunity, he'd leap onto it.

Now aged 21, he and Doreen were renting a house in Donaghmede, North Dublin.

'I reckoned I would buy it when a mate who owned it emigrated. But at this time, you had to have a third of the price for a deposit and to have been saving it for four years with the bank.

'However, a pal who worked for the Corporation said he could get me a Corporation loan. The house was nine thousand quid and he said he'd fix this up, no problem.'

But there *was* a problem.

'The next week when we met up he said he couldn't get me a loan. I asked why and he said, "Because you've already got a mortgage."

'"What?"

'"Yes, you own a house in Finglas that you're paying up."

'It was my mother's house, of course. And I offered to pay off the loan on my mother's but I was told that as a citizen you can only get a Corporation loan once, it was designed to give people a start on the ladder.

'So I told me mammy the story and said, "What shall we do?"

'And she came back, immediately, with, "Here's what you do. You and Doreen move in here." Of course, I had mixed feelings about this. So I said to me mam, "Look, I don't want to stay here. I want to move up. And when I move up I want you to move up with us."

'She asked where I was planning to move to and I told her about the dream house in Ashbourne, seven miles up the road from Finglas, but a world away.

'I said, "Look, Mam, I want us to live in a house with central heating. We've only got one fire in this house."

'"Well, Jaysus, I'm with you, Brendan."

'So we put the house up for sale and got twenty-one thousand pounds for it, putting the whole lot into the new house, at Ninety-Two Deer Park, with underfloor heating, the lot. And a very low mortgage.'

The mammy and son – and his new wife – in the same house? Well, it didn't, as you would expect, run entirely smoothly.

'My mam did her own thing but there were times when she and Doreen were at loggerheads.

'In the early days it was tough because I would come home and me mam would say, "There's your dinner." And then Doreen would come in from work later, cook, and ask me, "Why are you not eating your dinner?" So I used to eat both.'

They all managed to coexist, the biggest downside being Brendan's expanding girth.

'And I got to talk to my mother more and more. We had great discussions.'

Brendan and his mammy would still argue ferociously. 'But not about anything trivial. It was always about something major.'

The family triangle had moved up in the world, but the income had to support that. And Brendan, now 21, badly wanted a career beyond waiting tables.

'One of the things I did shortly after I got married was to try and become a farmer. So I rented out some acreage in North County Dublin and began to grow things.

'I knew from the hotel business that the most difficult part of being a chef was preparing the vegetables, so I bought myself a peeler and peeled the potatoes for the hotel. And I also did ready-prepared vegetables such as sprouts, chopped carrots and turnips, the sort of things you can buy in supermarkets now.

'It was one of the nicest jobs I ever had, out in the field in the summer, delivering the produce to the hotels, and I loved watching everything grow, picking the celery or whatever at the right time.

'But at the end of the year I did all the sums and broke even. Talk about naive. I didn't realise that most businesses struggle to survive the first year and to break even was pretty good. I had the ideas, but not the wherewithal to make it all work.'

He had to make it all work. Doreen announced she was pregnant. Brendan was thrilled at the idea of becoming a father. But now the pressure was on him to provide.

His next venture was into the world of publishing.

'I got a job selling advertising with a company called *Soccer Reporter* and they produced a football magazine. But we also had the contract with the Irish Football Association to sell advertising into their 15,000 programmes, which we'd make and give over for nothing, but we'd get all the advertising revenue.'

Brendan loved the challenge.

On 23 February 1979, Doreen gave birth to a son, whom the couple decided would be called Brendan. But the tiny little boy was born with hydrocephalus spina bifida.

'The doctors said, "Your baby is in The Holy Angels' Ward." They had had to operate on him while he was still in the womb, to remove fluid from the brain. But every time they removed fluid, it would damage him. As a result, he was born blind. Then the next thing we discovered was that he was paralysed, and I remember kneeling and begging God to take him – for selfish reasons, because I didn't think I could cope. I didn't even want to see him because he had no longer become the baby I had pictured in my head. Then the doctors let me see him. I saw he was lying on his side with tape running down his back covering the spine, and his left foot was badly turned and his head swollen. God love him, he was a mess.

'Then a voice behind me declared, "He's a beautiful child, Brendan." I said, "He doesn't look so bad." The doctor let me put my two hands into the incubator and hold Brendan, who had the biggest blue eyes I'd ever seen. And he *was* beautiful. Just beautiful. I held his little hands and of course bravado kicked in. And I said, "Well, when can I have him home?" And the doctor said, "Mr O'Carroll, you'll never have him home. Brendan could live for three days, three weeks, three months. But I hope for your sake it's three days. And if he ends up an angel in God's garden, he's a lucky God."'

A day later, Brendan, who doesn't believe in organised religion but does believe in a God, prayed. 'I was in the Shamrock Lodge, went into a cubicle in the toilet and cried.

I got on my knees and prayed God would take this child because I couldn't cope with the baby and the fear that Doreen would never walk again.'

Doreen had had two epidurals, and still had no feeling in her legs. She was also having dreadful dreams about the Devil trying to pull her out of bed. Brendan feared his wife was going to die.

On the third day, the doctor announced, 'Mr O'Carroll, I have bad news for you, your son died at three o'clock.'

He said it, but can see this may make him look callous. Yes, Brendan replied 'You frightened the life out of me. I thought it was going to be something really serious.'

He was joking. It was his only way of coping. Brendan was absolutely devastated. He now shudders at the memory.

'And when God did take him, it was my fault and I thought, "Oh, Jesus. What did I do to deserve that?" But you see I had prepared in my mind the white picket fence, swing in the garden, taking him to the zoo. I had all these things planned and all the plans went out the window. And I couldn't find peace in myself.'

The doctor suggested Brendan told his wife the tragic news. But he couldn't, at first.

'But then I finally told her Brendan was dead. We had a mutual cry. A few days later, Doreen began to walk again.'

His world in turmoil, Brendan left the magazine. There was now an incredible strain on the marriage. Doreen was struggling with a deep depression that was to last six months.

'We nearly had a major falling out. It was so hard. I was working my guts out and coming home to complete chaos, and I felt I couldn't take it any more. I had to explain that I was feeling that way because I'd lost a son too, and I, finally, wanted the right to mourn, to focus on my grief.

'One morning, Doreen woke up glowing, a changed woman. She'd had an incredible dream where this nun came around carrying in her arms what seemed like a bunch of flowers, or sometimes a baby. And Doreen said, "Brendan, everything's going to be okay." From that moment, she never looked back.'

THE MAMMY'S FINAL BOW

BRENDAN had been trying a range of jobs. He'd returned to waiting, had a go at window-cleaning; he did whatever he could to earn money. Nothing lasted long. Then, on 14 September 1979, Doreen O'Carroll gave birth to a gorgeous brown-eyed little girl. The couple named her Fiona, after Brendan's sister.

The new arrival stretched the family purse further.

'I was sitting out in the back garden one afternoon, reading a newspaper and wondering what to do. I'd sold my car and bought a van, thinking it might be useful. Just then, Doreen came out and said, "We've no money."

'"But you've got the unemployment benefit. I gave it to you on Thursday."

'"It's all gone."

'"Shit."

'So she went back inside and I had this idea. I picked up the phone and rang the *Irish Independent* newspaper and asked for the circulation section. A voice came on and I asked who the boss was while I could hear the machines going in the background. I got the answer "Tommy Curran". So I asked for Tommy and this voice came on the line.

'"Hello Tommy, it's Brendan O' Carroll."

'"Who?"

'"Brendan. Brendan O' Carroll. You asked me to give you a shout if you needed any labourers."

'"Oi did?"

'"Sure, you did. But listen, if there's nothing going don't worry about it."

'"Oh well, I don't want to let you down."

'"Don't worry about it . . ."

'"Look, I'm all right for tonight, but ring Bob Naylor in the *Sunday World*."

'So I did. And said, "Bob, it's Brendan O' Carroll. Tommy said to give you a ring about some work."

'"Can you operate a saddle-stitcher?"

'Now, I hadn't a clue what he was talking about. "Sure I can."

'"Well, I'll see you in here at seven o'clock."

'I turned up, and Bob explained there was work going on the collating machine already. Would I mind stacking pallets for the time being?

'I said, "No, not at all." Stacking pallets was easy. So I stacked and I was fast. I worked hard. And all the time I was watching the bloke work the saddle-stitcher, the machine that held the papers together. I realised it was all about how you fed the machine, fanned the paper, and so forth.

'Later that night Bob said to me, "Right we're puttin' you on the saddle-stitcher."

'And I was shittin' myself. If the machine was fed wrongly, the whole line broke down.

'Well, I don't know where God is, but that night he was watching over me. That night I got through it. And I got paid.

'My social security at that time, a married man with one kid, was thirty quid. But Bob came down with a cheque for fifty-eight quid. For one night's work. I was in raptures.

'Bob then asked me if I was available for a Wednesday shift, working on the *Farmer's Journal* and the other magazines. Later in the canteen he came up to me and asked if I was the bloke with the van. I said yes, and he asked if I fancied doing a run, near Finglas. He said there would be sixty quid in it for me. I said, "Load the feckin' thing up."

'I came home with one hundred and eighteen quid for a night's work. And I kept on doing the paper work, even when I got a proper job.'

The mind was never short of an idea.

'In Ireland at this time we had the *TV Times*, the *Radio Times*, *RTÉ Times*, but we had no *TV Guide*. So I came up with this idea for a magazine that would cover all of the television stories, with all the TV programmes.

'The next stage was to get a meeting with Fergal Quinn.'

Fergal Quinn Senior has a chain of supermarkets in Ireland. In fact, the Superquinn store in Finglas had been the scene of the Sellotape and bicycle-lock robbery that had landed the young Brendan in the reform school.

'I managed to get a meeting with him – I'd once worked at his house as a waiter – and I walked into his office and he said, "Brendan – you've got three minutes."

'And so I pitched him the idea and he asked how much I was going to charge for the publication. I said nothing. It would be given away free at the supermarket checkouts.

'The idea was he would get exclusivity in his supermarket alone. And at the end of the three minutes he said, "Okay. Let's do it." There was only one condition, that if he had an ongoing legal dispute with any of the advertisers, then I couldn't give them space. But that didn't represent a problem.'

Brendan was in. With an incredible idea he was set to become a millionaire. Offices were rented and Brendan went to the bank and secured a loan. He worked hard on designing the magazine, using the grid system of daily reference that all magazines use today.

'We got the first dummy issue produced and it looked amazing. We got it round to the advertisers and they were blown away with it.'

But when something looks too good to be true, it usually is. The Friday before the magazine launch, a courier arrived at the office door. It was a notice of impending legal proceedings. RTÉ were suing Brendan for breaching the copyright on their programmes. And they sent the same legal notices to Superquinn.

'The problem was that the BBC and ITV owned the rights to publicise their programmes. Now, we could have taken them on in court and perhaps won. And it's since been shown that every magazine on the planet can show TV listings. But to establish the precedent would have meant using up all our money. And all that would happen is then someone else would put out the same magazine.'

What else to try? Especially as, on 15 October 1983, Doreen gave birth to a healthy little blue-eyed boy, Danny.

However, Brendan's mammy wasn't enjoying the best of health. Now 71, she certainly wasn't old, but her general tiredness had increased and Maureen would take to her bed more often. And not for dramatic purpose. Doctors diagnosed heart problems.

'I could see my mammy was becoming more and more worn out,' he says, the voice still echoing the sadness of the time.

One afternoon, Maureen O'Carroll took baby Danny upstairs to lie down with her. She never woke up.

'And nothing could be done. But before she died she made me promise that I'd do two things for her.

'"Ma, like what?"

'"Sure, don't let me die in hospital. I don't want to die amongst strangers. I want to die with my family around."

'"Sure Ma, if I can organise that I will."

'"And I want to die on a sunny day."

'"Hell, Ma, I don't have any control over that."

'Danny was ten months old at the time and she died cradling him in her arms. And yes, it was on a sunny day.'

Brendan has never had a day since when he hasn't thought about his mother. They were bound together with a connection that's unbreakable. When Agnes Brown talks about loving her kids so much, even if they are 3,000 miles away, she says there is still an umbilical cord attached.

The inspiration for Brendan's stage show moment comes from real life. That is Maureen O'Carroll speaking.

'At least there was nothing left unsaid. We knew exactly how we felt about each other. I wasn't standing over the coffin saying, "If only." It doesn't get better than that.'

Brendan's thoughts on the death of his mother are contained, conflated, edited. He strives to give the impression he's at one with her passing, accepting of the belief this was a lady who'd had a good life, was loved by her family and had made a mark – and has moved on.

But that's not the reality. It's rare to spend time with Brendan without Maureen O'Carroll appearing in the room in the form of an anecdote or a reference such as 'My mother would have feckin' loved seeing a character like Agnes Brown on stage.' Whenever he offers up nuggets of wisdom, he will all too often reveal his mammy to be the source. He says he had enough time to share his thoughts with his mother, but it's hard to believe that now. Brendan shares his thoughts with his mother every day, believing she can hear them, believing they are still connected. Brendan doesn't grieve for his mother, and that's perhaps because she still hasn't departed his life. And she never will. Maureen O'Carroll left her mark outside the family. Her political legacy is recorded in the history books. And there's no doubt her shoulder was one of the strongest in pushing the boulder of women's rights up the hill.

Meanwhile, what was Brendan to do? He'd tried his hand at farming, publishing, window-cleaning, just about anything that would keep him away from the 1980s dole queues. And steady, well-paid work had dried up and life was a struggle.

One night, he was given a real clue as to where his future might lie. But it was small, and it escaped him.

'I went along with a group of friends to attend one of these murder-mystery nights, but instead of being supplied with a script to act out, I wrote it myself. It was full of colour. I gave all the characters big descriptions. And you wouldn't believe the threads I included in that story. It got to the stage that there were so many clues and red herrings that not even the murderer knew he was the murderer.

'I'd never felt so satisfied in my life. Of course, I hadn't worked out why I'd enjoyed this occasion so much. But the idea of holding the interest of a group of people was really satisfying. I knew when I was telling this story I had my pals in the palm of my hands. Honestly, it felt fantastic. Yet, feeling that and knowing what to do with that sort of skill is something else.'

In 1984, however, Brendan seemed to have exhausted his business ideas and was back waiting on tables at the Department of Foreign Affairs.

'I didn't feel it was beneath me. Nor was I intimidated. I always had the ability to accept my position in any situation. And I knew I would always do my best. While working in the department, my feeling was that these guys were getting the best waiter they could on that day.'

However, some people believed he was destined for greater things. 'Once I waited at a function attended by Dick Spring, the Deputy Prime Minister, and he was on his way to Foreign Affairs where I was serving lunch.

'Now, of course my Mother had been a TD. And as Dick passed the kitchen, he called out, "Brendan!", gave me his business card and said, "If you ever want to run for your mother's seat, give me a shout."

'I was taken aback. I was a waiter. And here was the Deputy Prime Minister telling me he would help me to become an MP if I fancied the idea. This was all too surreal.'

Brendan would later think seriously about moving into politics.

Meanwhile, his work at Dublin Castle was to bring him into contact with one of the most challenging customers he had ever served. The Iron Lady. Ireland was offered its third presidency of the EEC in 1984, and Brendan was hired by the Department of Protocol to work on the event in which Ireland played host to heads of state from around the world.

But he was halted in his tracks when he discovered he'd be serving the UK Prime Minister, Margaret Thatcher. He hated the woman's politics. How could a working-class boy from North Dublin brought up in near poverty not hate them? Or even begin to like the woman?

'And it was an odd feeling for me. I didn't even have a car at the time, so I'd have to hitch a lift to be able to wait tables for the likes of the President of the United States.

'That first morning, I got into this Volkswagen minibus, and I jumped in and said, "Thanks, lads. I'm off to Dublin Castle. Where are you headed?" And one bloke replied, "So are we."

'"Great. Let's go."

'So I closed the door, looked around and realised I was in a van with Sinn Fein. It was full of placards protesting against Reagan and so on. And I thought, "I can't get out of this van at the castle with this lot." So I said, "Lads, could you drop me off before the castle?"

'So they dropped me off at Christchurch a couple of miles away and I walked all the way up to the castle.'

At the castle, Brendan had to go through security training.

'Once we had been cleared by security we were told, "One of you six will be serving the top table." What this meant was, if President Reagan, for example, wanted something, it would be relayed via the head of security, who would then signal the head waiter who would then signal the waiters. It was all about waiting for signals.

'But this didn't sit right with me. As we were being addressed I said, "Excuse me, can I bring something up? I'm a waiter and if I hear someone say, 'Excuse me, can . . .' my first instinct is to say, 'Yes, can I help you?' What if I do that?" And the security man said, "You'll have one hole there," pointing to my forehead, "and about six bullets in your body."

'I'm telling you, some of the waiters rattled with nerves carrying the soup course to the top table.'

Though Mrs Thatcher managed, surprisingly, to calm Brendan's nerves.

'I gave her the first-ever drink when she arrived on Irish soil at the President's Palace. But although I wasn't predisposed to like her, there was something about her that I thought was class.

'I was introduced to her by the head waiter, George Buckley, who said, "Mrs Thatcher, this is Brendan, who'll be looking after you." And I offered her a drink and she said she'd love an Irish whiskey. Now, there was a little interval as she was having a sip and she said to me, "Now, tell me Brendan. Will you be with us for the next four days?"

'She asked if I had a family. And I said, "Yes, two children," and I told her the kids' names, Fiona and Danny.

'She smiled and said she would try not to be too much trouble.'

He remembered two things in particular about Mrs Thatcher. 'She ordered hot milk and pepper, to be taken in her room, for her indigestion.' (More than a decade later, when offered an entertainment show with Irish broadcaster RTÉ, Brendan had to think of an off-the-wall title and said, 'Just call it "Hot Milk And Pepper".')

'And the second was I've never seen anyone work so hard.'

He was also struck by her grace, but reveals he tested it to the limit.

'On the final day, the catering staff were really pressed for time, trying to get lunch finished because Mrs Thatcher had to make a one o'clock speech that would be on the news, filmed during this lunch.

'It was a nightmare, with four hundred people there, and my job was to make up the dessert, which was fresh strawberries.

'And as I served her Mrs Thatcher said; "Excuse me, Brendan, could I have some caster sugar?" I ran into the temporary kitchen, found a dessert dish, and cut open the white bag, stuck a spoon in it and put it in front of Mrs Thatcher just before the cameras came on. Just then the head waiter announced, "Clear up!" and we were moved back into an adjoining room as the Irish Prime Minister began to speak.

'At this point I looked at Mrs Thatcher on the television monitor. She picked up the teaspoon and sprinkled her strawberries. She swallowed a mouthful, and I watched her expression and she held a smile on her face the whole time. But I just knew there was something wrong. I looked back at the bag I'd taken the sugar from. It was salt.

'The blood drained from my face as I watched her pick up a strawberry, dip it into the salt, and swallow it. And she got up, made a speech that brought the house down. And you know, I never heard a word of complaint about that.

'At the end of that trip, Mrs Thatcher and Geoffrey Howe were sitting at reception in one of the rooms at Dublin Castle, waiting for the helicopter. I asked her, "Prime Minister, would you like a drink before you leave?" She ordered a coffee and, as she sipped it, she turned to me and said, "I bet you're glad it's all over, Brendan. And I'm sure Fiona and Danny will be delighted to see you."

'Well, I was taken aback. I had told her the names four days before. Once. And I thought, "That's class."'

While Brendan rated Maggie's manner and professionalism, not all of the heads of state merited the same praise.

'The King and Queen of Denmark were grand, but I remember Robert Mugabe (the Zimbabwean President) was something scary. He walked in surrounded by his ministers and cohorts and you never saw a group of people that looked more like a gang of thugs. They wouldn't be out of place as bouncers in the worst nightclub in Glasgow.'

Brendan never sought to climb the catering ladder, despite his diplomatic skills and popularity. 'All I was thinking was, "I'm going to get up today and make someone's day."'

Did he really love waiting on tables? He didn't want to be where he was, hence the constant movement. He was looking for options. Continually. He'd already confessed his desire to become a comedian to Hal Roach. And he had worked with Brendan Grace to the same end. Deep down he wanted to become an entertainer. But he couldn't entertain that thought. Waiters can't just suddenly become performers.

What he seemed to be doing was living life day by day.

'I'm not sure,' he says, smiling. 'I suppose I might have thought I'd like to own my own restaurant someday. But you just didn't look beyond what you knew. I certainly didn't have a grand plan.

'And if there was ever a Plan A, when I was at school or whatever, it never happened. I'm on Plan J or somewhere, way down the alphabet.'

He might not have had a grand plan, but he admits he's never been content.

'Should life always be about chasing the dream? I knew a guy who was a roofer, and in the morning he went off and fixed his roofs, got home, had a bath, watched TV and went to bed. This routine would continue, except for weekends when he'd have a couple of drinks. And he was perfectly happy with that. He knew his life routine. And I used to look at him and wish it were me. Just so I could relax.'

Brendan will never relax. He needs to be moving forward, trying out new schemes, new strategies. He was always driven.

'You feel out of sync with the world until you realise it's just the way you are. You need that new challenge.'

And it would appear. A Herculean one at that.

BETWEEN BEIRUT AND BAGHDAD

BRENDAN, despite his reservations about being promoted, had spread his wings a little and in 1986 was working as a restaurant manager in the Ashbourne House Hotel, close to his home.

'We had a bar manager there, Kevin Moore, and Kevin was brilliant,' he recalls one night in Derry, many years later, after a Mrs Brown show.

'He was great with people, really likeable. Great at keeping things together. Then, one day, one of the customers in the hotel, a bloke called Grimes who ran an auctioneer's business and knew me from Finglas, came over to me and said, "Look, you're probably the best waiter I know. And everyone from Finglas says good things about you. So I've an offer for you. Have you ever heard of the Finglas Castle?"

'I knew it was a new business, a lounge bar/club built in the shape of a castle, right on the border between Ballymun and Finglas.'

Brendan adds, grinning, 'Now, that was like having a pub between Beirut and Baghdad. It was in a war zone. These two places did not see eye to eye.

'So Grimes and his partner had built the pub – but they couldn't run it, with the gangs around and all. It was an almost impossible task. And it was taking its toll on them, physically and financially.

'This developer said to me, "Look, we want you to take it over." I said I had no money, but he was adamant that there had to be some way to make it work. So I designed a deal whereby we would agree a price for the pub, which would be about three hundred and fifty thousand pounds. Kevin and I would rent it off them for three years, at a rent of four thousand a month. And we got the first three months rent free.

'And at the end of the three years we'd buy it, but with a reduction of twenty-five per cent of all the rent we'd given them.

'So we shook hands on the deal. It made sense for everybody. This made the deal self-financing. We could get credit from the brewers, the food suppliers, and we knew we could do well.'

The sums added up, but what Brendan also had going for him, besides the ability to construct a deal, were two things: his popularity in the community and the fact he wasn't afraid of a little friction. He'd boxed as a teenager. He could handle himself. And he knew how to handle the bad boys.

It all looked fantastic. Brendan, a local boy, who had built up a great reputation in the catering industry, was someone the brewers could trust to run a tight ship, and he and Kevin knew what they were doing.

The first thing Brendan did was change the name to something more neutral. The pub became The Abbot's Castle.

'Now the abbot is a priest and no one could take offence at a priest. We also opened a nightclub in the building called The Jolly Friar and, to make sure it worked, we stopped the bad boys coming in.'

'Of course when the bad boys were denied admission there were threats of the "Do you know who I am? I'll be back to shoot you!" kind to deal with.

'There were loads,' says Brendan, his voice reflecting the mild indifference he'd displayed at the time.

'There was one really bad family, and I barred them. All of them. I was told the place would be burnt down and I'd be shot. I said, "Make sure you get me first time. Because you'll only get one chance."

'I never heard from them again but, about eight months later, I was taking a booking from a nice family for a wedding. And a couple of days before the function I was called up and the bloke who'd booked the function declared that the bad family were his relations.

'I said, "Oh, then I think we could have a problem."

'"I know, but we want to bring the three brothers along. And I can guarantee nothing will happen."

'"You don't have to guarantee me anything. I know nothing will happen. But the easiest way we can both make sure of having a good night is to not have them here. And you don't have a problem because you can tell them it's not you, it's me that won't have them here."

'"Brendan, we really would like them at the do."

'"Okay. For one night only. But I'm telling you now. If they cause any trouble I won't be going after them. I'll be coming to find you."

'So he took responsibility. But that night of the wedding yer man who'd first approached me was watching me and I was watching him.

'Later that night he came over and said, "Listen, that night you barred me. I was putting a gang together to come up and burn this place down. But, and this is a compliment to you, I couldn't get anyone to join me. Everybody I asked didn't want to know. They were either afraid of you or you had helped them out. Fair play to you."

'"Am I supposed to be complimented by that?"

'"Listen, you've seen what we're about tonight. We've behaved ourselves, we're a family who likes to enjoy ourselves. Are you going to lift the ban, Brendan?"

'"No. After tonight you're gone."

'And he was. I never saw nor heard from him again.'

Brendan had created Switzerland, a neutral territory in which people could enjoy themselves. It was that simple. He worked for almost four years, putting in every hour possible, without taking a single holiday. And The Abbot's Castle began to make money. The former waiter was well on his way to becoming a successful businessman.

He'd also found a new friend in the charismatic Gerry Browne, a tall, talented musician who would come to play a part in shaping Brendan's future life and career. (In fact, the pair would become so close that Brendan would dedicate his first book, *The Mammy*, to his chum with the line, '*A man I care about. And one who cares about me.*')

But the pair didn't hit it off straight away. Brendan reckoned that Gerry Browne came from a family of 'gobshites' (Gerry had ten brothers, one or two of them rather vocal in their opinions). And they had grown up in opposite ends of Finglas, the line between west and east separating the two tribes who were often going to war.

'I wasn't too sure about a couple of Gerry's brothers,' says Brendan with a wry smile. 'Gerry was a musician, a talented fella who had formed his own show band, Tinker's Fancy, and was part of the local music scene. But such was the feeling that existed between us, when Gerry first came to The

Abbot's Castle looking to play there, I told him no. I wanted nothing to do with him. Then one night, about three weeks later, I turned up to a party in a block in Ballymun where Gerry was playing guitar and entertaining people. And he was good. Very good. When Gerry took breaks I'd crack a few gags and win them over.'

The Finglas tribal war was being played out in a tower-block party.

'I reckoned I had the audience,' says Brendan, with a grin. 'Anyway, later on I was in the kitchen making myself a coffee when Gerry walked in.

'"Sure. I'll have one of those, Brendan. Two sugars."

'"See that? Coffee. Spoon. Kettle? Make your own."

'"You don't like me much, do you?"

'"What gave you that idea?"

'"Look, you don't know me, to be making these judgements. Let me tell you about myself . . ."

'And he did. And we got to talking for the longest time and I came to realise he wasn't a bad sort of fella at all.'

Gerry wasn't. And the friendship developed after Gerry and his band came to play at The Abbot's Castle on Sunday mornings.

Brendan was still casting around for new directions, and appeared willing to take guidance from any source, however unlikely.

'My sister Eilish lived in London at the time. And she was mad about spiritualism. And so was my former boss in Ashbourne, and she'd given me this phone number, saying to pass it on to Eilish as she'd found this spiritualist brilliant.

'Now, I happened to be in London, with some time on my hands. I'd never been to a spiritualist in my life so I thought

I'd give it a go. I rang the number, a woman answered, and I told her who I was and asked if she were available for a reading.

'She said, "Would you believe it. I've just had two cancellations and I'm free now."

'I took a taxi to this lady's place. She was called Joyce Rawlings. I told her I didn't believe in this sort of thing, but she didn't try to convince me, just said we'd have a go and see what happened. And I liked her.

'So we went into the front room and the first thing that struck me was that there were two armchairs and a series of religious pictures. Now, this may be a sad indictment of my experience of the Catholic Church, but for some reason I'd never equated religion with spirituality.'

Sitting down in front of the pictures of St Francis and the Virgin Mary, Joyce asked if Brendan would mind if she said a prayer before beginning. And Brendan, who hadn't prayed for years, decided to pray also. He decided to pray to Jesus that he should not be hoodwinked by this lady who seemed so nice. Brendan then asked if he could take notes. Joyce agreed.

'Joyce said it might look a little awkward, but she would stare at me until she "visualised my aura". And she explained to me about the different colours around the body and what they represented. Then she sat back and stood behind me, looking at me and waving her hands around. Finally she let out a yell and said, "Oh my God!"

'I said, "What's wrong?"

'"Nothing. It's just that you only have one colour in your aura."

'"Is that bad?"

'"I don't know. I've never seen it before."

'This seemed to me to be a pretty bad start, but Joyce said, "No, wait. There are spirits flying past you. And they're so happy for you. They're all dropping golden keys onto your lap. Now I don't know what you have coming, but it's huge and you so deserve it."

'Then she starts waving her arms around, fending off these spirits and I'm thinking, "Okay, great. But you haven't told me anything specific here."

'Then she says, "This one spirit wants to know who's the woman who bakes the brown bread?"

'Now, I wasn't going to tell the woman lies. But I wasn't going to help her. If she were being specific I would have. So I told her that most of the women in my family bake brown bread. It's an Irish tradition.

'Then she said, "But there's somebody who bakes a specific type, a soda bread, a 'tea brack'?"

'Now I'm thinking, "My mother."

'She said, "She's in God's garden now. And your father's there too. Walking behind your mother, holding onto the back of her apron. Would that be in keeping?"

'But I'm thinking, "This is all still so vague." Then she said there was a spirit that had a message from a man for me to deliver.

'I wouldn't take the message – it all felt too odd to me, so we agreed that she would write down the message anyway. It was, "I love you, I've always loved you, blah, blah."

'We moved on. And then she said, "I've come across a child in the spirit world. And I think he's yours. Can I bring him through?"

'Well, I was starting to feel a bit strange at this point. But I agreed. Then she started to talk about this child.

'"Oh God, almighty. He is the spit of you. Did you know that children grow in the spirit world?"

'"No I didn't."

'"Well, he has. And he said to tell you that he'll be ten shortly."

'Now, I was riveted. Brendan would have been four days short of his tenth birthday on 23 February.

'"Brendan, he said to tell you that you should have no regrets. No guilty consciences. He is meant to be exactly where he should be."

'"Jaysus."

'"But I'm getting more, Brendan. You're here in London for something to do with music. I'm getting a recording studio. A band . . . Something to do with a cannon?"

'This was amazing. The reason I was in London was indeed to promote a local band; I had a meeting scheduled with Bruce White at Creole Records. And the name of the song we were going to try and sell was "Jump The Gun".

'"That's what you're here for, Brendan. But that's not what is going to happen. I can see a studio and a microphone. Oh, and you love that microphone."

'"That won't be me in the studio. It's the band."

'"No, Brendan. It's you."

'"But I'm not in the entertainment world."

'"I don't care what you say. That's where your future lies."

'"Right."

'"And I want you to remember something. Glasgow. Glasgow is going to be so important. And it's you in the studio."

'So I wrote all this down. I was actually frightened by this point. Not visibly, but she took me in the kitchen, made me a cup of tea and then called a cab.

'I went back to the hotel. Still shaken. And I went over the six pages of notes. Was it waffle? I was worrying that some of this stuff would become a self-fulfilling prophecy.

'Anyway, the thing with the band didn't work out. But I ended up taking Joyce back to Ireland to read fortunes. And did they come true?

'During the stint, I watched as she made the hardest of men weep. But – and there was indeed a very large but, which I didn't pick up on till some time later – a pattern began to emerge. I think she knew how to get the genie out of the bottle, but not to get it back in. Ninety per cent of the people who took sittings with her had the most amazingly good news. And then had the most horrible five years that followed. Some went into bankruptcy, suffered serious illness. It was a terrible time for so many.'

What did it all mean? Was Brendan headed for a showbiz career? Was he destined to suffer incredibly bad fortune?

Has he formed this theory retrospectively because of the horrendous events that were to follow in his own life, looking back at the world with black-tinted glasses?

Brendan never saw Joyce after that trip. Nor has he since visited a spiritualist.

'I don't believe in them. I don't,' he says, not entirely convincingly. 'But I admit she stunned me. I just don't know how she could have told me what she did.'

In the meantime, he wouldn't worry about predestination. He would follow his gut instinct. Wherever that would take him.

PUB BOMBS

BACK in Dublin, The Abbot's Castle was ticking over nicely (Brendan was now driving a purple Jaguar XJ6) and Doreen, a mother-of-two, found time to work the door (the logic – correct, as it happens – being that tough guys would accept rejection from a slight female before they'd back down to a man). And Brendan and Kevin were easily making the payment terms.

In September 1989, Brendan reckoned he was due a holiday. His Toronto-based sister Fiona was getting married and he could take off and relax and enjoy himself in the knowledge that all was well back in his Dublin bar.

Kevin had had his problems in the past, mostly substance-abuse-related, and had spent some time in rehab. But he reassured his partner he could leave the bar in safe hands.

'Brendan, this is the biggest vote of confidence anyone could give me. I'll do you proud.'

Brendan and Doreen had a great two weeks in Canada and, returning to Ireland refreshed and invigorated, he felt ready to take the business up to the next level.

But it didn't happen. When Brendan walked into The Abbot's Castle on 12 September, he was frozen to the spot.

All the fixtures had been removed, the furniture, the lamp-shades, the stock. Everything.

'Kevin was gone and he'd even sold the plates and light bulbs.'

There was worse to come. When Brendan had a look at the bank account, he saw it had been wiped out. Clean. Desperately, Brendan made phone calls, spoke to friends to try to figure out what had happened. No one knew where Kevin had disappeared to, but acquaintances revealed they'd bought the furniture, the bits and pieces. Legitimately, they said.

Brendan was furious. A few months later, when he heard Kevin had come home for Christmas, Brendan was so angry he drove his car to Kevin's mother's house and sat outside waiting for him.

He sat there for hours, until common sense descended. Brendan realised he had a wife and kids at home, and it was Christmas Eve.

'Later on I thanked God I couldn't find him. I went back to my family and we focused on celebrating the day as best we could.'

The pub was closed. The dream was over. Brendan was disconsolate. He owed £96,000 on the business and it might as well have been £96 million for all the chance he had of paying it back. And with two young kids to look after.

Brendan had to face the New Year believing he had lost his one chance.

'It was gone. I was finished. Or so I thought. I've learned since in life that you get lots of chances. You've just got to be able to spot them. For example, if you have a massive debt with the bank, you need something to happen to pay it back.

And say that thing doesn't happen, you think you're in trouble. But then you realise you're not in trouble. It's the bank that's in trouble. So you say to the bank, "How can I help you get out of this trouble?" And you make a suggestion, to trade out, to borrow more money, whatever . . .'

But he hadn't yet learned that Zen-like approach to dealing with angry creditors. Brendan spent the next year in court, losing case after case after case against suppliers and finance companies.

'At that stage, if you'd put my name into the computer, you'd have sworn that I'd murdered the bank manager's wife, the credit rating was so bad.

'I owed so much money that I had no means of paying it back. What destroyed me was knowing we both could have come out of the pub experience as seriously rich men. But he sold us out for about ninety-odd grand. It was nothing.

'But then it's easy for me to say that.'

Three years later, Brendan discovered Kevin had been involved in the drugs scene, was gay and had contracted AIDS. Those days he'd disappeared now made sense.

When Kevin had realised he was dying, he'd taken all the money, everything, and headed off to Brisbane for a last hurrah.

But he came back. And he went to his mother's house. And the night after he arrived back at his mother's, he hanged himself.

Brendan was arrested the following day. Which wasn't surprising, since he'd made it clear to everyone how furious he was with Kevin.

'But the enquiries didn't last long. It was soon established Kevin had killed himself. 'Yet, I often reflect on it. One thing I think about is that I have no idea what it's like to be dying of AIDS. To be totally afraid. And even to be gay. Being gay can be a very lonely life.

'And then I have to think, "What does it take to hang yourself? How much desperation must you feel?" But you can't let it affect your faith in human nature. If you carry grudges, they weigh you down.'

He adds, ruefully, 'And anyway, it's one of those ironic twists. If he hadn't fecked off to Australia with the money, I might still be running a pub.'

Yet, he now had no job and a wife and two kids to support. What would he do?

STANDING UP

ONE afternoon, a gypsy woman came to the door of Brendan's four-bedroom terraced house selling clothes pegs.

'This woman had made lots of stuff to sell, so I would buy something from her like a comb and give her a fiver, and I'd normally give her daughter a tenner for her Holy Communion.

'And she said nice things, like I was the most generous person in the street. And then she said she had some really good news to tell me.

'"Great. What is it?"

'"Look, somebody put a curse on you a few years ago but it's nearly over. It's just about over. I just wanted to tell you that."

'Now, was it true what she was saying? Well, I reckon there's as much chance of it being true as not.'

Brendan didn't believe that Joyce had placed the curse on him. But part of him at least worried that those who had had their fortune told were in for some bad luck.

Meanwhile, Brendan knew that going back to waiting jobs alone wouldn't begin to pay off the debts. He needed to earn more. He tried all the usual outlets for temporary work but these were recessionary times. Brendan was desperate.

As for his luck changing, there was no sign of a leprechaun appearing in the corner of the living room of his Ashbourne home. In fact one would later appear. But in an unexpected form.

Meantime, Brendan saw another possibility, an idea that would have a major impact on his fortunes further down the line. He spied an ad in the *Evening Herald* with the catchy headline *How To Earn A Thousand A Week*. And he was curious. So he called up the company that had placed the ad, and he learned they were selling accident insurance.

'But the intriguing part was that they were offering this training course in Positive Mental Attitude, which lasted a week and took place in a hotel in Athlone.

'And so I went down there, was introduced to the main man whose name escapes me, and there were eight of us on the course. On that first morning, I took my place at the head of the horseshoe-shaped table, and the bloke in charge was full of energy. Right from the start he had us all up on our feet, and then the music struck up and he had us dancing to "It's a Long Way to Tipperary".

'I thought, "This is interesting. He's off to a great start, getting us all up and jigging around." And then he turned and looked at me, caught sight of the earring in my left ear and said, "Love the earring, Brendan. Not sure it's right for this course, but love it anyway."'

That night, almost subconsciously, Brendan took the earring out.

'Looking back, it was so clever how he'd managed to flatter me and have me do what he wanted me to do.'

The next few days involved training in Positive Mental Attitude, psyching the team up to believe that they could sell policies to just about anyone. Brendan loved learning how to get inside people's minds.

'The first thing this involves is the mantra, "Get up in the morning and look in the mirror." So effectively they use your mirror image to give you the PMA course every morning. You are taught to recite the Three Rs: Recognise something in somebody that's beneficial, Relate it to yourself and then Reuse it for your own benefit.

'Now, the irony was that those who learned PMA often became so good they left the company, moving on to big sales jobs. But the course does change people's lives. It gives them the sense that they can conquer the world.'

And, for a boy brought up to believe he could fly, the possibilities were limitless.

Brendan did very well selling medical insurance. And those who opened their doors to Brendan liked the cheery banter. They bought into his oh-so-positive sales pitch.

However, Brendan didn't stay with it. He was uncomfortable that he was milking friends and acquaintances. And the PMA had given him the confidence to walk away.

'It certainly focused my mental attitude,' he says, smiling. 'I thought I could do more.'

But what? The leprechaun arrived at his door one afternoon, in the form of Gerry Browne. Gerry took Brendan by surprise when he said he was delighted at the news of the pub's demise.

'I'm actually thrilled,' he told Brendan.

'Why?'

'Because now you'll be able to do what you should have been doing all your life.'

'And what's that, Gerry?'

'You'll go on the stage.'

Brendan's mind had already flirted with the notion of a career as a performer. He'd won the talent competition. He'd worked with Brendan Grace. And hadn't the spiritualist implied he would one day stand in front of a microphone?

Now, Gerry's declaration, combined with Brendan's PMA thinking, opened the gates of possibility in his head.

What if he *could* make a living at this game?

Outrageous Comedy

COULD Brendan make it as a comedian?

'I'd loved my little Sunday morning stints at The Abbot's Castle, informing the punters of upcoming events, doing it in the form of a little comedy routine. And now, with Gerry's thought in my head, I figured maybe I'd do a little stand-up, get seventy-eighty quid that the taxman wouldn't see. And I could start to pay off a few debts.'

Gerry Browne invited Brendan to appear with Tinker's Fancy – Jimmy (Dicey) Riley, Brendan Harrington, Paul Leech and Gerry Browne – in their regular gig at Slattery's Bar in Cable Street. (All had day jobs, working as chefs, mechanics, and so on; Gerry Browne was a milkman and Brendan was back working as a waiter.) And the extra money certainly came in handy.

The act featured the musicians performing for a section, and then Brendan would perform his own act, a Billy Connolly-like set of observational material and hilarious stories. Indeed, the show with Gerry Browne and co. was not far away from Billy Connolly's early folk music-and-comedy stage relationship with Gerry Rafferty in their band, The Humblebums.

'I went on the stage on 10 October 1990, aged thirty-five.

'I just opened my mouth and it all came out, like verbal diarrhoea, but everyone seemed to think it was funny.'

The new addition certainly proved popular with the audience over the weeks, although a couple of the Tinkers weren't too happy about sharing the spoils, nor the limelight, with the new boy.

So at first, the relationship didn't run smoothly. Early on, the group took off to London.

'We were offered a few gigs in London suburbs such as Leytonstone, Walthamstow, Kilburn – the tough Irish clubs filled with guys with tractor parts in their pockets.

'Now, the Irish who emigrate tend to be in a time warp. That's why the Irish bands who'd died ten years ago at home then have a life abroad. The émigrés tend to think of them as stars still.

'So we went over and the band did the ballads, and I did the jokes.'

'But at the end of the tour, the social club convener spoke to the manager, who was Gerry, and said that they didn't want the comedian. Me.

'God, I felt hurt. But even more so because by this time I had said to Gerry that I wanted to go full time in the business with him and the band, to really make a go of it.'

Brendan had hoped Gerry would say the club boss was an idiot, but what he actually said was that he and the band were thinking about going it alone anyway.

Gerry and his Tinkers continued to play in England, but on their return came back to play a gig in Ashbourne, in a bar near Brendan's home.

'I went up to see them and discovered the money for the Ashbourne gig was to pay for a new backdrop for the band. Then, after the gig, I spoke to Gerry and asked how the English gigs had gone.'

'"They were fuckin' phenomenal! We're going to be so big."

'"So you've made a final decision then about us?"

'"Yeah, we should go our separate ways."

'"Well, best of luck to you."

'And I went home, feeling really down. But the next day I got a call from Gerry.

'"Hi, Brendan. Look, do you still want to be part of the band?"

'"Yes, I do."

'"Okay. Let's do it."

Gerry believed in Tinker's Fancy. But he also believed that greater success lay with appearing alongside Brendan O'Carroll. And Gerry loved comedy. He loved writing comedy songs, parodies.

'So I rang a bloke called John Sweeney, a guy I'd known from the Ashbourne, who now ran a pub called the Rathmines Inn, and he was a bit taken aback when I said I fancied doing a bit of comedy.

'He said, incredulously, "Here? Look I could have Glenn Miller on in here and this lot would talk right through it."

'"No, John. I think it could work."

'"Brendan, the pub is always packed. There is no way anyone will listen."

'"Look, John, just give me a chance."

'And he did. The only night that was a possibility was a Tuesday, when it was a little quiet. But John said, "Look, don't *just* do comedy. Come up with something different."

Brendan thought for a while and then announced he had an idea.

'I said to John Sweeney, "All right. I'll do *Blind Date*." The idea came right out of nowhere. Brendan knew how popular Cilla Black's ITV show was, and simply thought to transfer it onto stage. It was a little moment of genius. Of course, being Brendan, he was never going to transfer the idea without O'Carrolling it to suit the occasion.

But then there was another problem. 'About a week before the gig, John rang me and said, "Just a wee question: what time is your band starting?"

'"What band?"

'"Well, you just can't stand up on the stage and go 'Howareye? We're going to do *Blind Date*.' You need a bit of build-up entertainment."

'"So I've got to provide that?"

'"Yes, it's your show."

'That's where Gerry Browne and Dicey out of Tinker's Fancy came in. They did a two-man warm-up and I paid them twenty-five quid each. I paid fifteen pounds for the rent of the PA. And that left me a tenner.

'And there were forty people in the pub.'

When it came Brendan's time to take the stage, he really hadn't a clue what he was going to do.

'I got a fellow up and I blindfolded him, and he would have a choice of the three girls who came up on stage.

'And the first question was, to the girls, "What's the first thing you notice about a guy when you see him?"

'Now, I had two girls from very posh areas, and one from a less posh town.

'The first girl, from Stillorgan, said, "Shoulders, Brendan. I like the way a man moves, his deportment, his swagger."

'And the audience didn't crack on. I thought, "God, make me funny, please!"

'And then onto the next girl and she said, "I like a man to be tall. With brown eyes. Because eyes are the window to the soul."

'Still nothing from the audience. I was feckin' dying up there. And then I got to the last girl, who was a cleaner in St James's Hospital. And I said, "What's the first thing you'd notice?" And she said, "I don't give a fuck so long as he has a big, swinging mickey."

'And the forty people in the audience laughed louder than you could imagine. It brought the house down.

'And what they were laughing at was the fact that this girl was herself, while the other two had been acting.

'Now, without any shadow of a doubt, the PMA experience had given me the self-belief I needed to hold an audience's attention for a couple of hours. I'd always had the feeling at the back of my mind that I could entertain. But it had remained there. PMA brought this positive feeling to the forefront. Now I felt, "Yes, I can tell jokes. Yes, I can make this crowd laugh. Now just go out there and do it." But at the same time I thought, "This is a lesson to learn. Brendan, just be yourself." And it made me think about honesty. I realised I'd spent years being someone else, so I should really try and be myself.'

He realised being funny on stage was like a drug.

'I felt a feeling of warmth and acceptance and, yes, power. I was the guy with the mic. I could say, "Look over there" and everyone looked. I loved it. And I was good at it. And I knew I could do it again.

'I loved that feeling. I was the little guy who could go up there and be noticed. I was the one everyone was looking at, everyone was talking about. I was the one who was getting the big smiles. When I paused, you could feel the sense of expectation. And when I told a story, they listened hard. I was in heaven.

'Meanwhile, the Rathmines asked me to do a show every Sunday morning, a stand-up. I took seven hundred and fifty quid at the door, on top of the seventy-five pounds. And that week I twigged that this could be a very lucrative business if it was managed right.'

The posters originally read *Tinker's Fancy . . . featuring Brendan O'Carroll*, but it soon became apparent that Brendan, with his fast wit and comedy persona, was the main attraction. He was also seen as the godfather of the outfit.

'We made an arrangement that in our organisation Gerry would be the management – on the face of it – and go in to negotiate. But if, for example, we were offered three hundred and fifty quid, he'd be able to say, "Oh Brendan won't do it for that. He wants five hundred. And he's a bastard. He really is." And he'd use me to play off one person against another.'

Meanwhile, Dicey dropped out, to be replaced by Colin Goodall, and the show became *Brendan O'Carroll's* Blind Date *. . . with Gerry Browne and Colin Goodall*, and ran successfully for almost two years, appearing right across Dublin and in towns such as Cork, Waterford and Wicklow.

A bass player joined the outfit, Willie De Mange, and the name was changed to *The Outrageous Comedy Show*. At times *The OCS* could be risqué. In fact, it was once described as 'bluer than a frost-bitten penis', and praise was delivered in similes that reflected the 'toilet' humour.

'*The Outrageous Comedy Show* got people's attention, but those who thought that that was me on the stage were wrong. It wasn't the real me. I was doing my job really well.

Me, I'm a waiter. I'm a father. I'm a husband. I'm Victorian in my own way. I've got Victorian values.

'I can go up there and talk about sex and get laughs. I can talk about the size of someone's mickey and get laughs. But this wasn't who I was. If I were at home or at a party I'd never crack a joke about genitalia. It just isn't me. What the audience were getting was what I thought they wanted. And they did laugh. And yes, some people didn't like it. They reckoned I was a filthy little bollix and maybe they weren't wrong. But you've got to find your level. And this was the level I thought I should be aiming at on stage.'

When Brendan was on the end of a stinging crit in *Hot Press* magazine for being too crude, he actually wrote the critic a letter. 'You're right,' it said. 'I'll change my ways.'

It's not surprising that Brendan's humour attracted some strong criticism in Catholic Ireland.

'I'm not a devotee of the Church; I'm not a devotee of any organised religion. I was christened a Catholic but I'm certainly not a supporter of the Catholic Church. The closer you are to any organised religion, the further you are from God. But I have a good one-to-one relationship with Jesus, which I've had since I was a kid.

'I've always tried to love my neighbour, which is the one Christian law that counts. I don't go to Mass at all but every time I hug my child, that's a prayer. As for, "Thou shalt not take the name of the Lord thy God in vain"? Great idea, but which God are we talking about? Jesus? Or, Jaysus? Most people who use the word "Jaysus" use it as a term of hope or a term of despair. If anybody who is in despair calls on Jesus, I think that's good, regardless of the situation. And Jesus can do with all the advertising he can get. I'm happy to include Him in my act.'

The Mammy,
Maureen O'Carroll.

Brendan's first school photo,
aged five.

Maureen arriving at the High
Court during the 'Batchelor's
Peas' Case, 1954.

Brendan back at the
original O'Carroll
home in Stoneybatter.

Brendan outside St Gabriel's School, Stoneybatter.

Finglas in the 1970s. The Drake Inn comedy venue is on the right.

Comedian Cecil Sheridan with the women of Moore Street.

Gay Byrne, a key supporter of Brendan O'Carroll's career, pictured here with another influence on Brendan, Hal Roach.

Brendan Grace, an early comedy collaborator.

The 'Outrageous Comedy Show' team in 1990,
including Gerry Browne on the top left.

Brendan O'Carroll and Gerry host *Hot Milk and Pepper* in 1996,
with former Irish soccer players (from left to right) Liam Tuohy,
Eamon Gregg, Noel King and Ray Treacy.

One of Brendan's many appearances on *The Late, Late Show*.

Gay Byrne and Mrs Brown on a visit to Moore Street in 1997.

Shooting a scene from *The Van*, with Colm Meaney and Donal O'Kelly.
The film was released in 1996.

Capers with Gerry Browne and the cast of the radio show *Northside Blues*.

Brendan performing
in the play *Grandad* in
1997, with Gerry Browne
and Martin Dempsey.

Film director
Jim Sheridan.

Anjelica Huston with
Tom Jones in the *Agnes
Browne* movie.

Fans at the Moravian Bookshop in Bethlehem celebrate
Brendan O'Carroll Day, in August 2000.

Brendan transforming himself into Mrs Brown in a
dressing room in Glasgow in 2000.

Brendan reckons Jesus, a man with a great sense of humour, would be a fan of Mrs Brown's. 'He'd piss Himself laughing. I betcha if I'd been around, He'd have booked me for the Last Supper.'

Brendan certainly had his followers in Ireland in 1991.

The mix of music and comedy was so successful that Gerry Browne sold his milk round and he and Brendan became full-time entertainers.

Colin and Willie, both musical purists, left to be replaced by Gerry Simpson and Eric Sharp and seventeen-year-old Glen Power (now with The Script) on drums, but the success continued, with the act doing eight gigs a week.

Audiences loved the format; the band would do forty minutes and Gerry performed some parody songs. Brendan would perform a further forty minutes of comedy, and then they'd all perform the final third of up-tempo songs.

The band of brothers were having an incredible time on the road. And by this point Benny (as Gerry nicknamed his pal) and Gerry had made a pact: other band members could come and go, but they were the axis on which everything turned.

'I then suggested building my own stage, with backdrop and lighting. I reckoned with this set-up we could do a gig anywhere. And to do all this would cost thirty thousand pounds.'

But therein lay a problem. Brendan couldn't raise thirty thousand smiles, even if he stood naked outside the President's Palace with a shamrock clenched in his teeth. His name was still mud at the bank. However, he managed to find a finance company that was prepared to back him, so long as he managed to get receipts for everything. But he needed a guarantor. Gerry Browne stepped up to the plate.

'"And I said to him, 'If you do that, Gerry, you'll be my partner.'"'

The one-time adversaries were now blood brothers. They wrote together, coming up with an album of parody songs, *Yer A Sick Man, Da*, which attracted major radio airplay. And now two other key personnel were added to the team.

'When I started doing the Rathmines Inn, I used to carry the speakers down, unlock the van and put the speakers in, lock the van, go up and get the microphones, come back down, repeat the process, ten times or so every week. Until this night, this fella was standing there and offered to help me throw the stuff in the van.

'This process repeated every week. Now, after a few times I said to him, "Look, I don't have enough money to pay you," and in fact, at first he was lending *me* the price of a pint.

'Then, when we got the first bigger-paying gigs, I asked him to come along as a lumper.'

Former window-cleaner Dermot O'Neill, aka Bugsy, and so nicknamed because of his resemblance to the wise-cracking cartoon rabbit, had been a fan of Tinker's Fancy and now became Brendan's first lieutenant. (Bugsy's brother Tommy was married to Gerry's aunt and played football with Gerry.) Since that time, Brendan and Bugsy have been inseparable, with Bugsy going on to play Grandad in the *Mrs Brown* stage and television adventures and being the butt of many of Agnes Brown's gags. 'We give Grandad Viagra,' says Agnes to Winnie. 'It stops him pissing on his socks.'

Brendan then hired another stalwart in Pat Shields, aka Pepsi, who would also become an actor, playing both Rory and Mark Brown.

'Pepsi was a sound man and working for another entertainer, Paul Malone, at the time, and I asked this guy for a loan of his sound gear when we were doing a trip to the London clubs. He said he would loan me the equipment and the van, because he was taking a two-week holiday, *if* I used his sound man, and of course paid his wages.

'And the sound man was Pepsi. About a year later, when things got busier, I offered Pepsi a job, and he jumped at it.'

'Pepsi had never directed or recorded anything before. But that didn't matter.'

The success meant constant night work. Doreen, with two kids to look after, would look in when she could, but Brendan was now beginning to occupy a different world. He was now creating a business, a little travelling troupe of blokes he could depend upon and have fun with. And he was starting to make money, which helped salve his conscience about being away from home.

'Doreen came to realise I wasn't a waiter any more.'

He was a full-time comedian. And it meant he had to come up with a tremendous amount of material. He wasn't writing scripts as such, but he'd get an idea for a gag and write the prompter on the back of a beer mat, say an idea about airplane toilet sex or whatever.

As time passed, the writing improved, and greater success was just around the corner. But even the best clairvoyant couldn't have seen it coming.

Radio Days

THE BRENDAN and Gerry success story continued to the point they reckoned they'd have to make a background history up, to make themselves more interesting.

Newspapers and magazines were coming at them, asking for feature interviews, wondering how this fun act came together and what was the connection between the pair?

Obviously, Brendan couldn't tell the truth, that he had reckoned the Brownes were best avoided, so they massaged the truth a little. (In the same way that the word 'massage' is used by the backstreet saunas offering extras.)

'We needed some really good publicity material,' Brendan recalls, grinning. 'And the idea we sold to the media was that we had grown up together in Finglas (true), hung around the street corners together (false), that Gerry had an old guitar with nylon strings he'd strum, and we'd sing funny songs together and everybody thought we were hilarious (false).'

To add to the colour, the story they told was that Gerry was always looking out for his little pal, Brendan, and so they'd always had their Mice and Men relationship (false).

A relationship based on a lie perhaps isn't the most solid basis upon which to build. But what the hell? The pair got on like a whole housing estate on fire. This was a partnership that worked.

The act was now so successful that the pair recruited the services of showbiz agent Pat Egan, the man who'd set up gigs for Billy Connolly in Ireland, to line up the bookings.

In truth, Pat Egan regarded Brendan as the money shot, the one with the most commercial appeal, but Brendan maintained there were *two* main men in the show.

That's not to say Brendan sang his partner's praises continually from every mountain high.

'Gerry was a bit of an optimist. At one point he said to me, with a real positive note in his voice, "We're doing great, Brendan. We've got twenty-two grand in the bank."

'"No, Gerry. We've got a thirty grand overdraft and we've only used eight grand of it. We're actually eight grand overdrawn." But that's the way he looked at life.'

Still, they were moving forward. Thankfully, the comedy show grew in strength, and Bugsy was now taking the money in at the door and helping with stage equipment. (Bugsy is a gentle easy-going bloke. But when punters tried to get in free he showed his toughness; no one got in without paying.)

Brendan and Gerry were fast becoming local celebrities and, splitting the profits fifty–fifty, were on their way to making a decent living.

It wasn't a subtle act, but it worked. Brendan reckoned what it needed, however, was a little more publicity; someone to work the newspapers, to generate interest in the travelling showmen.

That's where Rory Cowan came in. Rory had worked in PR with EMI Records, looking after the likes of Diana Ross and the Pet Shop Boys, but he had left his job, fallen out with his partner and generally fallen on hard times. He was trying to get back on his feet working as a promoter when he approached Brendan to do a gig in a Dublin venue. Brendan agreed, but unfortunately the show took place in the middle of a glorious Dublin summer, and the gig failed miserably.

Brendan didn't lose out because he was on a guarantee of £500 for the gig, but they took only £550 at the door. Despite that, Rory still offered Brendan his £500 – which Brendan refused. He said, 'Look, we'll pay the fifty quid for the hall, we'll both take two hundred each and give a hundred pounds to charity.'

A delighted Rory agreed. And Brendan was so impressed by Rory he offered him a job as a publicist. It was a bold idea – pub acts didn't normally hire PR men – but Brendan and Gerry were determined to go to the next level, to play the big hotels.

However, Brendan was also inviting Rory into the 'family', the separate showbiz world he'd created and was having so much fun in. To include Rory in this world meant Brendan believed his new chum to be a bit special.

'Tell me something, Rory. How bad are things?'

'Well, the house is about to be repossessed, and I'm three months behind with the electricity.'

'Now, tell me, Rory. Are you gay?'

'Which answer gets me the job?'

'The truth.'

'Well, I am gay, as it happens.'

'Fair enough.'

And Rory was now on the payroll. But Brendan first suggested they do another gig, this time in Finglas; as a local, he knew it would be a sell-out.

It turned out to be a great confidence booster for Rory, and Brendan knew his new friend would walk away with a couple of grand. They took £4,500 on the night. Then Brendan issued his terms of contract to Rory.

'I said, "Look, here's what I want to offer you. I'll pay you five hundred a week, but I'm going to take two hundred and fifty quid a week to pay your bills. I'll speak to the finance companies and I'll sort it."'

He did. And Rory has worked with Brendan since, graduating to play the role of Rory Brown, Agnes's gay son.

Why did Brendan ask if Rory were gay? He's certainly not homophobic, and it's not the sort of question asked in job interviews these days. Was it tied to his disappointment over The Abbot's Castle?

'It was about honesty. I wanted to deal with someone who was direct, and I really liked the bloke.'

Brendan, Gerry and Rory pushed the envelope in terms of trying to become a brand name in Ireland. They managed appearances in a couple of small TV shows, but nothing major. What they wanted was a slot on Ireland's most successful entertainment show, *The Late, Late Show*, fronted by silver-haired, silver-tongued presenter Gay Byrne. And they made it, performing a version of a parody song, 'Hey, Paddy', about how the Irish were treated in England.

But the impact was minimal. What the team needed, desperately wanted, was for Brendan to appear on the show as a solo comedian. (While Gay Byrne loved to give newcomers a chance, his production staff deemed the often outrageous O'Carroll too much of a risk.)

How to achieve it? What Brendan and Gerry did was hang around the RTÉ studio canteen, just to be seen. And both being highly colourful dressers (Brendan, though balding, had braided, beaded hair extensions), they were certainly noticed.

They'd go along on a Friday afternoon, pretending to be working on imaginary scripts, hoping to make contacts, to be seen as a couple of important players.

The ploy worked to a degree. They managed to land a spot on one TV show, *The Beat Show* (sponsored by Pepsi, and where Brendan arrived wearing a 7Up T-shirt, which created a little rumpus), and they were moving in the right direction.

Back at home, Doreen was supportive of Brendan's bid for fame, but the relationship, he says, wasn't going well. Brendan was spending so much time on the road; he certainly wasn't the husband Doreen had married. But, in November 1991, the marriage was truly tested. Doreen announced she was pregnant again.

'This was nine years after Danny was born and I was taken aback, largely because at this time things weren't good between us.

'But I came round to the idea. Then, very quickly, within two weeks, her breast swelled. One day, Gerry Browne came in and gave her a hug, "Howareye, Doreen", and she screamed with the pain of it. The doctors took her in for examination and cancer was revealed.

'Doreen had a lump, which within two weeks had gone from the size of my knuckle to the size of my fist.

'But it turned out that being pregnant saved her life. The oestrogen was feeding the cancer, which was growing rapidly. And if she hadn't been pregnant with Eric, the cancer would have grown, probably unnoticed.

'So the doctors decided to do a full mastectomy, while Doreen was pregnant. But they assured her not to worry about the baby because it would spontaneously abort.'

Brendan battled hard to keep Doreen's spirits up. But it was tough. When he arrived home that night, there was a man sitting outside in a car. Moments after Brendan had gone into the house, he rang Brendan's doorbell.

'I'm from Dublin County Council, and I'm hereby fining you for putting your posters up on lampposts around Mulhuddart.'

'Listen, mister. I've just been told my wife has cancer. Come back again, will you?'

'God love the man. The blood drained from his face. It was an awful thing to say to him, but I was just knackered. I never heard from him again.'

Brendan carried Doreen through the chemo ordeal. He and Gerry would turn up outside the ward window at Dublin's Mater Hospital with guitars and sing to her.

The cancer was a nightmare for Doreen, but it also took its toll on him.

'Before going on stage at night I'd cry. People would say to me, "How can you go on stage and be funny for two hours every night?" But the truth was that for those two hours I didn't have a wife who was suffering from cancer. I didn't have a child who was certain to die. This was my world that I had created, a world in which no one could touch me.

'And I have to say while I was on stage, nothing would faze me. If anything, the tragedy at home concentrated my mind and so I had to think hard about being funny. I was desperate to be funny, to forget about everything else. And it worked. And it also made me realise the importance of comedy, for the person who delivers it and for those who receive it.'

But he couldn't hold it together at all times.

'On the way back from a gig in the country, I'd pull off the road and cry. I'd sit for hours and sob.'

Doreen went through the mastectomy and the chemotherapy. Incredibly, the baby didn't spontaneously abort.

'We did think of aborting the baby. From the beginning, the one thing I knew I wanted was Doreen. We didn't care if they'd to take a breast, an eye, nose, leg, whatever they liked, as long as they got the cancer.

'The doctors were reassuring, however. They were great. They said they could treat the cancer without harming the baby, although on Christmas Eve she lost all her waters. Yet, she begged me not to let the doctors do an internal examination because that would almost certainly lead to an infection.

'"It's over then, Brendan."

'"Okay, Doreen. I won't let them."

'And at six o'clock the next morning, the pain had ceased. And she clutched her hands between her legs for five months to hang onto this baby. Now I, as a man, don't have that kind of courage. Women have real strength. We're wimps when it comes to something like this.

'But the miracle was that the baby didn't abort. He was born at twenty-eight weeks, at two pounds two ounces on 6 May 1992. And he was called Eric.'

Brendan had persuaded Doreen to leave the flap of skin tucked up under the scar, where the breast tissue was removed, in case she could later have breast reconstruction. Doreen initially said no.

'She wasn't thinking straight at the time. But she eventually agreed, and it turned out for the best. She went on to have a full reconstruction.'

Doreen was given the all-clear by a Harley Street specialist. The cancer hadn't spread. And it was reckoned the type of cancer that could have been stress-induced (perhaps the strain of debt?) and not genetic.

'This suggested that Fiona didn't have that cross to bear. I was so thankful to hear that.'

The cancer trauma brought the couple closer for the time being. However, Brendan's developing celebrity status brought its own problems for his family.

'Eric's birth made the papers, who described him as "a special kid". One day, Fiona came from school and said one little girl said her dad had told her Eric was "a special kid" because she and Danny had been adopted. She was distraught. I drove her in the car to the register office in Lombard Street and filled out a form to get her birth certificate. Fiona took my word for it she wasn't adopted, but all it takes is a seed from a comment like that to set someone on the wrong track.'

Brendan's career was shortly to shift track, changing his entire future, thanks to an appearance one sunny July afternoon in 1992 at the Dublin radio station, 2FM.

Rory Cowan had been working on building up Brendan's profile, saying at the time, 'You couldn't have given him away free with a packet of Daz outside of Dublin.'

Rory had spoken to radio presenter Gareth O'Callaghan and Gareth agreed to have Brendan and Gerry on the show 'to do some funny bits from the papers.'

Yet, the stand-up comedian had no idea of what the casual chat with Gareth, the Irish version of BBC Radio 2's Steve Wright, was about to produce.

'Gareth was a really good presenter. Anyway, after I did the interview on the show, I had a coffee with him, along with Rory and Gerry, and Gareth said he was looking for something to give the show a lift.'

'"Look, Brendan, you're a funny guy. Now, we've got this idea for the show where we run a little mini-soap. Just two minutes long, every day. Would you have any ideas for a character?"'

Brendan looked at the DJ and smiled. Of course he had no ideas. He was a stand-up comedian. He played pubs around Dublin, telling gags as part of a show band with his partner Gerry Browne. He wasn't a writer.

But those weren't the words that came out of the astonishingly confident – and opportunistic – O'Carroll mouth.

'Yes, I do have a couple of ideas I've been working on, as it happens,' said Brendan, brightly.

'Oh really? What are they?'

'Yes, what are they?' asked a bewildered Rory, smiling.

'Well, Gareth, my central character is a Dublin housewife.'

'And?'

'And . . .'

Brendan's brain raced up the gears. A bead of sweat formed on his head. He could sense this was a real opportunity.

'And she's got seven kids,' Brendan added, with a rush of breath. 'She's a recent widow, and she's struggling to bring up the kids on her own.'

'I like it,' said Gareth. 'Is there more?'

'It's about how she looks after her incredibly colourful family. She's a typical Dublin mammy.'

'Love the idea, Brendan. Maybe we could do something with that. So what's her name?'

Brendan threw a quick glance in the direction of his show-band partner whose mother he'd seen that very morning.

'Agnes Browne,' he said, smiling. (Brendan would use the name Agnes Browne in books and plays until 1999. Thereafter the 'e' would be dropped.)

'Nice. How soon can you come up with a script for us?'

'Sure, I've got some ideas at home,' said the comedian, almost believing his own line.

'Great, get them in, and if they work out we'll start the series next week.'

Brendan went home that night and told Doreen what had happened. She couldn't believe her husband had had the balls to fib to the radio guys. She worried too about how he would come up with a script. Brendan was dyslexic, after all. He'd never written anything longer than a shopping list or a poem. How could he dream up a radio series?

But Brendan didn't worry. He sat down with a jotter and a pen and the words came fast and furious. The dialogue was already in his mind. He knew Agnes. He knew her sons and her daughter. He immediately knew the situations they'd find themselves in.

How did he know Agnes so intimately? When the radio presenter asked for ideas, Brendan knew he needed to create a character who was larger than life, but entirely believable. So he thought of the women who'd made most impact on him. He thought of his mother, the indomitable Maureen O'Carroll, the former nun, who'd renounced her vows in order to marry, and produced a family of eleven, who'd had to cope alone when her husband had died. He thought of Moore Street, of Dublin's street market and the tough, battle-worn women who worked all day in the worst of weather and always showed the best of spirits. He thought of the mammys of Doreen and Gerry Browne.

What Brendan didn't appreciate at the time was that Agnes had been locked away in his head for years, just waiting for the day she would be let loose. She was his very own Old Mother Riley. She was universal, the Jewish mama, the black mammy, the tough creature who'd kill to protect her kids.

But the chat at the radio station revealed the essence of Brendan O'Carroll: a man who could turn an opportunistic moment into a career move.

In later years, on stage and television as Mrs Brown, he'd reveal his talent as an ad-libber, how he could react to a situation and throw in a great, unscripted line. But back in 1992, he wasn't self-aware enough to realise his own talent for thinking on his feet.

Could he write a script? Brendan used some of the stories he'd told at live gigs and he developed other characters.

He came up with a policeman called Fluffy, to be played by Gareth, the presenter. Betty would be played by a lady called Siobhan Scott who worked in the RTÉ newsroom, Gerry Browne was to be Dino, Mark and Buster Brady, Buster being based on a real-life scamp from Finglas called Radar. Rory would play Rory, the gay son (that in itself was a bold move considering homosexuality in Ireland was still illegal).

But none of this mattered. When Gareth O'Callaghan gave the finished scripts to his producer Ian Wilson, the producer read the dialogue and decided it was 'too urban'. What he was really saying was they were unbroadcastable. He believed they might be popular in working-class Finglas, but not across Ireland.

Mrs Browne's Boys were never going to be invited to play in the broadcast world of RTÉ's 2FM.

Brendan was gutted. But he hadn't given up on the idea. The following week, Brendan and Gerry were back on the show doing their 'bits' and they appealed to the producer. Still 'no'. A little later, however, the lucky leprechaun appeared by Brendan's side. Ian Wilson went on holiday and

Gareth O'Callaghan was hit by a wave of sheer boldness. He took a huge personal risk and decided to broadcast *Mrs Browne's Boys* in his boss's absence. Would it work?

Meanwhile, Brendan and Gerry faced another problem when it came to recording in Start Studios. The actress hired to play Agnes, Maggie Mallon, hadn't turned up. She'd reveal later she was sick, but that was no comfort to studio bosses. The show had to go on, or be pulled from the schedule.

'We'll have to cancel,' said Gareth O'Callaghan to a disconsolate Brendan.

'Like hell we will!'

'But how can we go on without an Agnes?'

'Give me a minute. Let me think.'

Brendan's mind turned over. He remembered those who'd told him he could never run his own nightclub, aged thirteen. He remembered those who said he'd never amount to anything, yet he became the best waiter in Dublin. He recalled those who said he was stupid because he couldn't read properly, yet he'd built up a half-million-pound pub business, only to have it stolen from him.

And he could laugh at those who said he'd never make it as a stand-up.

'There's an easy solution, Gareth. I'll play Agnes.'

And he did. It was Irish luck mixed with a streak of nerve. Brendan stretched his voice upwards a little and recorded that first episode with the idea he'd then go back to using the original actress.

But, Brendan reveals, 'the guy who was doing the edit listened to that first recording and said, "This woman is good, who is she?"

'"That's me."

'"Feck off!"'

'"No, it is."'

And Brendan never used an actress to dub over his lines. He had his Mrs Browne. And he would save the cost of a wage into the bargain. A negative had been turned into a positive. A disaster had been turned into an opportunity. And it was emblematic of the way Brendan would live his life.

He also featured those who were part of his second family.

But would these working-class characters be popular across Ireland? Within minutes of transmission, the waiter and the milkman had their answer. The 2FM switchboard lit up like a Christmas tree. It was jammed with requests for repeats.

The show became so popular that the inmates at Wheatfield Prison requested they lose an hour of their recreation so they could remain in their cells and listen to the broadcast. Taxi drivers would stop at the taxi ranks at 4.25 and wouldn't take fares until the five-minute episode was over. Brendan and Gerry had gone from singing rude songs in bars to becoming national institutions.

They weren't making money from the radio show because they had to pay for studio time, but at the end of every show, the presenter would plug the upcoming gigs.

However, the demands of writing a daily show almost brought Brendan to tears.

'When you write something to go out five days a week, it's really tough. You spend every moment going around with a pen in your hand. I would go into the recording studio every Saturday to record the shows for the following week, record the dialogue, and put the sound effects on for each of the episodes, which lasted from five to seven minutes.

'But there were times when I'd be sitting there on a Friday

night, knowing the studio was booked, the actors were coming in, and I was staring at blank pages. I'd make a cup of coffee and sit there, desperate. Every episode had to have a conclusion on a Monday, from a story that started the previous week, going on to Wednesday and the start of a new storyline.

'And I knew I couldn't go to bed until I had those five episodes. End of story. But by five a.m., I'd have it. Invariably, we'd go in the next day to record this rather ordinary script and people would say, "This is your best yet!"'

Somehow, from somewhere, Brendan would come up with the goods.

'I was learning it was all about work. This was a real craft.'

But what to do next? *Mrs Browne's Boys* was successful, and now most of Ireland had heard Brendan's name. But no one knew what Mrs Browne looked like. She was a disembodied voice on the radio.

What could Brendan do to make sure he became a household face?

THE MAMMY BOOK

ONE Friday night in February, 1993, Brendan O'Carroll's life was about to change beyond recognition. And it all came about by incredible coincidence. While Brendan, Gerry and Rory had doggedly pursued a solo slot on *The Late, Late Show*, it turned out that Gay Byrne's production team actually came looking for Brendan. Why? Newspaper stories had emerged about Doreen almost losing the baby, while Brendan was out working the pubs and hotels, trying to make strangers smile.

Here was the hilarious Mrs Browne from the radio – who'd had to endure personal hell. The researchers asked Brendan to appear and give the world the chance to see the face behind the radio mammy. But they also wanted Ireland to see the comedian who'd battled personal trauma with the dramatic birth of Eric.

And they asked for Doreen to be in the audience and talk about Brendan.

'I was booked for a nine-minute interview on the strength of the radio show and people knew the Mrs Browne series, but not me. But I had never met Gay; I didn't know how far

I could go. But I told story after story and ten minutes later he was almost on the floor laughing. I kept going and it turned out to be the longest interview with a comedian *The Late, Late Show* had ever done. And at the end of the thirty-five minutes he was wiping the tears from his eyes.'

The chat with Doreen also worked incredibly well. She was nervous, but came across as sincere, and supportive of her husband.

And what happened next was the stuff of movie scripts.

'The next day everybody in the country knew my name - it was an amazing transformation.

'The night before we had gigged in McGowan's bar for £350 and four days later I did a hotel in Mullingar for £3,500.'

Brendan would go on to appear on the nation's favourite TV show a total of 24 times between 1993 and Byrne's retirement in 1999. And he'd continually praise the man who 'gave him a leg up'. Gay Byrne, in turn, would describe Brendan as 'One of the funniest men I've ever met.'

By now *The Outrageous Comedy Show* was gone. The act was now *The Brendan O'Carroll Show*.

'We were now gigging around the country, getting a thousand people at the door, paying a tenner a ticket.'

The next step on the road to success was to move up from the pub and hotel world. How? Easy. Just hire one of Dublin's major theatres for a week, and fill the 370 seats every night. So what if it cost £4,500 a week to rent the Tivoli Theatre in Francis Street for a week.

But would the rising comedy star, now sporting a pony-tail, be able to fill a theatre? Brendan's popularity had grown with the radio show. The 'family' moved into the Tivoli and sold out week after week. The shows were so popular that one was recorded and the *How's Your Wobbly Bits?* video outsold U2 in the charts.

At long last, Brendan began to pay off his pub debt and he and Doreen and the three kids moved to a larger semi-detached house in Ashbourne, County Meath.

Yet, Brendan had misgivings about the big-league success that had come his way. He maintains his wife wasn't prepared to leap aboard this new, faster train.

'Suddenly, I had more gigs than I could handle. At the end of one stint I went home with the earnings in a bag. I had £25 grand in cash and I put it on the table in front of Doreen.

'Doreen looked at the money on the table and with a look of horror said "Sure, I'm not taking any of that!"

'"What? You're kidding me!"'

She didn't think he'd stolen it. Worse than that. She thought he was a phoney.

'She said "I'm telling you now, they're going to find out you're only a waiter - and everybody's going to want their money back. And I'm not having any part of it."

'And Doreen's perspective never changed. I was always the waiter. I had to say to her "You married the waiter. He doesn't exist any more."'

Brendan certainly wasn't being treated like a big star at home.

'I remember the opening night of my one-man show at the Olympia Theatre in Dublin and Doreen couldn't make it because she was taking her mother to the bingo.

'I'd come in having sold out a show, as I did once on a trip to London, at the Lyric Theatre in London's West End, and I'd get "Oh, that's nice".'

After *The Late, Late Show*, Brendan was the best-known comedian in Ireland. But he reckoned it was time to end his radio show. After all, he didn't need the publicity any longer and radio paid very little. So he decided to kill off Agnes, the woman with a mouth like a drain and the laugh of a machine gun without a safety catch.

Brendan ended the second series with Agnes ill in hospital, surrounded by her children, with the last line of the show being a doctor proclaiming, 'I'm sorry. I have to turn the machine off.'

What happened next? The fans were furious and the radio station was bombarded with complaints. 'How can you kill off Agnes Browne?' It was like the outrage that greeted Sir Arthur Conan Doyle when he tried to kill off Sherlock Holmes at the Reichenbach Falls.

'I had no idea we'd get that reaction. I presumed it was a Dublin story for a Dublin audience. I had no idea that nationwide it was going bananas. It was only when travelling around the country doing the bigger gigs that I truly realised. So I agreed to do another series and I opened the new one with the doctor repeating his line about switching off the machine and then Agnes coming in with, "Excuse me, they're my children. If they want coffee they can have as much as they like, but don't turn off the coffee machine!"'

Mrs Browne's Boys would gently fade out in 1994, but Brendan was now a star, voted Ireland's Number One entertainer at the *National Comedy Awards*. (Gerry Browne was now happy to take second billing to his friend, although he was still a joint partner, on a fifty–fifty split of all earnings.)

The pair continued to appear at the Tivoli, still very much the talk of the town, and one night the talk reached the ears of Hollywood star Gabriel Byrne, of *The Usual Suspects* and more recently TV drama *In Treatment* fame. The actor came to see the show and loved it.

'Someone told me he was in the audience with his (actress) wife Ellen Barkin, and I was asked if he could come back and say hello. Of course, I was delighted. So we had a chat and then Gabe asked me to come back for a coffee to the Westbury Hotel, and he got talking about my performance. He happened to say to me, "You have a very unique way of telling a story. You should think about writing a screenplay." And I said, laughing, "Oh I will, Gabe."

'"No, seriously, you should, Brendan."

'"Oh, honest to God, I will."

'And I kept the smile of tacit agreement on my face for a while before I eventually managed to work up the courage to say, "Gabriel, I have to ask you. What the hell is a screenplay?"

'"A screenplay, well it's a movie story."

'"What do you mean? Is it a script? Is it a narrative?"

'And he explained it was a sort of combination between a theatre script and a narrative. To highlight what he meant, he went up to his room and brought me down a couple of screenplays that he was in the process of turning down.

'He then asked me to have a look at them, to see how a film script was set out. And at the same time he suggested I read a couple of books by a film teacher called Syd Field, *The Scriptwriter* and *Making a First Script Great*.

'What happened in fact was Gabriel sent me these books. And Syd Field had a really great way of thinking, which inspired me.'

Hopeful writers are always told, 'Write what you know about', and Brendan followed the maxim. He had boxed a bit during his youth and he came up with a story called *Sparrow's Trap*. It was the tale of a young boxer who has the world – and his opponent – at his feet, until something stops him dead in his tracks.

Brendan loved writing the script, but of course he wasn't a film writer. It was just a bit of fun, an exercise in writing, and *Sparrow's Trap* was consigned to a bottom drawer.

Meantime, in the summer of 1994, Brendan was asked by RTÉ to go to America to the World Cup Finals where the Irish national team were taking part. He took friends such as Gerry Browne with him, and son Danny.

'I was to go out to Orlando to stay with the team, to do a three-minute piece to camera every second day, interviewing the players, that sort of thing. I was the light relief in the serious business of football.

'Now, to be honest, even though I was there with Gerry, I was bored out of my skull. Can you imagine me only working for three minutes every two days?'

Not even the trauma involved in having his ponytail removed by Leeds United and Ireland footballer Gary Kelly could create enough excitement in his world. (The ponytail was subsequently auctioned for charity and sold for $15,000.)

'To pass the time I read more of Syd Field's book. And one of the exercises that Syd had come up with was to encourage you to write a twenty-page synopsis on your central character. Then you have a back story, and you know how your character will react to any given event.

'Syd pointed out that drama is all about getting someone from A to B and putting obstacles in his way. But with a back story, you know how he'll cope with each obstacle. So I thought, "What a great idea." I went to the shopping mall across the road, got some paper and pens, and decided to do a back story for Mrs Browne. Of course, she had been popular on radio, but I reckoned we didn't know anything about her really. So I decided to do twenty pages on Mrs Browne, just to pass the time.

'Then I had to think where to begin her story. Now, it should have been set in the Thirties, to kick off her childhood, but I wasn't around then, so I thought I'd start the story in the Sixties, in 1967, and I picked 29 March, my mother's birthday. Agnes's birthday is 6 December, the day Roy Orbison died.

'I began the story on the day her husband died. And a new life begins. But the twenty pages ran on to thirty, to forty, fifty. A hundred pages. Then I got to two hundred and fifty pages and I hadn't even got past the first nine months of her widowhood.

'I read over it and became a little bit excited and thought, "This could be a book!" So I rang my manager back in Ireland, Pat Egan, and said, "Listen, Pat, I'm thinking about writing a book."

'"What's it about?"

'"It's about Agnes Browne, the first nine months after she becomes a widow."

'"Go on . . ."

'"It's nothing deep at all. It's just light and frivolous."

'"Okay, well, bring it home with you."

'But the very next day he rang me and said, "Good news, I've got a buyer for your book."

'"Who?"

'"O'Brien Press."

'"You can't have a buyer for the book, Pat. No one has even seen it yet."

'"Yes, I know, but I put a couple of feelers out and O'Brien say they'll take it because the interest in the radio series is huge."

'"No, Pat, I don't want that kind of deal. I don't want them buying a book they haven't read, just because it has Mrs Browne's name on it. It might be crap."'

What to do? Dismiss the offer because the publisher hadn't read the copy? No, Brendan reckoned he'd go and meet Michael O'Brien and see what he had to say for himself.

And he was glad he did.

'I liked Michael. His company was based in Victoria Place in Rathmines, on the outskirts of the city, and had been set up by his dad on a bicycle. In recent times they'd been publishing children's books and now they were keen to publish books for adults. And I liked the idea of growing with a small company.'

So far, so good. Michael O'Brien in turn loved the world Brendan had created and offered the writer a £5,000 advance, which was a decent figure for a first-time writer. *The Mammy*'s Agnes Browne wasn't the woman who appears on television today, though; that Agnes is a heightened character, perfect for sitcom. The mammy of the book is more serious. Still funny, but more measured. And set in a world in which you can almost taste the desperation in her life.

The Mammy certainly suggested Brendan had a dark comic mind.

The story is set in Dublin in the Sixties and features Agnes, the mother of seven kids, who lives in The Jarro (a fictitious amalgam of areas such as Summerhill and Stoneybatter, which would later lead to confusion when American tourists tried to find it), and gets up at 5 a.m. to work at a fruit stall in Moore Street.

The tale begins just hours after the death of Agnes's husband, Redser, when she has to go to the Social Security office to claim money. She's that skint.

The officious lady behind the window pulls out the necessary form and asks Agnes how her husband died. Agnes says he was killed by a hunter. The lady is horrified and asks 'What, with a gun? With a knife?' Agnes looks at her as if she's stupid and says, 'No, it was a Hillman Hunter. He was feckin' knocked down.'

And the laughs and the pathos continue for the next 174 pages as we're introduced to Agnes's seven kids, her best friend Marion and her would-be suitor, Pierre.

'Anyway, the book came out and on the Friday I plugged it on *The Late, Late Show*. And by the Monday it was Number One in the bestseller charts. It stayed there for an incredible eighteen weeks. I was quite stunned.'

The book launch in Dublin brought about an added joy. Brendan's favourite teacher and inspiration Billy Flood was guest of honour. Years later, when *Mrs Brown's Boys* became successful on TV, Brendan again acknowledged his mentor. 'If you don't like *Mrs Brown's Boys*, don't blame me,' he joked. 'Billy Flood made me do it.'

Brendan's first novel (dedicated to Gerry Browne) had hit the mark.

Four weeks later, Brendan met with Michael O'Brien in the Halfway House bar, between Rathmines and Finglas, to discuss the future.

'He had started to increase the spend on marketing. He could see it was still moving nicely. But Michael said, "Listen, we need to have a chat."

'I knew what he was going to say and I pre-empted the conversation. He was going to ask me for another book, afraid I'd go elsewhere. So at the meeting, I said to him, "Look, here's the deal, Michael. I see this as a trilogy."

'"Oh, yes. So do I."

'"Well, here's what I'll do. The next two books are yours."

'"Fantastic, Brendan!"

'"Yes, but you've got to promise me you'll keep up the marketing."

'Now, as it turned out, I don't think he had the will or the wherewithal to market the book on a worldwide basis. It was me who would eventually get overseas interest and world-wide marketing.'

Brendan knew instinctively that Mrs Brown would sell outside Ireland.

'Mrs Brown is not an Irish story. It's a mammy story. If a book like this sells well in an English-speaking country, there is no reason to believe it won't work in every English-speaking country. That's why Cliff Richard sells albums in Australia.'

He wasn't wrong. But *The Mammy* didn't only sell in English-speaking lands. It would go on to make the Top Twenty in India and Brazil too.

'It was translated into Japanese and Polish, a total of twenty-eight languages. During the Bosnia conflict, it was the Number One book in the country.'

Brendan had proved he could write a novel. And he set out to write the follow-up for O'Brien. But he'd soon come up with a writing idea that was, even by his standards, quite audacious.

THE COURSE

BRENDAN had fun writing the follow-up to *The Mammy,* called *The Chisellers,* the title emerging from the alcohol-tinged tongue of Agnes Browne as she mispronounces the word 'children'.

Set three years on from her husband Redser's death, it features Mrs Browne's battles 'in being a mother, father and referee to her fighting family of seven.' But Agnes Browne is no longer living in the inner city area, The Jarro. She has now moved to suburban Finglas, the area where Brendan grew up.

Write what you know.

But while there was a real chance the book would replicate the success of *The Mammy,* what he needed was an idea that would present him with a completely new challenge.

'I had no idea what that was,' he says with a grin.

'Then, one day in January 1995, I was asked by a journalist what I planned to do in the year ahead, and I said, "I think I'll write a play for the Dublin Theatre Festival and stage it myself."'

Brendan had never written a play before. He hadn't actually seen more than a couple of theatre plays, apart from the

Christmas shows and revues. Nor had he ever produced one, or hired actors, booked theatres, etc. It was an entirely insane idea, particularly as he was still carrying The Abbot's Castle debt, and had a mortgage and family to look after.

So of course he had to go ahead.

'I was aware that a Dublin writer hadn't been premiered at the Festival in eighty-five years, so I thought I'd have a go,' he says with the casualness of a man who's just declared he's off to buy new socks.

Maureen O'Carroll was gone but she continued to influence her son's life. Brendan was once again looking over the edge of a crevasse, but his mammy gave him the courage to leap to the other side.

And, after all, he'd written a bestselling novel at the first attempt. Why wouldn't he be able to replicate this feat in Theatreland?

While making the announcement, Brendan had avoided mentioning the name of the play or indeed the subject matter. Not because he was being deliberately coy. It was because he hadn't a clue what it was going to be about. He was desperate for an idea. Think positive. Come on Brendan, it's all about having the right Positive Mental Attitude. That's what the course taught you, wasn't it? Yes, the PMA course you had to undertake as part of the job with the insurance company. When you walked away from that course you believed you could conquer a mountain range that Edmund Hillary would have walked away from.

Now, all you have to do is put on a play. You can come up with a premise.

And there it was. He'd call it *The Course*, of course.

And so he came up with the story of a group of 'losers' who sign up for a Positive Mental Attitude seminar.

The play's central character, Joe Daly, played by Brendan, gives courses to a motley bunch of seeming no-hopers, and he gets a good bonus for every person who passes the exams.

Everything is going well until the American supervisor, Burt Rubenstein, arrives, reckons Daly to be a scammer, and threatens to close down the course – unless everyone passes the exam.

'So I started all the basics, trying to work out how many characters I needed, writing them in, rubbing them out. And I realised that you become God when you write a play.'

Once he had the idea, the shape of the play began to form quickly, and he came up with his oddball cast of characters, which included a prostitute, a golf widow, an alcoholic, a resting actor and a country bumpkin. Brendan/God loved creating this new world, to be played out on stage later that year.

Meanwhile, during that summer, Brendan picked up the Entertainer of the Year Award at the National Concert Hall in Dublin. Brendan and Gerry sang 'Hey, Paddy' and Brendan forgot the words. It didn't matter; the pals had a great night. And were delighted to be introduced to U2. Gerry took the chance to mention to lead singer Bono that he used to deliver milk to his family home in Ballymun. It put a smile on his face to think he'd supplied the snap, crackle and pop to the pop star's Rice Krispies.

Brendan also landed his first film job, appearing as Weslie in Roddy Doyle's mobile-chip-shop adventure, *The Van*. Brendan loved the filming, and became pals with the writer.

During filming, however, Brendan received a rather unwelcome phone call.

'It was from the Dublin Theatre Festival office and the person on the end of the line sounded very serious. They wanted me to give up the theatre to some Italian Circus Opera.

'The Italian production had been booked into the town's Andrews Lane Theatre, which was too small. So they wanted me to swap. They wanted me to swap theatres.'

Producers rarely play musical theatres with their plays. Audiences don't like to migrate. Publicity has to be remounted. But the Festival office didn't see the problem.

Brendan did. He was hugely resentful. He felt that the Theatre Festival people were making him out to be the bad guy, forcing him into a very difficult position. And being cavalier. This was theatre royalty treating him like a Johnny-come-lately, a lowly subject.

Thankfully, Roddy Doyle was quick to encourage his fellow writer.

'Roddy took me aside and said, "You cannot let these people do this. You've got to do it yourself, outside of the Festival Theatre umbrella."'

Yes, why not? He still had the Tivoli. He still had the backing of Tony Byrne. Three days later, Brendan picked up the phone to hear a very friendly co-producer on the line.

'Tony was an avid golfer and he asked me to go for a round with him, at Holystown (the North Dublin suburb where Brendan would later live).

'So we started playing golf and we got to talking. At about the fourth or fifth hole he said something strange to me. He said, "You know, when I told people in the theatre business that I was going to co-produce this theatre play with you, a man with no theatre experience, they told me not to touch you with a ten-foot bargepole."

'And so we moved on to the next hole. But at the sixth hole Tony said to me, "I got a call from the Theatre Festival."

'And right then I knew. He had been leaned on. So he opened up a bit and said, "What do you think about their problem, Brendan?"

'"Well, exactly that. It's their problem, Tony."

'"I'd like to help them out."

'"If you want to do that, you'd better build a theatre very quickly, because you're not getting the one I have."

'"Well, I am joint producer."

'"Yes, Tony. But you came in as co-producer after I had rented the theatre. That rental arrangement stands. I rented the theatre and I'm lending it to the joint production."

'"If that's the case, Brendan, I'm pulling out of the joint production."

'"You're kidding! That'll leave me about thirty-five grand short."

'"Look, Brendan, that's the way it is. I have to think about my reputation within the theatre industry."

Tony certainly didn't want to incur the wrath of the theatre inner circle. Meanwhile, the golf match continued. And when the pair, now operating in something of a cold silence, reached the ninth hole, Tony was three shots in front. But by the end of the game, Brendan had won by five shots.

'I was feckin' determined to whup his arse. During the last rounds, he tried to talk about the play, but I just put him down saying, "Tony, from the ninth tee off, you were no longer producing the show. I don't want to talk about it with you."

'"Well, I want to explain . . ."

'"You don't have to explain. The show is nothing to do with you. Let's play golf."'

After the match, Brendan was furious, and desperate too, given he had to find the extra £35k to open his play. But when he arrived home there was worse news. He picked up the phone to hear a *Dublin Herald* journalist ask: 'Have you seen the paper?'

'And there it was in the Arts section of the *Irish Times*. It read: *Dublin Theatre Festival Rejects Brendan O'Carroll Play*.

'So I went through the story to see what excuse they had come up with. And the copy revealed the play had been rejected because it wasn't up to the standard required by the Festival.

The Theatre Festival boss Tony O'Dalaigh didn't expand on his reasons and Brendan had no idea why his play was turned down. It transpires however Tony O'Dalaigh thought *The Course* to be 'derivative', the idea a little too close to the 1975 play *Comedians*, by Trevor Griffiths, about a bunch of comedy losers who are transformed by a course.

Brendan meantime was in despair. The dream of writing a hit play seemed stuck in a bunker with Tony Byrne's last shot.

Thankfully, that same night the forlorn writer had a visit from Gerry Browne and Tommy Swarbrigg, who now arranged Brendan's stand-up bookings. At least he could rely on support from his right-hand man and one of his trusted lieutenants.

Or so he thought.

'Gerry actually seemed pleased at this bad news. Now, he wasn't trying to get one over on me; he had his own reasons for not wanting it to go ahead. I think it's because he really didn't want to do the play.'

It seems hard to believe Gerry didn't want success for his friend.

'He did. But he wanted our world to stay the same, to carry on with the comedy shows. His thinking was, "Stick with what you're good at." I wanted Gerry with me. I wanted him up there on stage with me and said to him, "Gerry, take some acting classes." But he never bothered. He was scared, I guess. Yet, I knew he could act. He was a natural.'

Gerry denies all this. He says he wanted to move forward with the idea of the play. He had no idea whether his friend could write a play, but he assumed it was possible. After the success of *The Mammy* books, anything was possible.

'Tommy was also accepting of the bad news. He said to me, "Now I don't want to add fuel to the fire, Brendan, but you have to accept that the Theatre Festival people have been in this business a long time. You have to accept they know what they're talking about."

The Theatre Festival pressure, and the fact that his friends weren't exactly stoking the fires of encouragement, took its toll on Brendan. Regardless, he went off and finished his play. And he felt he had written a decent comedy. But given the obstacles in his way, PMA just wasn't kicking in.

'I was so low. And by early September, just a few weeks before the play was to go on stage, I was seriously considering throwing in the towel.'

The metaphor was appropriate. Even a helicopter ride the following day to a World Boxing Championship couldn't lift Brendan's spirits.

'On this Friday, I had a helicopter picking me up to take me to Cork, where a friend of mine, Steve Collins, was fighting Chris Eubank for the middleweight title.

'It was their second fight. Steve had won the first because Eubank was out of sorts. And we all knew that this time around Eubank was going to kill him. Or we thought we knew.

'I had really been looking forward to this fight, but on the flight I was so low I never spoke to a soul. I was so gutted. I was the same during the limo journey. Wrecked at the thought of the play being pulled.'

At the ringside, an RTÉ producer approached Brendan and mentioned that Jimmy Magee, the well-known boxing commentator, had spotted him on one of the cameras.

'Jimmy knew I'd boxed and wanted me to go over and do a piece to camera, and so I did. It went fine, and I managed to sound upbeat, and we talked about Steve's new style, which meant throwing bombers, big punches that would upset Eubank's style. It was hoped to turn it into a scrap, because if that were the case the street fighter – Steve – would win.

'And as we were talking about the fight plan, I looked up at the monitors and could see the fighters arrive. And I found myself staring at the screen. I could see Steven's face under the hood, the close-up, and I could read his lips. And they were saying, "Still the champ. Still the champ . . ." And that was something I had told him earlier: "As long as you are still standing, you are still the champ. And you don't stop being the champ until that fight's over."

'And there he was, in that ring, saying to himself, "Still the champ." And at that moment it dawned on me. I thought, "*I'm* still the champ."'

Steve Collins certainly was. He bombed Eubank from every direction. Eubank was completely disorientated and Collins retained the World Championship.

'We flew back to Dublin the next day. And of course the press were now ringing me non-stop for a reaction to the news about the Festival dropping the play. I said I was disappointed, but added that since I had promised so many of the Dublin public they would see the play, I wasn't going to let them down. My thinking? "I'm still the champ. I can win here."'

What? How? His co-producer had walked off at the ninth tee. The Festival had announced they didn't want an O'Carroll play. And Brendan reckoned Gerry wasn't fully committed.

'I told the press the play would go ahead, at a little Fringe Festival, and it would be taking part in Francis Street, at the Tivoli.'

Tony Byrne freaked at the news. He pleaded with Brendan, saying he couldn't take the theatre show, that it would ruin relations with the Theatre Festival office. And the Tivoli boss argued the negative publicity would kill off *The Course*'s chances of success.

Brendan argued back that he *had* to take over the Tivoli, and that, rather than garner negative publicity, 'the neggie would be turned into a possie.' How? He worked out a plan with Rory. On every newspaper ad for the show he would be printing the tag line: *The play that Dublin Festival rejected*.

'And I added that I wanted to thank Tony O'Dalaigh for singling me out as the only unique play.'

The newspapers loved Brendan's sheer balls and ran riot with the story. Now, he had the most talked-about play ever to hit Dublin. And he talked it up even more. During a series of radio interviews, he turned the news of Festival rejection around, saying he was delighted his play had been turned down. The hopeful playwright stressed that the Festival plays were for the elite – while his plays 'were for the people who liked a bag of crisps and a laugh.'

Clever. And the impact of all this? Brendan O'Carroll became the People's Champion, the voice and soul of the little guy. The battle lines were drawn between working-class Dublin and the middle-class theatre establishment.

But hassles with the various theatre producers meant that Brendan was on his own mounting the play. Now all he had to do, apart from remortgaging his home to pay the actors' wages, was to deliver a piece of theatre that was powerful, incisive and hilariously funny.

After all this fuss, it *had* to be that good.

The Secret Millionaire

BRENDAN thought his play was funny. And, having read it, so did Gerry. But what did they know about theatre? (Gerry had only ever seen one play in his life.)

The pair decided to enlist the help of Lee Dunne, who'd written the classic Dublin book *Goodbye to the Hill*, which had been turned into a play. And so the waiter and the milkman took off to see Dunne's play performed in the Peacock Theatre, set under the main Dublin bus terminus.

'When I went along to check out the play, I was a bit late arriving. The play had already started and I tried to sneak quietly into the auditorium. But I was captured by the usherette, a blonde lady who didn't know me from Adam, who showed me in the direction of my seat and said, "Sit the feck there!" And so I did, thinking, "Jaysus, I wouldn't like to get on the wrong side of that one!"'

Brendan settled down to watch the play but, as the on-stage drama unfolded, his eyes suddenly opened as wide as the stage itself. The 'usherette' who had just given him a dressing down had made her way up onto the stage. She was playing the female lead.

'And she was good. Very, very good. And it turned out this was Jennifer Gibney, an actress I'd been tipped off about beforehand. She'd been waiting outside in the foyer because her character had to make her entrance from the back of the hall. And the reason she was so pissed off was she'd been told an important guest – me – was due to arrive, and became fed up with the waiting. So we didn't get off to a great start.

'But not only was she brilliant, she got a standing ovation at the end. And far bigger applause than any of the other actors.'

Though possibly it helped that Jenny, a statuesque blonde and also from Finglas, had been working part-time in a bank and a group of around twenty colleagues had come along to support her. Hence the huge cheer.

Yet, she was still very good. And Brendan had found the actress to play the downtrodden housewife, Emily Beauchamp.

He didn't look too far in recruiting the rest of the team. Brendan played Joe, the PMA boss (who, in fact, had few comedic lines; everyone else got the chance to shine). Gerry played Will Benson, the cynical, recovering alcoholic, and Brendan Keely, whom they had met during the Rathmines stint, was perfect for the fey, out-of-work actor, even though he'd never acted before.

Brendan Morrisey, Paul Lee (an established actor from the prestigious Abbey Theatre) and Ciaron McMahon completed the cast.

Brendan and Gerry, once again, tried to recruit from people they knew. The wardrobe mistress, Mary Cullen, had an alterations shop in Finglas, and had never worked in a theatre in her life. Brendan reckoned she'd soon learn what was required. And she did. The family was growing.

Did it matter that Brendan and Gerry had never acted on stage before? Not to them. The rascals from Finglas believed they could do anything, until proven otherwise.

However, rehearsals, it's fair to say, were not what the experienced actors in the cast had been used to. Jenny Gibney certainly wasn't overly impressed by the troupe. She thought Gerry a loud-mouthed irritant, a feeling no doubt fostered by the first thing he said to her. 'Let's rehearse the sex scene,' he joked. And the line might have gone down better had the play in fact contained a sex scene.

She wasn't overly impressed by Brendan Keely's raw approach to the craft, nor was she pleased by the cavalier approach the producers seemed to have towards theatre production.

Jenny was used to turning up for rehearsals at 10 a.m., and starting exactly on time. On this first day, Brendan and Gerry and co. 'were doing a lot of standing around, huddled together chatting and drinking coffee and looking like the Dublin branch of the Mafia. And it was now twelve o'clock.'

Jenny didn't immediately warm to the producer and the star of the show either. She thought Brendan was 'a little Hitler'.

'I thought Jenny was a mouthy gobshite,' says Brendan. 'Although she did the *Irish Times* crossword, smoked Consulates and drank coffee, which reminded me of my mother.'

But it was all very well employing friends, soon-to-be-friends and mouthy gobshites with Maureen O'Carroll traits. They all had to be paid during rehearsals, even when there was no income coming in. Brendan and Gerry were still gigging at night and making enough to pay their own bills, but this additional cost of eight wages, building a set, renting rehearsal space, wardrobe and stage crew soon gobbled up any spare cash.

By the second week of rehearsals, all the cash had gone. The People's Champion, the lover of crisps, hadn't the price of a packet of Golden Wonders to his name.

The waiter and the milkman might have had the self-belief of a legion of men on Prozac, but that didn't mean they could go anywhere near a cash machine.

But out of the blue, Brendan got a call from business magnate and Celtic FC majority share-owner, Dermot Desmond. He had read the story about the Theatre Festival pulling out.

'Brendan? It's Dermot Desmond. Can you come up and see me?'

Brendan set off immediately to Desmond's office. The multi-millionaire was seated at his desk.

'Tell me, Brendan, is the story about the play being rejected true?'

'Yes, it is.'

'But why?'

'Well, Tony O'Dalaigh said it lacks artistic merit.'

'Do you think it's a good play?'

'Yes, I do.'

'Are you going to go ahead with it?'

'I definitely am.'

'Okay.'

Dermot Desmond pushed an envelope in front of the hopeful theatre producer and said, 'Okay. You have to go now.'

Brendan left the office, opened the envelope, and inside was a cheque for £5,000.

It was enough to pay the wages through rehearsals. But Brendan, now just past his fortieth birthday, then came up with a strategy that had never been attempted by any theatre producer in the world.

He told his cast they weren't going to rehearse the play; they were going on a course, the very same PMA course that Brendan had embarked upon five years ago. The grinning producer announced he'd hired one of the PMA instructors to put them through their paces.

'They were a bit taken aback when I told them this, but the idea was so they could really understand the play. And I also wanted to have them psyched up for the whole experience of performing it. At first they thought the idea madness, but then they came round to it, and viewed it as a learning experience – and a bit of fun.'

At the end of the session, Brendan was taken to one side by the PMA leader and given some insight into his cast's performances.

'He said, "There's one girl in the cast who, if this play doesn't work out, has a real future in sales. She's a sales star in the making." The girl was Jenny.'

The play was due to open on Tuesday 9 October. On the Friday beforehand, Brendan sat the cast down and delivered his own inspirational speech.

'I told the cast what the play meant to me. I told them about my first theatre experience at the age of nine, what that had meant to me. I told them what I felt they had to give this audience. They were with me. I had them. They were psyched.'

Great. They were all set to put on a fantastic show. Surely nothing else could go wrong?

'Just then my director announced he was leaving. The lighting designer pulled out. Then my set designer walked out as well.'

And so the writer/star was pushed to make his acting, writing and directorial debut, all at the one time.

'I said to the cast, "Look, even if this is the greatest theatre disaster ever, this is the most high-profile play in Irish history. And no matter what happens, you are going to be part of it. So let's do it well."'

The production hadn't even sold enough tickets to fill the front row of the 600-seat theatre. Anyone else would have read the signs – and wept.

'I thought we were knackered. I thought it was all over. But we had to go on.'

And then a miracle happened. A moment worthy of any Hollywood film finale occurred that opening Tuesday night in 1995.

'I set off for the theatre around six, and headed into Francis Street,' says Brendan, his voice emotional as he rewinds. 'And you couldn't get into the street. The queue outside the theatre was running all the way down the road.'

Dublin had turned out in droves to see his play. Those who had seen Brendan perform stand-up wanted to see what the fuss was all about. And those who'd read in the papers that he was something of an outcast from the theatre establishment warmed to the council house rebel with the primary school education.

'I had misread my audience. They weren't all regular theatre-goers. They were not people to buy tickets way in advance. They go along on the night.'

And so the cast performed the play to a sell-out crowd. And when the final line was delivered and the lights went down, the biggest cheer Brendan had ever heard in his life went up. They took curtain call after curtain call. And when the cast walked off and stood in the wings, not believing their ears, the applause still boomed like thunder.

The Course went on to run for an amazing sixteen weeks. Word of mouth was incredible. The *Irish Independent* said, 'The Course is a few scenes short of a play', but, on the whole, newspaper critics loved it.

And for the two weeks during the Festival, *The Course* took more at the box office than all the other Festival plays put together. The fact that the play was about Positive Mental Attitude gave the tale an added piquancy.

'The rehearsals for the play carried me through it,' Brendan admits. 'I needed the PMA to get me over the hurdles.'

One of the smaller hurdles Brendan had to leap over was Brendan Keely. One night at ten to eight, Keely still hadn't shown up and Brendan called him, only to discover his actor was 20 miles away. What to do? There wasn't an understudy so they waited until they knew he was 20 minutes away and began the show, hoping he'd arrive by the time his character made an entrance.

After the show, an outraged Brendan revealed he was going to kill his namesake.

'You're a little bollix and I should sack you.'

'And if I were you I would. I am a little bollix indeed.'

And that admission totally disarmed the boss.

'What can you do with someone like that?' he says, rhetorically.

The likeable and entirely honest little bollix that is Keely would later go on to join the priesthood.

Dublin, meanwhile, couldn't get enough of *The Course*. After the play's eight-week run at the Tivoli, it moved on to the Gaiety Theatre (with almost triple capacity) and sold out for another eight weeks.

No other play had ever run in Dublin for four months. It was the biggest-selling comedy play ever and it would hold that record until five years later, when beaten by a new theatre show called *Mrs Brown's Last Wedding*. (And that record would be beaten by *Mrs Brown Rides Again*.)

The People's Champion had been crowned. He had created unashamedly populist theatre that was funny. And his subjects loved the fact that he was anti-establishment.

Brendan was a rebel and a fighter. He didn't negotiate. He hired non-actors. He didn't follow the rules. Not consciously, it was just his way. But he couldn't have cared less.

The financier Dermot Desmond never came to the opening of the play. And he never spoke to Brendan after that time in his office. But there's no doubt he would have smiled when he read of the massive success. He would have agreed that *The Course* being the best play in the land, it simply had to go on tour.

GOING WEST

THE COURSE toured most of Ireland's major theatres. The show ran well, and a tour of Scotland, England and Toronto was lined up. In the spring of 1996, just before *The Course* set off to go to Glasgow's Mitchell Theatre, Brendan was rummaging around in his office at home and found a CV from an actor, Michael Pyatt, which had been sent to him the year before.

'It was a really nice letter. It was very warm and humorous and it was from a bloke who said he lived in Stafford but his mother was Irish. The mother had seen me talking on *The Late, Late Show* about how I planned to write a play. And she had persuaded Michael to send me his CV and ask to be kept in mind if/when the play came to go into production.

'At the time I had already fixed up a cast, but I sent him a letter saying I'd keep him on file if ever anyone dropped out.

'Anyway, there it was and I rang up this bloke, and when he came on the line he could hardly speak. He told me the reason later. It turned out that at the moment I'd called, he'd been tidying out his desk, found my letter and had just crumpled it up and thrown it in the bin.

'During our conversation, he fished it back out and was smoothing it out as we spoke.'

It was one of those magical moments.

'And I said, "Michael, what are you working on at the moment?"

'"Well, I'm driving a van actually. I've been working in kids' educational theatre but the contract has just come to an end."

'"Well, how would you like to come up to Glasgow?"

'"It sounds great. But could you give me twenty-four hours to think it over?"

'"I can give you twenty-two. Because that's when we're leaving."

'"Okay, I'll call you before then."

'And he did. Eleven hours later he rang. "I'd love to come up for the audition, Brendan."

'"You don't have to audition, Michael. If you want the part it's yours."'

Incredible. Hired on the strength of a letter and phone call. But Brendan had liked Pikey, from the tone of the letter and the conversation. (Pikey would become a Mrs Brown regular on stage and on TV, playing Cathy's boyfriend Professor Clowne.)

In Glasgow, the cast assembled on the Monday for a week of rehearsals and Brendan replaced Paul Lee with Michael Pyatt.

In 1996, the show toured Ireland and then moved on to play in London, Manchester and Birmingham. Sales weren't great, but it was a new play. However, when the cast arrived in Liverpool, it was now the height of summer and 'gorgeous weather'. And the last place anyone would wish to be in was a theatre.

As a result, box office for an unknown Irish play full of unknown actors was dreadful. One night there were hardly enough people in the hall to fill the front row of the Royal Court.

Brendan was determined that it wouldn't affect the show, saying to his cast, 'Look, there may not be many people out there, but I want you to perform this play to the very best of your ability for every last one of them. They've paid their money, so they deserve to have a great night. And that's what we'll give them.'

But the box office was so bad that Brendan and Gerry couldn't afford to pay the wages. It was Jenny who offered to bail them out. She borrowed £8,000 from the bank and the travelling band of actors remained in business.

That didn't stop Brendan and his team from setting off for Toronto in August in a bid to conquer North America. Sure, the UK trip hadn't gone too well. But they believed Canadian audiences would find *The Course* funny, given the Irish contingent who'd emigrated to North America.

And it all looked hugely promising. The troupe arrived at Toronto's Pearson Airport, at the start of the Toronto Film Festival. Ordinarily, that would make no difference, but this year Roddy Doyle's *The Van* was the major film being premiered.

The papers had picked up on the fact that Brendan had been nominated for a 'Best Supporting Actor' gong for his part and journalists' requests for interviews flooded in. Since Brendan was the only actor from the movie who happened to be in town, it was all a godsend for the Toronto papers, a city that carries three major dailies.

Brendan couldn't believe his luck. And he felt he had to capitalise on it.

Brendan with Bryan
McFadden from
Westlife in 2003.

With Boyzone's
Keith Duffy and
Coronation Street's
Bruce Jones in 2004.

Brendan with
Peter Kay in
2008.

Mrs Brown in all her telegenic glory.

Giving Grandad a good scrub.

Rory Cowen (right) has worked with Brendan for over 20 years.

'We are not the Waltons, that's for sure…'

The loudest, proudest mother in Ireland . . .

Winnie McGoogan (played by Brendan's sister Eilish) is hypnotised.

Ding Dong Merrily on High – Mrs Brown copes with Christmas.

Recognition for *Mrs Brown* at the 2012 Baftas.

Brendan's cast and family at the Baftas 2012.
Jenny is standing next to Brendan in blue.

Another win at the National Television Awards in 2013.

Brendan took on the role of Mrs Brown when the actress due to play her failed to turn up.

Visiting today's 'Real' Mrs Browns at the fish market on Moore Street.

'We were booked to play in a small, six-hundred-seater theatre, but we reckoned that with the publicity we'd get, we had to move to a larger theatre. And we did, hiring the St Lawrence Theatre in the financial district, with two and a half thousand seats.'

The gambler was throwing the dice again. But there was a worrying sign that Brendan and Gerry's relationship was becoming strained. Gerry had suggested everyone take an extra suitcase with them on the trip, with everyone carrying their own wardrobe. And so the actors, including Brendan, arrived at Toronto Airport and picked up the luggage, soon laden like pack mules. Except Gerry. He leapt into a taxi upon arrival and headed straight to the hotel bar. Brendan was incensed when he realised what had happened.

'I phoned his room and got him and yelled, "I'm coming up." And I did, and when he opened the door I chased him around the room, throwing a television set at him in the process.'

It turned out that Gerry wasn't as badly damaged as the smashed TV set. But the incident highlighted the fact that the comedy partners weren't entirely on the same page.

Then major disaster struck. At the last minute, *The Van* was withdrawn from the Film Festival.

'It seemed Roddy Doyle and the director Stephen Frears couldn't agree on the final cut. As a result, the film was pulled.'

And with it went the miles of column inches that the interviews with Brendan would have produced. The tickets for *The Course* simply didn't sell. The first night was papered, which means tickets are given away free, in the hope word-of-mouth will encourage sales. But the second night saw only fifteen people in the audience. There were more in the cast and crew than punters in seats. More importantly, Brendan had fourteen people in hotels with no guarantee of their wages.

It didn't matter if reviews were good, Toronto just didn't turn out. Perhaps it was that the culture of the play was too un-Canadian. Brendan and Gerry lost £60,000 on the trip, and the Irish tour hadn't been successful either. The reasons? Hubris. Ego. And simple economics. It was all very well taking a troupe of friends around Ireland, but they had to be paid. *The Course* worked in Dublin without hotel bills to pay, transport and food costs, etc. Outside of the city, it simply wasn't viable.

However, there was another problem. The lack of cash had put a major strain on the Brendan–Gerry relationship. If their company balance sheet were a movie script, it would have been a horror, classified 'X' certificate.

By now, the pair were barely speaking. The blood brothers had developed anaemia.

Deal Or No Deal

BACK in Dublin, Brendan's relationship with Gerry Browne improved, although it wasn't quite what it had been before they had taken *The Course* to Toronto. Brendan had become closer to Jenny Gibney, though. It seemed she had now become much less of a gobshite in his eyes and more of a friend and a confidante. Their time on the road together had taught them that they had more in common than they'd first thought.

Meanwhile, the third in the trilogy of Agnes Browne books was released. *The Granny* went straight to Number One in the Irish bestseller list and the first print-run sold out immediately.

It was darker than the first two. With all the Browne children now grown up and leaving home to go their own ways, Agnes Browne becomes a granny at 47 when Mark and Betty have their first child. Some of the children have gone on to lead very successful lives, but Cathy is stuck in a bad marriage, and Dermot ends up in prison for manslaughter along with his best mate, Buster. Agnes finds the break-up of the family hard to deal with, but with her lover Pierre by her side, she copes.

Brendan's writing was believable because he had drawn from his own childhood. And the work was described by the *Sunday Independent* as 'a brilliant book' and by the *Irish World* as having 'language as rich as oxtail soup'.

The sales would help to make a little dent in Brendan and Gerry's personal overdraft, but Brendan knew the books should be more successful. He didn't feel his *Mammy* adventures were being promoted in the way they deserved. It was all very well doing great box office in Ireland, but he wanted to conquer the world. And he saw a chance to push Agnes Browne into the international spotlight one afternoon in a Dublin restaurant while having coffee with film director and producer Jim Sheridan (director of the 1989 Oscar-winning film *My Left Foot*, starring Daniel Day Lewis).

The pair had become friendly in recent months and were joined by literary agent, Darley Anderson.

'We got talking to Darley, who had managed to secure a book deal and film rights for Jim's brother, Peter, who was writing his first book. Jim pointed out I'd done three books but sales were contained in Ireland. Anyway, Darley asked me about the foreign rights and I told him nothing was happening on that front. He was astounded and said he wanted to become involved.

'Later that day, Darley rang Michael O'Brien, who then called me and told me the "great news".

'"Darley Anderson's been on to me, Brendan."

'"I know. I've been talking to him."

'"We really need to push sales abroad."

'Now, I'm thinking, "It's about time, Michael!"'

The result of the meeting with Darley meant that Brendan's work was showcased at the Frankfurt Book Fair.

Some weeks passed and the plan to promote *The Mammy* and her two offspring paid off.

'The result of going to Frankfurt was that it caught the eye of Penguin in America. And they wanted to release the three Mrs Browne books in America under a licensing agreement with O'Brien. Fantastic.'

Brendan went on a promotional tour of America, covering 22 cities in 30 days. And his books sold in their thousands. After that, he returned to his screenplay about boxing, *Sparrow's Trap*. His Dublin publisher, Michael O'Brien wanted another O'Carroll book, and when he read the film script of *Sparrow's Trap* he was convinced the story could be rewritten as a terrific novel. Brendan protested, rather incredibly given his success, that he wasn't a prolific writer, certainly not someone who could turn a screenplay format into novel form. And it wasn't a case of false modesty.

'I'm not a writer in a structured sense. I just sit down and have a go when the mood, or the idea, takes me. But in the end I agreed to try, to keep Michael happy. Yet it was such hard work.'

He slugged it out with *Sparrow's Trap* and won with a knockout. The book would become an Irish bestseller. And, out of the blue, during the writing process, Brendan found himself volunteering to step back into the boxing ring.

Jim Sheridan, coincidentally, was working on a boxing script for a movie, based on the life of Irish World Champion flyweight Barry McGuigan. And he wanted to make sure that there was no overlap. So the writer/director tentatively asked Brendan if he might be able to look at his script. When Brendan readily agreed, Jim Sheridan was surprised.

'People don't let you read their scripts normally,' he said. 'For all you know, I could steal some of your ideas.'

'Well, if you did I'd just write some more.'

What confidence.

When Brendan read the McGuigan story, he loved it. But not just because of Sheridan's clever structure and storytelling skills. He was struck by a thought. 'This is me. I'm the guy in this story.'

He had a point. Brendan had boxed as a teenager. He even looked like Barry McGuigan.

Then Brendan had a call from Jim Sheridan, who asked him to come up to Dublin as he was keen to talk to him. It all made sense. Brendan knew, instinctively, that Jim wanted him to play the Barry McGuigan role.

So they met back in Dublin and Brendan went up to Jim Sheridan's house. However, Brendan walked in to a surprise. Daniel Day Lewis was there. Rather taken aback, Brendan said to Jim Sheridan, in the nicest possible way, 'What the feck's he doing here?'

Jim Sheridan's reply threw Brendan onto the ropes. 'He's playing the lead in the Barry movie.'

'You must be joking!'

'I was stunned. There are only two boxing weights that translate into movie terms, that's stories about heavyweights and lightweights. This was a great lightweight story.

'I desperately wanted to play this part. And this was one of those great roles. So I said to Jim, "Look, you can't cast Daniel. I'm perfect to play this part. I even look like McGuigan. And I can box."

'"Yeh, well, I've done some boxing in my time too," said Daniel.

'I turned to Daniel and said, "Listen, Daniel. I'll tell you how we'll decide who's the best man for the part. We'll go down to Foley's gym and get in the ring and we'll put on the gloves and go at it for three rounds. The winner gets to play Barry McGuigan."

'At this point Daniel looked stunned, turned to Jim Sheridan and said, "I'm not fighting him!"

'Now, I know I would have knocked the shite out of him – and he knew it too. He wouldn't fight me. But he still got the role in *The Boxer*!'

Meantime, Brendan wanted some answers.

'"Look, Jim. If you didn't want me to play the lead in this movie, why did you call me over here?"

'"Endings, Brendan. I can tell from your books you write great endings. I wanted you to write the ending for my movie."

'So I took the positive from the experience. Jim Sheridan needed me to finish his picture. He needed me. That was a great compliment.'

Jim Sheridan's comment about Brendan coming up with great endings would prove to be ironic. Later on, the pair would argue over one of Brendan's film endings – to the point, says Brendan, of coming close to blows.

Brendan never did write the ending for this particular film. *The Boxer* ceased to be about Barry McGuigan, and instead became the story of an IRA man, a former boxer, who comes out of prison and refuses to return to the ring. Daniel Day Lewis played the lead role of Danny Flynn, and, it has to be said, did a typically brilliant job.

As Brendan got more and more involved in the film world and international book deals, he looked for support from those closest to him. But it wasn't Doreen he was turning to instinctively for support any more, it was Jenny. 'I guess we were on the same page, whereas Doreen wasn't overly interested in that world. She was making sure the family were all fine.'

The strain on Brendan's marriage would develop as he headed deep into the film world.

Hot Milk And Pepper

THE CANADIAN adventure had shown Brendan indeed had wings. But like Icarus he'd flown too close to the sun and been badly burned. He'd landed his international book deal and written *Sparrow's Trap*. But what to do next? Irish TV station RTÉ came up with an answer.

'After that major appearance on *The Late, Late Show* and the success of *Mrs Browne's Boys* on radio, RTÉ sent out a command to their producers, "Get O'Carroll into something. Get him in everything."

'I could have written my name on a piece of toilet paper and they'd have used it. But, to be honest, television didn't really appeal to me; my thinking at the time was it didn't pay that well and it uses up a lot of comedy material. So you have to limit yourself. However, RTÉ kept coming up with ideas over a two-year period, to front *Ireland's Funniest Videos*, that sort of thing. But I kept saying no.'

It was only during a trip to London, when Brendan turned up to the opening of *Riverdance* at the Hammersmith Apollo, that he began to rethink his attitude towards TV.

'At the break I bumped into the controller of programmes for RTÉ and he said, "Look, Brendan, we've offered you almost fifteen programme formats. And you've turned them all down."

'"Well, I don't think the time is right to do television."

'"The truth of it is, Brendan, RTÉ gave you your first break. In the past two years you've been on *The Late, Late Show* five times. There has to be some payback."

'The next day we were gigging in Manchester and I thought, "You know, he's right. I do owe RTÉ." So I made the decision that the next thing they offered me, I'd do it. And it wasn't long. About two months later I was offered a quiz show. I agreed to do it and RTÉ were stunned. And delighted.'

Brendan decided the name of the show would be *Hot Milk And Pepper*, a reference to the drink he'd once served Margaret Thatcher.

'We went through the format and it was okay and then I asked what Gerry's role was. The producer, Gerald Heffernan, looked at me blankly.

'Nothing.'

'Nothing? No, you don't understand. It's Brendan and Gerry. We're a team.

'So they came up with a device whereby Gerry read out the scores and announced the prizes. Gerry was delighted. And the credits for the show would read: *Starring Brendan O'Carroll . . . and Gerry Browne.*'

Brendan saw *Hot Milk And Pepper* as an experiment; it wasn't exciting television and it certainly never played to his strengths, i.e. allowing him to be himself. But it was an opportunity to reach kids and that section of Middle Ireland that might be offended by his stage show. He decided that in the next series he would be looking for more control.

'The best bits were edited out. I don't think it was done deliberately. The way it was edited made it very disjointed. But I liked doing it. In for two weeks, twenty-eight shows recorded, take the money and good luck.'

But Brendan was soon able to see the bigger picture. Almost literally. Thanks to *The Mammy*. The book had gone on to reach the bestseller list in 28 countries. The tale of Agnes Browne – mischievous, irascible and yet warm – was so popular, so universal a character, it would have come as no surprise had the publishers called to announce the book was to be translated into Apache. It was surely only a matter of time till Hollywood came calling.

Meantime, Brendan and Gerry were back touring Ireland with their comedy show (now far softer than *The Outrageous Comedy Show*), selling out 600-seater theatres. Brendan loved the live audience. This was so much more fun than the routine of the TV quiz show. And he loved to meet the fans and sign autographs at the stage door. Brendan was certainly attracting his share of female attention.

'Occasionally, a girl would ask you your hotel room number, for sure. But you'd put them off, in a nice way. I certainly didn't want to spend the night with the girl that wanted to spend the night with me. I wanted to be with the one that didn't want to be with me. At every gig, there was somebody who was mesmerised by this thing that's on the stage because, God love them, they don't have a fulfilled life of their own. They want to be part of your life. Now, I'd be a liar if I said I didn't look at some young women and think, "God, she's lovely!" But I wasn't into a quick bang-bang.'

And of course he had Doreen and three kids at home. But where was Doreen at this point? Life with Brendan had never been easy for her. She'd stood by her man through a whole range of traumas, from The Abbot's Castle to the financial crash of *The Course*. She'd watched Brendan climb ladders with book deals, make it onto TV with *The Late, Late Show* and *Hot Milk And Pepper*.

But Brendan was away from home a great deal and he was far from the man Doreen had married. He was forging his own path, dealing with the adulation of fans and the like. Although not all of Ireland was in love with him. Comedian Sean Hughes, for example, had made repeated derogatory references to Brendan at a recent Dublin show. But Brendan took the criticism in his stride.

Brendan, it seemed, at forty-one, couldn't win over the next generation of comedians who appeared in Dublin stand-up clubs such as The Attic and Lillies. Many were critical of the O'Carroll comedy show, claiming it to be old-fashioned, obvious and crude.

But as Brendan says, 'By this time we had made four videos of the shows, and between them they sold a quarter of a million copies. There couldn't have been a quarter of a million eejits out there.'

Brendan hoped a TV company would offer drama or sitcom work but, meantime, he had another, bigger idea. At the end of 1996 he began pitching his film script. *Sparrow's Trap* had sold well as a novel. It had a cracking storyline. Why wouldn't it make a great film? And indeed Brendan believed it could launch a series of RTÉ films.

But doesn't pride always come before a fall?

In Brendan's case the fall would be spectacular.

MAMMY MIA!

BRENDAN sums up his creative life pre-1992 (when Mrs Browne was born) with a succinct line.

'I'd done nothing really. Then I did the stand-up, the radio series and *The Late, Late Show*. Then, over the next five years, I wrote three plays, four novels, two screenplays and made four stand-up videos. Why the explosion? I think this was all a result of the dumbing down I'd imposed on myself. It was all inside, desperate to come out.'

He'd tried to unleash his comedy talent along the way. He'd won the talent competition, he'd tried pirate radio, he'd worked for a comedian, but never managed success. Then the radio show came about – and it all changed. Brendan was born on the same day as Agnes Browne.

However, he dismisses the notion that his talent was always there, waiting to boil to the surface. 'I've always been funny. That's not a boast, it's just a fact. People have always laughed at me. But it's not talent, it's attitude. It's about making the leap. Lots of people, for example, could write a play, or at least make a passable attempt, but they just don't have the attitude. It's about facing the sun, rather than turning your back and wondering why your face is full of frost.

'I think I'm lucky in that I've always seen possibilities, whether it's trying to grow my own food on a farm or setting up a company to sell videos. The ideas don't work out, but I've never been afraid of failure. Most people see the negatives as soon as they come up with an idea. I see the positives. And the ideas keep on appearing.'

It's true. Once when we were chatting over coffee, we were talking about writing short stories – we had both read each other's most recent efforts. Brendan suggested an idea for a book of great short stories that could go into hotel rooms, free, but sponsored, giving guests an option beyond the Gideon Bible. The idea was developed, until pressures of work saw it fade. Had Brendan had the time, his belief, his energy, could have made it work.

In January and February, Brendan was set to tour again with the show *The Story So Far*, appearing at the likes of Dublin's Olympia. Brendan also took off to New York for a stand-up comedy tour, with his entourage, and such was his success in the Big Apple that he could hardly move in the bar of the Fitzpatrick Hotel without being greeted by passers-by who had seen his performance the night before.

'Now, with all that comes a feeling of invincibility. But there is a huge difference between having a very positive mental attitude and being an idiot.

'Sometimes when you are that idiot, you just don't see that difference. So, by the start of 1997, in my own mind I was a god. I was invincible. And I decided I was going to make a movie.'

The one-time gambler would actually go on to make two movies, almost simultaneously. Whom the gods would destroy, they first imbue with rampant self-belief?

'I'm very aware of the fact that I have an excessive personality,' he admits. 'When I gambled, I really gambled. I don't gamble at all now. I wouldn't even back a horse on Saint Stephen's Day. I don't do the Lotto. I wouldn't even do the Grand National. I know now I have access to money and I could blow it all. I genuinely could. When you're gargling, you can only gargle so much before you pass out. But I could blow savings, the house, the kids' future, all in one day.'

The gambler didn't see the next two projects to come his way as high risk. Hollywood came calling. Not in a Cecil B. DeMille multimillion pound *Cleopatra* way, but not quite in a *Carry On Cleo* low-budget manner, either.

Back in the 1970s, film producer Greg Smith had read a bawdy comedy book called *Confessions of a Window-cleaner* and managed to convince the film industry it should be made into a movie. Now, having recently finished filming *Great Expectations* in the States and ready to fly back to Britain, while passing the time in the airport bookshop he happened to spot an interesting book cover. It was *The Mammy*, with the sticker '*The No. 1 Bestseller*' attached, and Greg bought it. By the time he arrived in London, he'd read of the adventures of Agnes Browne and her brood – and was hooked.

'This guy called Greg Smith called me up one day and said he represented the Disney Corporation. I said, "Feck off!" and hung up. I thought it was someone taking the mick. Disney and *The Mammy* together? I don't think so. But it turned out he was from Buena Vista, which is their adult arm. Then he called back and asked who owned the film rights to *The Mammy*.'

Brendan said he did. (He'd been smart enough to make sure that clause was in his contract with O'Brien.)

'Greg wanted me to meet with his partner Morgan O'Sullivan, who was based in Ireland with Admiral Studios.'

The pair met and one of the first things sorted out was what to call the film. *The Mammy* wasn't seen as a real possibility – it evoked thoughts of Al Jolson or colonial slave plantations to mind. And while the title *Mrs Browne* would have been a real possibility, Billy Connolly and Judi Dench had beaten them to it. So they settled on *Agnes Browne*.

But there were going to be many fights to be fought.

'They wouldn't let me write the screenplay (they didn't know I'd written *Sparrow's Trap* and probably would have cared even less), so they brought in a hired gun to write it, which was fair enough. He was English and had never been to Ireland. I wasn't arguing with that point. The blokes who'd written *Star Trek* had never been to space.'

John Goldsmith travelled to Dublin for a day to meet Brendan, who showed him around the world of Agnes Browne.

And so the writer set off to produce the first draft of the script based on Brendan's novel. Meantime, Brendan had his own writing commitments. He'd been working hard on his first book for Penguin, *The Young Wan*, which was released in the autumn of 1997. It was the story of the young Agnes Browne, before she was a Mammy, when she was Agnes Reddin, a young girl growing up in The Jarro in Dublin.

(The Reddins were the family who'd lived in Gerry Browne's house before the Brownes moved in.)

It told of how young Agnes manages to survive the indignities and demands of Catholic school, the unwanted births of siblings, days spent in the factories and markets, and nights in the dance hall as rock and roll invades Dublin.

A poignant line from the book summed up the spirit. 'She had watched her sisters over the years, each one trying to be more beautiful than the others, constantly dressing up and appearing at social events looking like a gardener's exhibit. The sole purpose of which seemed to be to capture a man just like their father – and then become invisible just like their mother.'

The book joined its predecessors on the bestseller list although, like the rest, it didn't make a fortune.

'At this point, I had a lovely office in the house in Ashbourne (replicas of a grinning Stan Laurel and Oliver Hardy lined the steps), but I'd do my writing in the kitchen, between midnight and 4 a.m., with CNN on beside me with no sound. I'd sit there and look around, and it was important to have a house like that. It reminded me why I worked so hard.

'My only indulgence, besides the house, was that I bought myself a twenty-six-thousand-pound car, a Renault Saffron. I despise drugs. I like a vodka, but not to excess. Doreen still collected the feckin' vouchers off the milk to get free flights to England. Every now and again, I needed to have a splurge, but only very rarely and under controlled conditions. I'd say to Doreen, "Let's go to Shelbourne Park with two hundred quid and blow it." And when we went, we blew it. If you go to the dogs for one day, you're gonna blow your bread. But I got great craic blowing it. Then, that's that. It's over.'

But Brendan was still gambling, big time, with his career. As if trying to develop *Sparrow's Trap*, writing *The Young Wan*, touring and getting Agnes Browne to Hollywood weren't enough, Brendan began work on another novel, *Eeny, Meeny, Miney, Mo*, an epic tale spanning several generations and incorporating themes such as racism and Church oppression.

It's still not finished, though, because other commitments got in the way – such as a new play he'd written. His late-night kitchen table sessions had produced *Grandad's Sure Lilly's Still Alive*.

The story involves Charlie, a recently retired deep-sea sailor, who arrives at the Kingfisher Retirement Home to be faced by a motley bunch of characters. The residents are bored and lonely until this auld fella, full of PMA, comes up with the idea of staging a play in the home – and rehearsals begin. But we discover Grandad mourns for his lost love, who happens to be a lady of the night, and he goes off searching for her.

The premise seemed fine, although it's always tricky portraying old people. But Brendan and Gerry had a more pressing problem: they had no money to mount the production. To the world they were two successful guys who lived in lovely homes in a lovely village with lovely fitted kitchens. But, in reality, they lived day to day.

The other problem was the play, like *The Course*, had a huge cast. (Though one particular delight was that Brendan's sister Eilish joined the team as wardrobe mistress. She'd gone on to live in England and had acted in am-dram, and was keen to come back to Ireland.)

Luckily, Brendan and Gerry pulled in a sponsor in the form of Brendan's friend Mike Nolan, who ran an electronics company. And when things got really tight they'd do a gig.

But first, Brendan had to be able to convince as a 90-year-old.

'I needed to be able to age up, so I rang a guy I knew in Dunleary College of Art, to ask if they had a good up-and-coming make-up artist. They had, and his name was Tom McInnerney, and he created Charlie. (Tom McInnerney would go on to work on *Star Wars* and *The Nutty Professor*. And Brendan also appeared, for the first time in drag, as a character called Maisie.)

The cast was similar to *The Course*, with Brendan using as much of his new family as possible, including Jenny, with Gerry playing Pius Lamb.

Grandad's Sure Lilly's Still Alive opened at the Gaiety Theatre, Dublin, in June 1997, with Brendan in the lead, offering up a great rendition of a doddery auld codger, capturing both the pathos and the comedy of old age.

'You can't have comedy without pathos. Comedy in itself is sad. I have to be honest and say that I laugh at dark things. I see an old woman walking down the street and the arse comes out of her shopping bag and I fall around the place laughing. Now, I'll help her pick things up, but I think it's so funny. People walking into lampposts – hilarious!'

He also admitted to loving happy endings. 'Steven Spielberg said you can do anything you like with an audience. You can have sharks eating people or aliens arrive from space. But give them a happy ending and you can do anything with them. This play definitely ends happily.'

Brendan's slapstick and shamelessly sentimental play didn't produce a happy ending for its producer, however. It certainly didn't hit the mark *The Course* had. The play enjoyed some initial success, but the short Irish tour didn't sell. The Irish disappointment didn't stop Brendan and Gerry from lining up an English tour, though, a position born out of a shared madness as much as confidence. (It's all very well staring in the direction of the sun – but be careful you don't get sunburn.)

Looking back, Brendan agrees they should have cut their losses. He should never have taken the chance on touring an untested play with such a large cast and costs.

Yet, he couldn't kill the production. He had tremendous faith in the play, the world he'd created. Cutting the production would have been like cutting a leg off. Brendan believed the play to be really funny. He loved the idea of older people revealing they had a real sense of fun, a theme he would later develop with Agnes Brown. As the producer and writer, he could create roles for friends such as Gerry and Jenny Gibney, and provide work for Bugsy and Eilish and the crew. Brendan had become an old-style actor/manager, who travelled with his troupe of performing players across the land.

However, he had to get better at arithmetic. By the time the troupe played Liverpool, Brendan and Gerry were once again facing financial ruin.

During one performance there were only ten people in the audience. And the cast, predictably, were so low they were almost in the orchestra pit.

The lack of cash was set to bring the curtain crashing down, but another disaster got in the way.

Gerry had made a day trip back to Ireland and on his return had been arrested after a minor altercation with an overzealous female customs officer, who'd assumed every Irishman was a troublemaking Celtic supporter in town to watch Celtic play Liverpool that night.

The case would never go to court and CCTV of the incident conveniently 'went missing'. But Gerry was badly beaten up by four security men, suffered concussion and the play had to be cancelled.

Yet, while Brendan was losing money on his theatre productions, he was never tempted to go cap-in-hand to Ireland's art theatre Establishment.

'I know that if you entertain people, they will come. They

won't come if your idea of theatre is a couple of actors on a stage wanking each other off.'

Perhaps he had heard of the South American production of *The Marquis de Sade Story* which played at the Edinburgh Festival in 1998 and did indeed feature two blokes performing self-love in front of an audience.

No matter, Brendan's Darwinist approach to theatre survival meant he was more than prepared to take his own losses on the chin. But the *Grandad* loss meant his chin was very sore indeed.

The gamble, on this occasion, didn't pay off. What to do next? RTÉ would come up with the short-term answer, offering a new series of *Hot Milk And Pepper*.

At least that would pay the bills. But in the longer term his ambitions lay in Hollywood, where all the streets are paved with gold.

They are, aren't they?

WHO'S AGNES?

THE DISAPPOINTMENT of *Grandad* was tempered slightly when Brendan was offered the role of Rissoll in the Irish movie *The Tale of Sweety Barrett*, starring Brendan Gleeson as Sweety, a large man with a childlike innocence who is forced to leave his job in a circus and ends up in a fishing village, making and smuggling bootleg whiskey.

Then it was back to RTÉ for the next series of *Hot Milk And Pepper*.

'I got a call from the producer who said the TV station really wanted to do a second series, but without Gerry Browne.'

There are those stars who would have left their right-hand man out in the cold and, given Brendan had had to crowbar his chum into the show in the first place, he could perhaps have been forgiven for doing so. But fortunately for Gerry Browne, Brendan O'Carroll didn't see it that way.

'I said, "Look, I don't work without Gerry. That's the way it is."'

The waiter and the milkman were a team. Yet, Brendan felt he and Gerry weren't always on the same wavelength.

'I heard he was cancelling offers to do things I didn't know about. Too much was happening and I think Gerry was panicking. It was getting out of his control.'

Brendan has a theory about why Gerry wasn't behaving as he'd hoped.

'People aren't born to enjoy success. We're programmed to hunt and then sleep. Success is an unnatural state. The problem with success is that some people can't cope with it – and they also worry if they can hold onto it. I think Gerry saw success looming and just couldn't take it.'

But Brendan couldn't jettison his friend. He had been half of the partnership. He owed him. Yet, what had been an equal partnership was now unbalanced. Brendan maintains he had grown in ways that Gerry hadn't.

'I think he was happy when we were gigging around the country and we'd get a thousand people at the door, paying a tenner a ticket. I was having to push him all the time.'

Gerry disagrees with this theory. He argues he was incredibly happy *not* to be gigging around the country, singing comedy parodies night after night. He was all too happy to ride whichever new showbiz horse came along.

Regardless, the TV series recorded, Brendan could focus hard on the movie deal. But there was a more immediate problem to overcome: who to play Agnes?

Buena Vista Productions never considered for a moment Brendan himself could play Agnes in a film. Sure, he'd played the part wonderfully on Dublin station 2FM but, despite the fact film companies often miscast (John Wayne as Genghis Khan comes to mind, or Sean Connery as an Irish cop in *The Untouchables*), Disney reckoned film audiences wouldn't buy into the fact that Mrs Browne could be played convincingly by a balding 44-year-old.

On the other side it could be argued that Buena Vista weren't considering the legendary screen cross-dressing successes of the likes of Alistair Sim, Alec Guinness or Dustin Hoffman. And Agnes Browne wasn't a comedy as such. It was a drama with comedy.

But no, they felt they needed a star to play Agnes Browne, and that's why Brendan ended up on a plane headed for Tinseltown – to meet Anjelica Huston.

Buena Vista people in LA had suggested the role to the actress, who'd read the book – and loved it. What also heightened her interest was she'd lived in Galway as a schoolgirl, with her famous director dad, John. Anjelica, she said, felt a real affinity with the Irish.

Now, Brendan knew instinctively that the pale-faced, dark-eyed Anjelica, who'd once played Morticia in *The Addams Family*, would be perfect for the part of Agnes Browne – had Agnes been Transylvanian and lived in a Gothic castle instead of a Dublin council house. At least Huston's Irish accent was rather more believable than that of Tom Cruise in the cinema turkey *Far And Away*. But that didn't matter so much. What mattered was that Brendan was cash-strapped, thanks to the cost of staging *Grandad*, and had to pay his debts. And here, after all, was one of the biggest names in the movie world agreeing to a meet.

'I didn't know much about her at the time. All I knew was that she'd been with Jack Nicholson for years and that she was really part of America's royal family. But what I did know was that if she agreed to make the movie . . . well, her name alone would create massive interest. The film couldn't fail with a Huston attached to the project.'

Meantime, director Jim Sheridan had come on board the project as co-producer, and Brendan was delighted to have a fellow Dubliner and high-profile film industry figure to help steer the film through tricky waters.

Now, all Brendan and Jim had to do was to convince the pallid actress with the intimidating presence that she should sign up with the film.

'We drove down to Venice Beach in Los Angeles, where Anjelica owns a whole block, and her office is part of that block. The first thing she did when we met was light a cigarette and I thought, "Thank, God." I didn't think you would be allowed to smoke anywhere in LA.'

Anjelica began the chat by telling the Mrs Browne creator that the *Agnes Browne* script was a work of genius, that the little Irishman was the funniest writer to come out of the Emerald Isle since Oscar Wilde. Or, at least, that's what she would have said had they been living in a parallel universe.

'She told me that the script was shit. And I just smiled. The script had been written by the hired writer, and I didn't really think it captured the essence of the book.

'Everything was wrong with it,' says Brendan. 'The pathos was gone. There was no rhythm, no flow. But I was told that it could be modified, that another draft could be done.

'So the next night we had another meeting, and when we got out there Angelica had rung the production office. She was demanding to know what had happened to the original book she'd read.

'John Goldsmith wrote a second draft and again her reaction was, "What the hell is this?" At this point Jim Sheridan announced to me, "We need to have a bash at this," and then he announced to me, "You don't know what this film is about."

'"I think I do."

'"You think you do, but you don't."'

'"Well, considering I wrote the book, I've a feckin' fair idea what it's all about."

'I was hearing this from a director who had won an Academy Award. I wasn't talking to a nobody. But on the other hand I couldn't understand what he was saying. It just left me thinking, "What the hell have I got myself into?"'

Brendan came back to Ireland, to tour again with Gerry, leaving Jim Sheridan to sort out the problem with the script and Anjelica Huston's vision of how it should read.

But it didn't look as though a happy solution could be found.

'I came up with the idea that the only solution was for me to go back out to LA with the co-producer, Greg Smith.'

And at the start of this trip a little magic moment occurred.

'I was doing a guest spot on the *National Song Contest*, filming the show in Cork, then had to get to London for a connecting flight to LA. But when I got to London, eventually, because the flight was held up with really bad fog, I got to the Aer Lingus terminal and I was handed a note. It was from Greg Smith, who was also late, and it said since we'd missed the LA flight, he suggested we should take the Virgin flight instead.

'So I waited in the American Airlines lounge, until three p.m. when the next flight was due to leave, and I happened to have a look at Greg's note again. It had been written on a telex, and I turned it over, and on the other side there was another printed note. It read: *Miss Jennifer Gibney is arriving in Heathrow, but has been fog delayed. She will be taking a taxi from Heathrow to Gatwick and will be flying on to LA. But she has forgotten her passport, which is being flown direct from Dublin to Gatwick. Please make sure she gets her passport on arrival.*'

What were the chances of Brendan being handed a note with details of Jenny's holiday plans? And it being on the other side of his message from Greg Smith?

'How weird is that?'

Very weird. And it transpired that Brendan's Virgin flight was the same plane Jenny was now travelling on.

'But I was in first class, and she was in coach, so I didn't go back,' he says, laughing.

'However, we spoke in the airport. And I rang her a couple of days later, at her sister's, and we met for a drink.'

The pair were growing closer. There was a real connection. But not an affair. However, it's fair to say Doreen didn't feature too often in this new world Brendan was creating for himself. And part of that creative process involved keeping Anjelica Huston happy.

'I spoke to Anjelica on arrival and agreed with her comments about the film. Then she asked how we should go about getting the script right, and I offered this basic idea that we'd take the fifty best bits of the book and make them into a movie. She thought that made sense and we agreed the best bits. And we played out scenes, where she would be Agnes and I'd be Winnie, Agnes's friend. And we'd swap around.

'Every night I'd go back to the hotel and I'd work on the ideas we'd come up with that day. And the next day she'd be so impressed that I'd worked overnight. As a result of working with her every day, I was in heaven. It had to be one of the most exhilarating experiences of my life. That entire week's work was just breathtaking.

'However, at the end of the first day, co-producer Greg Smith came to pick me up in a limo. And as we headed back to the hotel, he asked how it was all going. And I said, "Great,

Greg. But I have to tell you. I'm not getting actors' notes off Anjelica. I'm getting director's notes."

'"What do you mean?"

'"I don't get the feeling she wants to play Agnes. I get the feeling she wants to direct."

'"No, no. She's in every page of the script, Brendan. She can't direct and act. And we've got Emma Thompson down to direct."'

As they worked together, Brendan could see Anjelica become more absorbed with the life of Agnes Browne. The book's ending sees Agnes meet the man of her dreams, who happens to be Cliff Richard. And indeed the Peter Pan of Pop was written into the script to play a cameo. But Anjelica had a thought; she said that – rather than the original Bachelor as the dreamboat – surely Agnes Browne's fantasy man would more likely be Tom Jones?

'I said, "You know, you're right. I wish I had thought of that at the time. Agnes wouldn't be into a cuddly mummy's boy. She'd be into a Tom Jones, a bit of a rascal."

'As it turns out, Disney had already asked Cliff if he would play the part, but Cliff wanted a guarantee that none of the kids would say "fuck" in the film, as they had done in the book. But Disney said, "Sorry. The dialogue stays as it is," and Cliff turned it down. When Anjelica heard this she just picked up her phone straight off and called Tom Jones. "Tom, Hi. Want to do something with me? . . . A film . . . Great! Yeh. Maybe two weeks." And she turned to me and said, "Tom's in."'

Brendan's excitement soared. He was working with a Hollywood star who'd just pulled a music icon into his movie. Maureen O'Carroll would have been delighted to know her youngest child was headed skywards.

'I just felt this screenplay was going to be brilliant.'

But was Anjelica committed to the project as an actor, a director – or both? Brendan had to find out. However, he couldn't call her agent and ask; that would seem to be disloyal, so he had to subtly coax the truth out of her.

'I said to her, as we were having coffee in this lovely restaurant on Malibu Beach, with Greg Smith, "Just a little thing, Anjelica. When you get to Dublin, would you prefer a house – or an apartment? It's just that if you had people coming over you might prefer a house . . ." Now, if she'd replied, "Well, we'll see closer to the time . . ." that would mean she wasn't about to star in this movie. But she didn't. She said, "Erm, we haven't really discussed a director yet."

'Greg chipped in, "Well, Anjelica, as you know, we have Emma Thompson as director."

'"Oh, she's completely wrong for this."

'"And I watched as Emma Thompson flew right out of the window."

Did this mean the film was doomed? Brendan looked at Greg Smith. There was a moment's silence and then Greg said to Anjelica, 'Would you consider directing it yourself?'

'Yes,' came the reply. 'We'll give you your movie. And we'll cast Agnes as someone else. When I think about it, I'm too severe-looking to play Agnes.'

In reality, this was the best possible news. Anjelica wasn't right for the part and she knew it. But she was still part of the project, and her association would open cinema doors. Win-win!

And to seal Brendan's delight, Anjelica had someone in mind who was perfect to play Agnes.

ROSIE

ROSIE O'Donnell, one of the biggest stars in America, not only had Irish heritage (and an authentic accent), she had that mix of cosy warmth, vulnerability, toughness and stoicism that Agnes had to have. It was a great casting suggestion which, aligned to Anjelica as director and Brendan's script, made this a film that couldn't possibly fail.

Yet, would Rosie be interested in playing the part of Agnes? O'Donnell was an extremely busy woman, with a chat show on Fox Television and a new baby she had adopted with her female partner.

O'Donnell made a hundred shows a year and it was claimed she'd turned down 'trillions' to make *Flintstones 2*. However, when she received the *Agnes Browne* script sent over by her pal Anjelica, she read it – and loved it. Rosie reckoned her own mother, even though she'd grown up in the Bronx, was Agnes.

'She agreed to take our meeting,' says Brendan. 'And we knew that was tantamount to acceptance. Rosie clearly loved the Agnes role so much she'd change her life plans for the year. I thought, "We're laughin' here!"'

The plan was that Brendan, Anjelica Huston and Jim Sheridan would fly to New York to meet up with the former Betty Rubble and club her over the head with charm and persistence.

But the trip looked problematic before the trio even set off. Brendan and his fellow Dubliner weren't hitting it off, despite the fact that Jim Sheridan's production outfit were effectively rescuing the project.

Brendan reckoned Jim was 'too sure of himself'. Then again, Jim had every right to be. Sheridan was a major player in the film business. That first night in New York, for example, Jim invited Brendan out to dinner with 'a couple of interesting people'. Brendan later regretted having turned down the invite. The 'interesting people' turned out to be Marlon Brando and Lauren Bacall.

Meantime, back in New York, it was time for Brendan, Jim Sheridan, Anjelica Huston and some of the production team to travel up to Westchester to meet with Rosie O'Donnell.

'She lived in a lovely big house in the country. And she was great. I really liked her right from the start, and when I looked at her I thought, "Now, this is Mrs Brown." She'd read the book, which she loved, and I discovered she'd learned a bit about me, which was nice. She was delighted to hear that I was a stand-up comic; she'd started off in stand-up too. So we had that in common. And it all went so well. Rosie added she had some great ideas for the film. For example, she had this idea of an early scene where Agnes is in the bath with all of the babies. And it was great because it would have been so Agnes.

'Then she said, "Let's get down to business! Now, I can only do this film if my stuff can be shot in this fixed period of time. I understand how difficult this is. And I don't want to create problems for anybody. But what I have arranged is that Fox will let me use their private jet, to fly me to wherever you want me, at no charge to the production company."

'Now, I'm thinking, "Thank the Lord! We are so home and dry here."'

Money wasn't an issue either. The film company offered Rosie $1.2 million, a drop in the bucket for the actress, but it wasn't about cash. She simply loved the Agnes Browne character.

'Then we went on to add more ideas, when one of the production team threw her the possibility of Bette Midler playing Agnes's best pal, Marion. And I got a real measure of Rosie's belief in making the story as real as possible, because a little while later during a coffee break she said to me, "You cannot have that woman in this movie, Brendan! She just doesn't fit!" So I said, "Relax. There have been no decisions made on that, Rosie. Let's just get you in, and between us we'll call the shots." But she looked at me cold and said, "Brendan, don't let them fuck this film up."' (Whoopi Goldberg also read the script, fell in love with it and wanted to play Marion. But the presence of a black female in 1960s Dublin would have been a little difficult to explain.)

Back in Rosie's living room, Brendan reckons Jim Sheridan rocked the boat by saying to Rosie, 'I want you available whenever I want you.'

'Now, I was completely panicking when he said this because you can't lay down rules to a star like her, especially one who's doing the film for relatively little money.

'"Well, then," says Rosie, "in that case I can't do the movie."

'"You can't just set out your own conditions."'

'"I'm not setting out conditions, Jim. I'm just telling you when I'm available."'

'And the meeting became very heated. So I cut in and said, "Look, let's all take a breath of fresh air. Guys, I'll make coffee."'

'I was panicking at this point but tried to keep it all together. There was no way I was going to see Rosie O'Donnell walk away from this movie. So I said, "Rosie, calm down. It can be sorted. Trust me." And I left her making the coffee while I went into the garden to talk to Jim.

'I said, "Look Jim, we're within a hair's-breadth of tying this all up. Listen to what she's saying. She's not saying she doesn't want to do it. She's just saying when she's available. And if she's available for thirty days spread out over these weeks, we can schedule it. It can be done."'

'"Okay, we'll see what she says when we go back in."'

Brendan had saved the day. He'd calmed the star and the co-producer. He had his movie with the best possible lead.

Or so he thought.

'When we sat down, Jim turned to Rosie and said, "Okay. We'll up your money."'

'Rosie said, incredulously, "What?"'

'"Yes, I know what this is about. We'll give you two million."'

'At this point Rosie stood up and yelled, "You'll up my money? You'll up my money! Let me tell you something. I do a hundred shows a year for Fox, I'm paid extremely well for them, and I'm contracted for five years. You cannot UP my money."'

'And at that she threw everyone out of the house.'

Jim Sheridan's rewind on that scene doesn't play out the same way as Brendan's. He maintains Rosie began walking backwards the moment Bette Midler was named. Regardless, the Rosie O'Donnell dream was over. Brendan's heart sank. He knew how much he'd lost. But who would play Agnes now that Rosie had walked? Or was Agnes Browne being killed off before the script had even been completed?

COULD THE SPARROW FLY?

BRENDAN had never given up on the idea of turning *Sparrow's Trap* into a movie. After RTÉ passed on the idea, he became even more determined.

And now, with *Agnes Browne* in development, albeit without an Agnes, he was part of the film world. He had an understanding of the process. So why not use this understanding to make another movie? Wouldn't it be fantastic to have two Brendan O'Carroll films coming out within months of each other?

The other attraction in developing *Sparrow's Trap* was that it represented a sharp contrast to the oestrogen-driven world of Agnes Browne. Agnes Browne's story was grey at times, but never black, thanks to the raw humour. *Sparrow's Trap* was different – a story about making the wrong decisions, about a boxer who throws a fight and ends up working for gangsters. It was a story about how life could change in a matter of seconds. Brendan knew of this dark, precarious Dublin existence. He had friends from Finglas who had taken the wrong path.

'If I hadn't become successful, I could have ended up a

bank robber or a drug addict,' he admits one night at his home in Dublin. 'It could easily have happened.'

Sparrow's Trap was a good story that would make a good film. Brendan and Gerry reckoned they could make the film themselves, using some of the family and friends such as Jenny, Fiona, Danny and Eilish to help with production. They came up with the idea of making a guerrilla movie, a low-budget film in which a director shoots scenes quickly at real locations – streets, railway stations, shopping centres, parks; anywhere they can.

The pair reckoned they could make the movie for around £150,000. But after a meeting with a producer from the Irish Film Board, they were persuaded that only a bigger-budget movie would do the story justice, and they should be thinking about something in the region of £2.2 million.

As optimistic as ever, Brendan and Gerry weren't daunted by that figure, especially after Agnes Browne's original producer Greg Smith and film partner Morgan O'Sullivan had read the script and loved it – and announced they would consider becoming distributors for the movie, making sure it got a cinema release.

And if that happened, it would be likely to recoup the £2 million-plus investment. But they laid down some conditions.

'They wanted a name to play the lead role. They said they needed a star in the credits to make it easier to distribute.'

Brendan, of course, would have been perfect for the role, had he not been aged 42, and with a public profile that didn't go beyond the Eire borders.

'What I wanted to do was ask for four million quid to produce this film, and make a few bob for myself.

'When I talked to Greg and Morgan about finance I told them I'd approached Stephen Rea and Aidan Quinn and neither of them had said no. Greg said, "If you get either of those, we'll give you the four million."'

Great. All Brendan had to do was sign Stephen Rea or Aidan Quinn on the line that was dotted.

'I met up with Stephen Rea, and found him to be a lovely guy. I hadn't a lot to offer for the lead part – around fifty grand, which wasn't a huge amount – but it would cover a few bets on a Saturday. Stephen was interested and I thought, "Great!" But then he called and told me he had just started on another film and he couldn't do mine.'

One down . . . but Aidan Quinn was still a real possibility.

'I sent a copy of the script to Aidan Quinn via his management company, CAA, in Los Angeles.

'Now, we were scheduled to begin shooting at the end of January 1998, so on New Year's Eve I found myself on a plane to LA, trying to track down Aidan's agent.

'I finally got him on the phone and he agreed to meet me on 2 January. And I got to the agency – and it was closed.

'So I thought, "Okay. I'll come back tomorrow." And I did. And I met the agent and he said Aidan loved the script, but that he was doing another Irish film and he didn't want to compromise one against the other. But I wasn't for giving up. I said, "Look, I appreciate you won't make much money on this, the budget is too small, but I'm looking for your permission to talk to Aidan, that's all."

'So he said, "Okay, sure."'

Doreen didn't take off with her husband on the trips to Hollywood. Brendan reckoned his wife didn't want to be a part of the politics of getting a movie made. And there's little doubt the gulf between them was now becoming a gaping chasm. It seems they were staying together more for the children than their own relationship.

Gerry Browne didn't fly to Tinseltown either. Yet, Brendan, at the time, was saying his right-hand man was with him every step of the way in the project.

'If I'd said to Gerry that I wanted to paint the moon green, he'd say, "Right, I'll go out and price the paint." That's the kind of support I get from him. He's an incredible friend.'

Meantime, there was a little problem in Brendan meeting with Aidan Quinn. The actor lived in New Jersey, on the other side of the country. Brendan managed to get hold of Aidan's number from a friend, though, and rang him. The actor answered.

'"How do you do, Aidan? You don't know me. It's Brendan O'Carroll. I'm a writer from—"

'"Yes, I know you, Brendan. I'm sure I saw you when I was home in Ireland. Was it on *The Late, Late Show*?"

'"Grand. Well, Aidan, I'm just getting your thoughts. I'm making the movie *Sparrow's Trap* and your agent said you liked the script but that scheduling could be . . ."

'"What movie? What script?"

'So I told him about the story. And Aidan was interested. And as it turns out I had a guy in New York who had three copies of the script.

'I got one sent out to Aidan while I was on the flight and I let Aidan know which hotel I'd be at. So I got in at ten o'clock that night and Aidan promised he would ring me, before midnight, once he'd read the script.

'I had a bath, called Jenny to fill her in on the news, and had something to eat. And then I looked at the clock and it was ten to one. I thought, "Well, that's that." But then I realised the light on the phone was flashing. It was a message from Aidan. He said he'd meet me the next day in a coffee shop in the village at two o'clock. Well, my heart lifted at this. And I rang Jenny back and told her.

'She was curious. "Do you think it's good news?"

'"Well, Jenny, he's not meeting me to tell me he doesn't want to do it."

'"Do you think he's in?"

'"Sure, I do."'

As John Lennon said, 'If you want to make God laugh, tell him your plans.'

The next day, Brendan was picked up and taken to the Princess Hotel and he met with Aidan Quinn as arranged. The meeting began well enough. Aidan complimented Brendan on the script.

'It'll make a nice little movie, Brendan. But listen, my agent wasn't lying. I'm doing a little Irish project myself, me and my brother, based on my father. And I wouldn't do anything that would compromise that project.'

'Does this film compromise it?'

'No. It's a million miles away from it.'

'Great.'

'But I have a couple of difficulties.'

'Well, run them by me. As long as it doesn't change the basic tenor of the story, I'll be glad to make changes . . .'

'No, no, it's not the story. It's fine. It's a personal thing. My wife is about to give birth. So I've got to run it by her, to make sure she's okay with it.'

'Sure, Aidan.'

'Look, I'll let you know by midday, Monday. Irish time. Is that okay? And I have to say I'm predisposed to do this.'

'Great, Aidan. I really appreciate that.'

Brendan could have flown home without the plane. Aidan Quinn was as good as signed. That meant he had his star. And that meant he had the £4 million he needed to make the movie – and make some serious money.

'On the Monday, we set about auditioning kids in Jurys Inn in Dublin, and a few adult actors. But what a horrible day we had. Jenny's hairdresser's pal Paul, we discovered, had been killed crossing the road while on holiday in Spain. And she was devastated. And I was trying to console her. But while doing this I looked at the clock and it was half past twelve. No word from Quinn.

'I thought, "I can't wait any longer." So I rang his office. And a secretary answered. I said who I was and she said, "Oh, hi. Did you get the message?"

'"No, what message?"

'"I left a message on your answer phone."

'"No, I'm not at home. What is the message?"

'"Aidan can't do the film."

'My chin dropped to the floor. "Is there nothing I can do to change that?"

'"I don't know. All I know is that he can't do it."'

This didn't mean the film was cancelled. No, Brendan hadn't lined up a star name, but the deal was so far down the line it couldn't be halted now.

And the day wasn't all about bad news. Just ten minutes later, purely by chance, Brendan took a phone call from actor Bryan Murray, who starred in the TV series *The Irish RM* and in Channel 4 soap *Brookside*, in which his character, the evil Trevor Jordache, came to be buried under the patio.

'Bryan had heard about the film and was asking if there was any work going. He said that just because he was in England, directors in Ireland had forgotten about him.

"'Any chance of a crack at something, Brendan?'"

"'Crack at it? You've just got yourself a leading role.'"

"'What? With this phone call?'"

"'Yes, can you be here next Monday?'"

"'I most certainly can.'"

So Brendan had a terrific actor in the cast. But not one the film company would back with £4 million. It didn't matter, though. A deal with a distribution company had been agreed verbally. Brendan and Gerry would still be able to cover the cost of making their movie.

But three days before shooting, the letter of guarantee from the distribution company hadn't arrived. They'd pulled out at the last minute.

Brendan wasn't sure if he should be worried, but rang again repeatedly until he finally spoke to someone. To his horror they blithely told him they'd changed their minds and Brendan's reaction was understandably furious. Now, Brendan had a major decision to make. He had a movie and cast standing by, which was budgeted to cost £2.2 million. But he had £25,000 in the bank. Disaster. Major disaster.

And the film was cancelled. The dream of bringing Sparrow McCabe's story to the screen was over. Or at least it should have been.

Brendan refused to throw in the towel. This was just another challenge, he reckoned. He'd make this movie somehow. Think PMA. But who to play the lead role? He'd do it himself. So what if he were a little old? He looked like a boxer. And he could play Sparrow McCabe wearing a wig.

But what about the money to make the movie? He got on the phone. He and Gerry Browne called everyone they knew with cash to invest. They asked friends, Dublin businessmen, anyone they could think of to get the film moving. And they told them they'd not only get their money back, they'd make a few bob. It meant begging and borrowing – if not stealing – money to make the movie.

Dublin responded. The money emerged to pay the basic costs of film production, of hiring cars, Winnebagos, use of venues, etc. And his cast responded. Brendan called in the actors' union and told them he wanted to make the movie. He said he would direct the film himself, but asked permission to get the actors to work for next to nothing until he could get backing.

The actors' union backed him. Then Brendan spoke to his cast and crew and explained the situation, and said he would understand completely if anyone chose not to work on the project.

Incredibly, such was their belief in Brendan, very few walked out. The scene was so powerful it could have been part of a movie in itself.

Brendan was incredibly touched by the backing, but he also had support from close quarters. Eilish stepped up to the plate, doing whatever necessary. Jenny became Brendan's assistant director. And between them they determined to make the worst of times something close to bearable.

'I'd get up at five a.m., be on the set at six, start shooting, acting and directing. I'd shoot till six, then I'd go and watch rushes till eight, and by half eight I'd have dinner with guys who were potential investors. And I'd schmooze them until ten, half ten. And then I'd go home to sleep.'

The money came in, in 'dribs and drabs', something close to £450,000.

'But I wasn't holding it together. There are scenes in the film where Sparrow has to look dreadful because he's a man on the run. But I do look dreadful. I look out on my feet. I was knackered.

'I remember on the third week of filming, on a Thursday, we were waiting on a payment of thirty grand and it was to pay the wages. And the money was due to come from Cork, by midday. Now, that day there was a minute's silence all across the UK and Ireland for peace, ten years on from the bombing of the cenotaph in Enniskillen.

'So, at midday, I was waiting for a call from the bank. And I asked everyone to stop for the minute's silence.

'And I looked across at Jenny. And she was as worried as me, knowing we desperately needed the money. And the silence over, I got back to shooting the scene and she waved over and gave me a thumbs-down sign. The money hadn't arrived.

'One day, I asked Robert Quinn, who was my first assistant director, now a great director, to get all the heads of department together. I said, "I want everybody to assemble in the function room of the hotel at two o'clock."

'And I told him why – that we had no money.'

Up until this point, Brendan and Robert had been at loggerheads. Robert Quinn in fact had left a movie set in Romania to come and make *Sparrow's Trap*.

'So he said to me, "Right, as far as I'm concerned, don't think about paying me. I'll finish this movie whether you pay me or not."

'I said, "You've no idea what this means to me."'

Brendan was attempting what few had ever managed in film history. Jim Sheridan points out that Orson Welles received great plaudits for acting and directing, but Brendan was starring, directing and producing a movie, trying to make it all look good on screen while calling up greengrocers and the like, asking for cash.

Meantime, during the eight weeks' filming, Brendan was still trying to move the *Agnes Browne* project forward. There were script meetings in LA to attend, casting decisions to be made.

With Rosie O'Donnell having thrown the production team out of the door, a new Agnes had to be found. Anjelica Huston stepped back into picture. 'Looks like I'm going to have to play Agnes myself,' she declared.

Sparrow's Trap, somehow, was finished. But it never did get a cinema or a video release. As a result, it was worthless.

'*Sparrow's Trap* was a disaster. It broke me, and not just in financial terms.'

There were many actors and extras who struggled to feed their families as a result of the movie crash, and there were some very angry investors too. Incredibly, Jim Sheridan stepped in with a cheque for £40,000. He and Brendan might have had their differences over the Agnes Browne story, but that didn't stop the writer/director putting his hand in his pocket, for a film he wasn't even part of.

Meantime, Brendan was flattened. He certainly wasn't in the mood for doing comedy gigs.

'My confidence disappeared.'

Brendan didn't realise his resolve hadn't yet been stretched to breaking point.

Mammy Films

BRENDAN had worked on *Sparrow's Trap* for eight long weeks and, looking back, he knows his initial belief in the project was, at best, misplaced.

'I should have stopped right there and then when the plug was pulled by the distribution company. But I didn't. The ego was so big I kept thinking another company would pick it up. I guess I had become a bit arrogant. You think you can walk on water. I guess at this time I had the belief that if you read out a shopping list I could put it on stage or turn it into a film and it would be a success.

'But then it all fails and on the day you learn the worst, you are less than an ordinary mortal, you are a failure. And the day after that, you are less than a failure, you are a bum.

'So, all of a sudden, you are afraid to get back on the horse. You are terrified.'

Maureen O'Carroll would have been devastated to see her youngest so desolate. Sure, Brendan had had disappointments; *The Course* didn't travel well and *Grandad's Sure Lilly's Still Alive* had cost the production company £80,000 – and didn't get the audiences it needed for a second run. But those were irregular blips in the O'Carroll heart monitor. The *Sparrow's Trap* fiasco had lost £2.2 million. This was flatline. A situation far worse than The Abbot's Castle collapse. Brendan vowed somehow, someday, to pay back those who'd backed him. But that's not to say the experience didn't knock the stuffing out of him. (Or that the bank didn't put him on the blacklist.) Brendan suffered severe depression and his balance of mind was seriously affected. On top of that, he had to contend with the ignominy; here he was a national figure, a huge comedy star, and all of a sudden no one was laughing.

'I was well and truly fecked,' he says, succinctly.

But he had to pull himself together. He had to come up with a way to rescue the situation. The bills had to be paid. The family had to be fed.

'I started doing stand-up gigs again. It was a time of sheer desperation. What else could I do?'

The next few months saw Brendan and Gerry tour, raking in as much money as possible. But it's fair to say relations were strained. Both were as miserable as every sin they'd ever committed.

Then filming for *Agnes Browne* was confirmed for July, and production offices set up in Sir John Rogerson's Quay in Dublin, on the south bank of the Liffey. It should have been a wondrous occasion but Brendan couldn't become excited, given the recent film failure. To compound matters, three and a half weeks before shooting, Brendan and Jim Sheridan still hadn't agreed over the script.

'Jim didn't really like my screenplay. He's very much into subtext and there wasn't enough subtext for him. There certainly wasn't enough confrontation in it. Jim wanted the mother and the eldest son to be fighting all the time. But that's not what happens with mothers and eldest sons. Mothers and eldest daughters, sure.'

Brendan argued that everyone had loved the script he'd developed with Anjelica Huston. Indeed, he had recently read a story in the *Irish Times* by international movie critic Michael Dwyer, in which the writer spoke of being at the Cannes Film Festival, and how Princess Caroline of Monaco had revealed to him she'd read *The Mammy*, and declared it to be 'the best storyline she'd ever read.' What? How? Princess Caroline? It transpired that Grace Kelly's daughter had an Irish butler and every time he came home he bought Brendan's stand-up videos. He'd also got a copy of *The Mammy* that he'd taken back to Monaco. The princess became a Mrs Browne/Brendan fan and had managed to get hold of the film script.

But Jim Sheridan was adamant. 'The script needs more.'

And for the next ten days there *was* more – heated debate, that is.

'Jim's basic problem with the script was the ending. He believed Mrs Browne's desperate plight to keep her kids fed and watered and nurtured would be solved when a wonderful man comes into her life and saves the day.' Whereas Brendan argued that Agnes could very firmly stand on her own two feet (lace-ups, with a small heel).

As a result, the producer and writer developed 'creative differences'.

'We agreed to try and settle the problem with the ending. Then, one day, when I was on the tenth draft of the script, Jim came up with the idea of getting out of Ireland. He said, "Let's go to LA, take five days. I've got some meetings there and we'll work and we'll get it done." So we took off and landed in LA and moved into the Chateau Marmont Hotel.'

Brendan adds, laughing: 'Jim wanted the room in which John Belushi committed suicide. I don't get that. Not for me, thanks. I was happy with a room where Tracy and Hepburn had their love affair. I wanted to have a vibe of passion, not of someone vomiting to death on a carpet.'

There was no love lost, however, between the collaborators. 'We couldn't agree on anything. And I was ready to hang myself. Well, not really. But I'd had enough. And I left the hotel one night, for a walk, which of course no one does in LA, but I reckoned I looked as odd as anyone else. And I really was depressed and I called Jenny, who was still just a friend at the time, on the mobile, and began to rant to her. "I can't do this! I'm comin' home." And it was eight in the morning in Dublin. "I'm getting the first flight out of here, Jenny! I don't want to see this little bollix ever again!"

'"No problem, Brendan. I'll meet you at the airport."

'And I said, "Thanks." And then she added the footnote, "But I have to say this to you, Brendan. It's not like you to give up."

'"No, but this is different, Jenny."

'"Yes, I'm sure it is. But I'm just saying, it's not like you. And I'd hate you to come home and then maybe regret walking away."

'Well, I asked Jenny about this tactic later, if she were using reverse psychology, but she said she wasn't. She really did mean to meet me at the airport. But she also believed I wasn't myself, that I must be in a bad way. Anyway, I hung up the phone and started to walk back towards the hotel. And I reckoned it was pointless going out to the airport at this time. I'd fly home in the morning. So I got back to the room, turned on the telly. And I thought hard. I needed a way to turn this problem around. But how? Jim had me by the bollix. He knew I had massive debts. And he knew he had me cut off from the film pack. As a producer, he was in control.'

What was interesting about Brendan's story was it revealed Jenny had been the person he'd called in his moment of crisis. He felt she had the answers. In an ideal world he'd have been calling his wife at home. The line between Brendan and Doreen hadn't been disconnected, but it was becoming increasingly crackly.

Meantime, Brendan and Jim were not on the same line at all. What to do? Brendan's mind flashbacked to the Positive Mental Attitude course.

'I tried the PMA, to look at the negative and see the positive. But where was it? Then I realised it. Jim Sheridan had me isolated. That was the neggie. But it was also the possie. I had been trying to hang on to my script with all my might. And nobody knew what he was trying to do to it. So what could I do?

'I let Jim win. I let him have his way, then faxed off the script and went back to bed for a very long sleep. And how I slept.'

But around two p.m., Brendan was awakened by the sound of the phone ringing. It was Anjelica Huston, on the line from Ireland.

'Hello—'

'Don't hello me, you little bastard. I sent you over there with *It's A Wonderful Life* and you sent me back some mother's *My Left Foot*!'

'Just a second, Anjelica. Jim? Can you hear me? Line Six. It's for you.'

'I got a taxi to the airport and flew back to Dublin. And I had a smile on my face for the length of the entire journey.

'The script that had gone to Anjelica's office after the all-night session was Draft Thirteen. The one that was finally shot was Draft Four. The one I wanted to film.'

Not quite. When Brendan read over Draft Four he realised one glaring omission: himself. So he wrote in a cameo, where he plays Seamus, an ever-present town drunk, a nice bit of comic relief.

'I thought, "I'll be fecked if I'm making a movie that I'm not in." I wanted to bring a few more laughs.'

When filming commenced, there was a heavy atmosphere on set. Many of the crew had worked on *Sparrow's Trap* and hadn't been paid.

'I was seen as the failure on the set. And here they were filming my next movie straight away.'

Brendan borrowed from Tom Cruise during the filming. Not in an acting sense, but the wig, one of the hairpieces Cruise used in *Mission Impossible*. But while Brendan's head was a little warmer, Anjelica Huston blew 'hot and cold' during the six weeks' filming.

'She was like the rest of us. She can laugh a lot. And she had the will to make the movie. But I felt the process had chipped away at her. Some days she wouldn't come out of her trailer until I went to talk to her. I'd have to say to her, "Hi, Angel, here I am. I've got a coffee for you. Why don't you come out? There's a whole big world out there waiting for you. And there's a big machine that's depending upon you. We all need you." And she would say, "Are you sure, Brendy?" "Yes, I'm sure." "Well, I'll come out, then."'

The director, it seems, was stressed to the eyeballs with the pressures of filming and acting.

'You just don't get time to think, really, or time to be alone,' she said at the time. 'The moment I'm on the set, I go into hair and make-up, because I've got to get ready for the scene. And everyone wants to know what's going on. "What are you going to do for the next scene and do you want her to sing? And what should the child wear?" You literally do not have a second in which you are not preoccupied with some immediate problem, or having to plan, or having to figure out yesterday's mistakes. And you have about five hours' sleep a night and most of those hours are spent dreaming about it.'

But the star didn't quite grasp Irish culture in the Sixties and saw Dublin through Hollywood glasses. Brendan explains: 'One look at the set and I could see the film was no longer about Moore Street. Anjelica had created a completely new market, a compromise between a west of Ireland horse fair and Petticoat Lane in London.

'In one scene she has a ceilidh band playing outside a pub in Moore Street. If we'd seen a ceilidh band in Moore Street in 1967, we'd have set them on fire for the craic, just to see how quick they would play.'

He would get his chance to make another Agnes Browne movie, given the success of his BBC sitcom. But for the moment, everything was a compromise.

'Gerard Depardieu, for example, was set to play Pierre, Agnes's baker friend. But he had a motorbike accident in Cannes two weeks before the shoot and broke his leg. So we had to get Arno Chevrier at the last minute. Arno was great, but he wasn't Depardieu.'

One big star, Tom Jones, did come good, however, belting out 'She's a Lady'. (Close to production time, Cliff Richards offered to do the movie, but by that time Tom was signed.) Ray Winstone was great as the local loan shark.

Brendan can be more relaxed now about the fate of the

film. 'It's still a nice little movie. But you have to accept the first thing to go when you make a movie is the book. The other problem was that we lost the first gag from the book, the Hillman Hunter gag from the Social Security office scene, which really told us what Agnes was all about. Now, you needed that gag. It tells us Agnes has a real contempt for authority, she'll play with people, and doesn't trust them to pay her out. Again, she's Che Guevara in a dress.'

Yet, Brendan learned from the film experience.

'The movie wasn't bad. It was a cute little movie. And people have said they enjoyed it. But I just know that it could have been so much better. From a writer's point of view, I saw things happening in it that left me dismayed. I knew that wasn't what I wanted to say. What I also learned from the film experience was the realisation I'd nearly given up at one point, and I had to watch that. My thinking had to be: "Don't ever get into a situation whereby anyone can undermine your decision-making process. And don't let them change your script."'

Those words would stick with him years later when BBC producers would try to tell him how to write his hit sitcom, *Mrs Brown's Boys*.

Meantime, Brendan was still insolvent. It would be two years before *Agnes Browne* was released, and in financial terms it would do little more than take up space on the DVD rental shelf.

Any money that arrived from his share of the film company advance was swallowed up by *Sparrow's Trap* debts.

He had to come up with a new plan.

THE LAST WEDDING

BRENDAN'S career was in meltdown and in the autumn of 1998 his personal life was now in crisis. Since the success (and financial failure) of *The Course*, his time had been spent on the road, in Hollywood, in bank managers' offices, with his troupe of touring players or in television studios.

And during this journey the distance between Brendan and Doreen became unbridgeable. They no longer lived in the same world. Brendan was living his life at a speed Doreen couldn't possibly match.

Was there one moment when he knew all was lost?

'No, well, maybe the more I got into show business . . . But there was something else. Couples, as they get older, look back and say, "Remember when we lived in that one room in Tallaght and there was just the two of us and we had no money and robbed milk off somebody's doorstep? Weren't we so happy then?" When you start saying, "Where did that go?", you know it's a warning sign.

'And that happened to Doreen and me. Couples are at their happiest and best working against adversity. When that's gone, you take a long look at your own life. I did. I didn't look at Doreen and say, "It's her fault." I looked at myself and said, "I'm not happy." Basically, my marriage separation happened because I wasn't happy. I couldn't even explain why. Yet, for years, I was afraid to tell Doreen. I hid those feelings, wondering how you can love someone and feel hollow inside.'

Brendan had pots of adversity in his life in the form of massive debt. But adversity has to be shared to keep a couple strong. Brendan wasn't sharing his problems with Doreen. In fact, he wasn't sharing much of anything.

By this point, Jenny had become a major feature in Brendan's life, appearing with him on stage and on film. And she was now his best friend and business confidante. He maintains they hadn't become a couple during their working time together, but there's no doubt they had a strong emotional attachment. It was Jenny he had called from LA when he was in the doldrums. And Jenny had backed Brendan not only with cash, but unstinting loyalty.

'When you are an artist – and I am an artist – and you are out and about, your greatest wish is for everybody to know you. That's what you are trying to achieve. But Doreen felt she was living in a goldfish bowl.

'It wasn't because of Jenny that we separated, it was because of the pressures of show business. Doreen would be at home lonely and I would be away lonely. The two of us just went in different directions. I felt as if I was standing on the edge of the Grand Canyon and there was no one standing beside me to share the exquisite view.'

But break-ups of 23-year-old marriages are seldom less than awful.

'It wasn't that I was saying, "I don't want to be Doreen's husband," I was saying, "I can't be anyone's husband. So much to do, so little time." But sitting down with someone you love and admire and saying, "I'm not happy here," is bad enough, but trying to explain, "It's not your fault," is even worse.

'Many wives, in this situation, would feel, "It must be my fault", or say, "You're lying. If not to me, then to yourself," as Doreen did.

'But what I was saying was, "I'm not happy with the whole thing. I've got to step away from it." The rot was a basic unhappiness I hadn't sorted out. And, remember, we were fourteen when we met. Maybe it wasn't about love back then. Maybe we got married because I felt it was about keeping a promise.

'Whatever, when the end came I felt guilty, especially about the manner in which we'd broken up. I'd rather I'd been more honest, told her what I was feeling. I was arrogant. I thought she'd fall apart and I should have gone earlier.

'I knew I was taking the first step by leaving Doreen. Yet the loneliness at the start, in my apartment, was dreadful.'

Brendan had bought an apartment in the city's Temple Gate. As if being insolvent weren't enough, he had to cope without his family life and seeing his three kids on a daily basis. And he admits he simply couldn't cope.

'This really was the most depressing time of my life. I sat in my living room for two days with my arms crossed. I couldn't move. Eventually, the second night I got down on my knees, and I prayed, like I did when I was a child. I prayed to my mother. "Mam, I hope you can hear this, but if you can, I know that you can help me. Give me the answer to how I can get through this."

'And that night I went to sleep and I had the most incredible dream. I dreamt I was in my office, an office I didn't even have at the time, and the phone rang. And the secretary buzzed and said, "That's your mother on the phone, Brendan."

'And I said, "Sure, I've been expecting the call." So I took the call and it was my mother. And I told her I needed help. And she said, "Sure, Brendan, if you have the strength to get down on your knees and pray, you can get back up again and get on with life. Now do it!" And I woke up the next morning and I did.'

Brendan's tone turns upbeat as he continues the story.

'We have an old saying in Ireland: *God doesn't give you a cross to bear that you can't carry.* And really what we're saying is, life is preparing you for every little thing. And rarely do you come across something that completely devastates you. You've had preparation for that somewhere along the line.'

What to do, though? The comedy gigs paid the mortgage on the house in Ashbourne and the rental on the flat. But there was the company debt the size of Dublin Palace to consider.

One September morning, a magic moment occurred in the form of a phone call from John Costigan, manager of one of Dublin's most prestigious theatres, The Gaiety.

'John had loved *The Course*, and he liked me. So he asked me to have a coffee with him in a café in Chapel Street.

'He said, "Listen Brendan. I've got three weeks free in the Gaiety in February. And Denis (Desmond, the owner of the Gaiety and the most important man in Irish showbiz) says he wants you to scribble up something for that time."'

Scribble up? What that very loose language translated to was that Denis Desmond wanted Brendan to write, hopefully, a hit play that would fill the theatre. But Brendan couldn't take on that sort of task. He was flattened. He didn't have the confidence to write a postcard, never mind another hit play.

'I said, "Jaysus, John. I don't know. I really don't know."'

To complicate matters, John said they would agree upon a joint production – split the costs and, hopefully, split the box office. Now, to most theatre producers, this is a perfectly reasonable suggestion. However, the set-up costs to Brendan would be around £50–60,000. Now, Brendan didn't have fifty/sixty pence. In reality, he owed more than £2 million.

'I was feckin' fecked,' he says, summing up his financial position with clarity and colour. 'And I told John this.'

However, John Costigan had envisaged this problem and had a plan.

'Look, Brendan. Denis says he will advance you the money. And he will later take it off the top of the bestseller.'

'Bestselling what? I haven't even an idea.'

'Ah, but Denis says you'll come up with something.'

'So, I said okay. And I really appreciated this. Denis is a really kind man. But then over the next couple of months I thought and wondered what the hell I would write about. And I realised I had to look back at what had failed, and bury it in my head. But I also had to look back and realise what had succeeded.

'And it came to me. Mrs Browne had succeeded. The radio stories had been a great success. And the books had done great business. And I thought, "What about a Mrs Browne play?" Then I began to think what would give an Agnes Browne play a device, an obvious backdrop for tension. And I thought, "A wedding. That could be the answer!" And with that in mind I wrote the play in four days.'

It was a phenomenal effort. Typing eighty pages of script alone could take a couple of days.

'I suppose the character was already in my head, and I found her so easy to write for. I'd go to bed at night and dream up storylines for her. I just knew how she would react in any situation.'

Of course he did. He was writing about his own life. He was writing about his mammy. He was writing about the relationship between a mother and her kids, which could change in a heartbeat from 'loving the very bones of them', as Agnes would say, to trashing them with a wicked one-liner. When Brendan came up with the storylines he only had to think about the confusion in his own house, of how his mother was so switched on, but couldn't switch on a fridge. He only had to recall the wisdom, the philosophy of Maureen O'Carroll, and transpose it into another frame. He also knew of the depth of the relationship between an Irish mother and her sons, and he knew the debates that came about as daughters grew into their mothers. He only had to think about how his mother could be a little hoity-toity at times to come up with Agnes's telephone voice, or the faint hint of deference she'd show when meeting Maria's posh mother. Brendan might not have realised it at the time, but his mammy was looking down on him as he battered the typewriter keys. But the real reason Brendan found it so easy? He loved writing about this world, his own world, which he could now recreate in fictional form. And, as for the supporting cast? Brendan based them on characters he'd known as a kid, taking elements of personality and amplifying them.

Brendan already had his key characters. Jenny played Cathy, Derek Reddin played Rory, Dino was played by Gerry Browne, Dermot was Simon Young and Mark was played by Ciaron McMahon, who played Tony in *The Course*. Eilish played Winnie McGoogan.

The storyline is simple: Agnes Browne is trying to plan her son Trevor's wedding to the posh Maria, aided by her gay son Rory and his lunatic hairdresser boyfriend, Dino.

Audiences are invited along for the hen party, a stag party and a dinner party with a difference. And when Agnes tries to impress her son's prospective mother-in-law by installing a new downstairs toilet – well, you can just imagine.

'So I rang John Costigan and told him I'd written a script and I offered to send it over. But John and Denis said they were happy to see it on opening night.

'That, to me, was a massive vote of confidence. And I will never forget Denis for giving me that lift.'

Yet, while Brendan was able to capture Agnes's voice on radio, how could he possibly look like a 60-year-old woman? He rang Tom McInnerney, who'd worked on *Grandad's Sure*.

'I said, "Look, you know Mrs Browne, you've read about her, I want you to make me up as Mrs Browne."'

But there was a slight catch. Brendan didn't want any mirrors in the room. He didn't want to see the transformation take place. He wanted to see the complete, finished result.

'I was made up and I began talking as Mrs Browne, using the voice saying, "Mary had a little lamb . . ." and as I talked I walked towards a mirror, looked up and said [Mrs Browne voice], "Hello!" – and she was standing there in front of me. I thought, "This is going to work."'

Writing the play had given Brendan confidence. He sensed he had a winner. The plan was to open *Mrs Browne's Last Wedding* in Cork, at the Everyman Palace Theatre, for five nights, before moving on to Dublin.

Brendan didn't want to open the production in Dublin: that would be too risky with an untested play. Far better to open out of town, take the opportunity to iron out wrinkles, see if the cast all gelled, and make the mistakes that wouldn't matter too much.

That said, he desperately wanted the Cork run to work. He knew that good reviews would reach his home town.

The next step was to call Gerry in and ask him to arrange dates in Liverpool, Glasgow and Manchester. Brendan knew he had to tour. He *knew* he could make money.

But then everything seemed to be going mad. Things weren't helped by the reception the cast received when they arrived in Cork, on the day before the Monday show.

Brendan was met by the front-of-house manager, who announced that the sales were 'disappointing', which is a trade euphemism for 'You may as well open an artery and let the blood flow into the stalls.'

Brendan was knocked by the news, but he took an upbeat line, saying, 'Don't worry about it.' He tried to console himself with the fact that this was just a warm-up for Dublin. And he desperately hoped the week in Cork would at least pay for itself.

There was another worrying sign, however. Good first-night reviews are vital to the success of a play, but on opening night, the reviewer for the *Cork Examiner* was ill, so the paper sent their opera/culture critic.

'The house manager was shitting himself when she arrived.'

Brendan was truly nervous. He was dragging his old debts around and was also risking having to pay back Denis Desmond's investment, should the play go belly-up. The last thing he wanted was for the first review to be negative.

Bizarrely, given how skint Ireland's two Likely Lads were, Brendan and Gerry decided to donate the profits from their world premiere show to the Chernobyl Children's Project.

And it wasn't uncharacteristic of the pair. They gave money over to charity projects on a regular basis.

The *Cork Examiner* described how 'the partners and life-long friends would be making many young children happy.'

But would they put a smile on the faces of grown-ups that week in February? The production was already facing a minor meltdown.

'We didn't even have a dress rehearsal, and we were so far behind with the technical rehearsals when the lights went up for that very first scene, with me in Agnes Browne's living room, the cast saw me as her for the very first time. Jenny says from that moment, she never saw me as Brendan O'Carroll on stage, she just saw The Mammy.

'I also wanted Agnes to be totally believable to the cast. This wasn't as it had been in rehearsals, with the cast speaking lines to a bloke with a moustache. They had to be speaking to their mother.'

And they were. Brendan's Agnes was bang on the money. She looked like Maureen O'Carroll and she had many of her mannerisms. On top of that, Brendan had unconsciously added little bits of Gerry Browne's mammy, too, and of Dolly Dowdall and Cecil Sheridan's stage dames. This wasn't a woman up there on stage, although she had the walk, the demeanour, the presence. But it wasn't a caricature either. It was as close as you can get without removing the Adam's Apple and the usual male instrumentation. The Monday night audience bought into Brendan's performance completely. His stage version of the character he'd created on radio was hilarious, and the audience loved her from the moment she shuffled onto the stage.

They also loved her friend, Winnie. What the audience didn't realise was that Winnie was far from the doddery old lady she appeared on stage; that Eilish O'Carroll had done a fantastic job of getting into character. She had achieved it by creating a picture in her head of who Winnie should look like, based on her mammy's friend, Nancy Pimley. Nancy was a bright Winnie, but always in awe of Maureen O'Carroll.

And all the other characters gelled. A standing ovation followed the curtain drop and, after the show, the cast celebrated like it was Christmas and New Year combined.

All except Brendan. He had other matters on his mind.

'At this time, Fiona was sixteen and she was working on the ships to Le Havre as a receptionist. She called me in tears. She was being worked for twenty-two-hour stretches and had had enough. So I said to leave the ferry when she came back and I'd pick her up in Wexford. And I set off at four a.m. to collect her and took her for breakfast and to cheer her up, and she was grand.'

The newspaper reviews were also grand.

'The *Cork Examiner* review began, "I was met at the door of the theatre before the show started by the front-of-house manager, Vincent. He obviously wasn't expecting to see me. He said, 'Welcome to the show, but let me just forewarn you. This is not Shakespeare.' But you know, I've seen this play and I have to say this is Shakespeare. Shakespeare wrote for the Penny Circle. Shakespeare wrote for people who have dreary lives, who get to come and watch their lives being lit up on stage and have the opportunity to laugh at themselves. This is what Shakespeare did. And this is indeed Shakespeare."'

The review helped box-office sales, but word-of-mouth was the major factor. By lunchtime on Tuesday, that night's play was sold out. And the rest of the week quickly sold out too. Brendan's wings began to appear again.

'The theatre manager asked us if we would extend the show to Saturday and Sunday. And we didn't want to let him down – he'd shown faith in us – so we agreed. And we weren't opening until the Tuesday in the Gaiety, so it was all feasible.'

But there was a problem to overcome. The actress who played Betty said she didn't want to perform at the weekend. She said she wasn't signed up for the weekend, and she'd made plans to go out with her boyfriend.

'I said, "Look love, this is the acting business. You have to work when the opportunity is there. And, even more importantly, if this play does well, and I think it might, we could extend our run. And we're going to Dublin for three weeks. Who knows what will happen?" But she stuck her heels in. "I'm not doing Saturday and Sunday," she argued. And I said, "Okay, no problem."'

Brendan came up with a ready solution. Once again he decided to pick a wild flower from the garden. In this case it was Sheila Carty, who ran the theatre bar. Brendan reckoned she had a great personality, which came across after the shows when she would get up and sing with the jazz band.

So why not put her up there on stage?

'I said to her that night, "Sheila, I want you to watch the play tonight really closely, in particular the part of Betty. Because, on Saturday, I want you to play Betty."

'She looked shocked and said, "Oh, I couldn't, Brendan. I've never acted."'

But she could. And she did. Sheila would go on to tour with the cast as Betty for the next two years.

The next stop was Dublin. And the play took the town by storm, going on to run at the Gaiety for an incredible 15 weeks, beating the audience records for *The Course*.

Yet, Brendan says he was a little more subdued by success this time around.

'I didn't ever go back to the thinking that I owned the sun,' he says. 'I came off stage feeling thankful that we'd gotten away with it, that we'd had a wonderful day. And that's the way I've felt ever since.'

He adds, 'I'm always saying to Jenny, "Hey, it's the end of the day and we're still alive."'

Now, all Brendan and Gerry had to do was take Mrs Browne on tour. But they were both entirely aware that having a hit play in your home town doesn't guarantee success anywhere else.

However, Brendan believed he had to take the gamble.

AGNES BELONGS TO GLASGOW

THE IRISH success of *Last Wedding* wasn't the only highlight of 1999. Brendan had a small part in the hit movie *Angela's Ashes*, playing an undertaker, although he admits he found Frank McCourt's book about his Limerick childhood a little depressing and didn't make it past Chapter Ten. (*Angela's Ashes* also offered work to a hopeful young actor, Danny O'Carroll. Now 16, Danny would eventually join his dad on stage playing the Buster Brady character.)

Director Alan Parker and star Bobby Carlyle were great to work with. But Brendan found filming *Angela's Ashes* traumatic.

'I accepted the part immediately. But it was only when I looked at it more closely did I realise that I would be burying children in their little white coffins. Suddenly the colour drained out of my face. All I could think about was little Brendan.

'After the funeral scene, Bobby asked me to come out for a pint with him and the rest of the cast, but I turned him down. After filming a scene like that, I just wanted to go home. It was so emotionally draining I couldn't bear to go out and enjoy myself, even though in retrospect it would have prob-ably been a great way to unwind.'

Brendan's next focus was on the upcoming *Last Wedding* tour. This time he was more than aware of the risks of taking out a huge production, with so many hotel rooms to pay for and mouths to feed. He knew he had a hit play. But would the UK give Mrs Brown the time of day?

Gerry Browne was dispatched to Glasgow, a hugely impor-tant city in that it was home to the Pavilion Theatre, a former variety hall and a 1,600-seater with a distinctly working-class audience. On the face of it, the Pavilion was the perfect home for Agnes and co. And so Gerry arrived at the theatre door with a plastic bag in his hand and a look of desperation on his face. But, in the Superquinn bag, he felt, lay hope. What it contained was a dog-eared copy of *Mrs Brown's Last Wedding*.

But what would the no-nonsense, short-fused Pavilion manager Iain Gordon think of this Irish invasion? When the phone rang in his upstairs office to herald the arrival of a Mr Browne, Iain Gordon studied his closed-circuit camera to check out the man in the foyer. And the sight of a tall, slightly scruffy, slightly desperate-looking man clutching a super-market plastic bag didn't impress him.

Upstairs in the office, Iain Gordon told Gerry Browne straight off he'd never heard of him or Brendan O'Carroll. And why should he even think about staging an unknown Irish play in his town?

But he liked Gerry Browne's upbeat attitude, and loved the fact he seemed a trier, and said he would read the script. He did – but the result wasn't good. The theatre boss reckoned the play was 'as funny as piles'.

Gerry persisted, arguing how well it had gone down in Dublin. Iain Gordon listened, but didn't agree. It was only when he brought in an actor friend to read it aloud in an Irish accent that it seemed to make sense.

The Glasgow theatre boss agreed to take the chance on the play, splitting the box-office receipts. But there was a problem. The Pavilion manager reckoned a new play needed £25,000 spent on advertising, which Brendan and Gerry would pay half of. But Brendan and Gerry, still with massive debts, had no money. Zero. Gerry was in fact sticking the travel costs on his Visa card.

Gerry asked Iain Gordon for an advance. It was highly unusual, but the gruff Glasgow theatre boss put his hand in his pocket and gave the Irishman the money for the hotels.

The Pavilion boss also paid for the radio and newspaper advertising. But the strategy didn't work. Ticket sales were disastrous.

And when the Irish hopefuls turned up for technical rehearsals the day before the show opened in June 1999, the Pavilion boss was dismayed by what he saw. He reckons the set was the cheapest, tackiest, ever. And Brendan and co. 'looked to be a team of losers'.

To make matters worse, ticket sales for the week were dreadful. June is not a great month for theatres anywhere, but this was disastrous. A few hundred tickets had been sold for the opening night, but that was in a two-for-one deal.

The entire ticket sales for the week were just £5,000 (an average production would take in from £50,000 to £80,000 for the week) and the Pavilion boss was all set to pull the production.

'I wouldn't have blamed him,' says Brendan. 'The advertising hadn't worked. No one had ever heard of the Mrs Brown character. Why would they come?'

However, Brendan made an appeal to Iain Gordon.

'I walked into his office and said, 'If you stick with this play, I will make you a million quid.' Now, the truth is, I didn't have a clue what I was talking about. But it turned out to be true.'

The theatre boss announced to Brendan and Gerry that he'd run the show until the end of the week, and then it would be pulled. He was cutting his losses.

On opening night, however, the theatre boss was amazed by what he witnessed on stage. It didn't matter if the set looked a bit ramshackle, the audience simply loved *Last Wedding*. And Iain Gordon, a man who guards his emotions more carefully than the box-office takings, says he laughed louder than he'd ever laughed in his life. By the end of the week, a minor miracle on Renfield Street was taking place. Those who'd seen the first few nights had gone home and told their friends. The box-office phone sparkled like the generators Brendan, John Breen and Jimmy Matthews had once slept near. And the theatre boss kept the doors open for a second week. On one day alone, the Pavilion till took £20,000.

'You have to take your hat off to Iain Gordon. He didn't know us from Adam. He gave us the theatre with no rent and no guarantees. He showed a lot of balls.'

This was *The Course* all over again, except it set a pattern of success that would continue for the next decade.

That run at the Pavilion alone saw *Mrs Brown's Last Wedding* pull in £400,000. Brendan had conquered Glasgow, which would become his favourite venue in the UK, with the Agnes Brown plays going on to pull in millions.

(Bugsy made his first appearance on stage at the Pavilion, playing the role of Grandad, in a cameo. The former window-cleaner, now instantly recognisable, is today besieged for autographs wherever he goes.)

Thankfully, Liverpool and Manchester followed suit. Not quite in the same numbers as Glasgow, but the Mrs Brown train, packed with friends and family, was now funded – and off and running.

However, in London, at the Lyric Theatre, Hammersmith, it came off the rails, in terms of the broadsheet reviews and box office.

'It is potentially a fine enough comic set-up, and gets plenty of laughs,' said the *Financial Times*. 'However, the thing is, most of the laughs are titters of genteel shock that O'Carroll has taken a mildly smirksome line and inserted the word "fuckin" into it. I began to keep a tally of the number of laugh lines he gave himself which did not include that or another expletive; by the end of the show, I had spotted a grand total of five.

'The audience, on the other hand, were by the end so ready to laugh at anything that they giggled through the climactic mother–daughter sentimentality.'

The reviewer added, 'The play exists somewhere between Roddy Doyle-land and the territory of Caroline Aherne's *The Royle Family*, with a cousin of Les Dawson's Ada in charge.'

The review highlighted a couple of important points: the broadsheets weren't keen on what they thought was lowbrow entertainment; yet, those in the audience loved Brendan's broad comedy strokes.

Sadly, *Last Wedding* played to houses little more than a third full in Hammersmith. Brendan and Gerry didn't have the money to back the full-scale advertising campaign needed in London.

Yet Brendan wasn't overly worried.

'Fuck London,' he said at the time.

And, after all, the northern cities loved Agnes. But sadly, overall box-office success didn't cement the relationship between Brendan and Gerry. Gerry was dealing with his own problems. He'd had enough of travelling with the O'Carroll circus and decided it was time to step off the carousel.

Gerry decided he would break up the partnership on the night of the premiere of *Agnes Browne* in Dublin in November. At the time, the former milkman had a broken ankle he'd sustained in a football match but, more importantly, a broken spirit. He had spent too many years living in a metaphorical tent and he reckoned his wife and two kids were paramount. He'd watched Brendan's marriage break up and didn't want his to go the same way.

Even though Gerry was desperately broke, he chose to walk away from the upcoming plays, the Mrs Brown royalties, everything.

What had happened between the pair to break up such an incredible friendship? Two men going at different speeds, sometimes in different directions? Perhaps.

Or perhaps they were like many seemingly inseparable double acts such as Dean Martin and Jerry Lewis, Abbott and Costello, Little and Large, there simply comes a time when they have to separate.

'It was on the cards, I guess. During the difficult times we would have rows and Gerry would get angry and say, "You bastard! I've looked after you since we were kids . . ."

'And I'd yell back, "You didn't, Gerry. We made it up!"

'"Well, I would have . . ."

'It had all become confused. We simply weren't on the same page any more.'

The pair had loved each other like brothers. Somehow, life got in the way.

Film director Jim Sheridan landed Gerry a couple of small roles in movies, but Brendan's former best friend was not after the limelight – he happily went from making a movie with Anjelica Huston and Tom Jones to gigging in a hotel bar for £200. However, he was content to be living a life he could control.

Brendan believed it was time to go it alone.

'What I do think was that Gerry believed his own publicity. In his own way, though, he was a lovable guy.'

Brendan had lost his best friend. Benny and Gerry, who'd shared debts, reviews, holiday apartments with their wives (and even beds back in the touring days when they were skint), were no longer an item.

But Brendan had greater problems to contend with.

THE SPECIAL ONE IN BETHLEHEM

THE GLASGOW success story continued on to Newcastle, Manchester, Liverpool and Glasgow – *Mrs Brown's Last Wedding* returned to the city in October 1999 and sold out. And the play went on to tour in Canada and Australia.

But that didn't mean Brendan was home and dry as far as the banks were concerned. He had a long way to go.

Yet, at least he now had stability in his personal life. What had changed in recent times were his feelings for Jenny. She had been a semi-permanent fixture in his life since 1995 – they had been working together, sharing problems, sharing the cost of keeping a troupe together – and it was obvious, if not to themselves, but certainly to those around them, they would become a couple.

However, when they made their announcement, there were seismic shockwaves. After all, Brendan was now a national figure.

At the time of his marriage break-up, Brendan had called the papers in Dublin and informed them that he and Doreen had parted. He asked that they refrain from writing about the story, in a pre-emptive strike, because of how vulnerable the kids were feeling. And Brendan said he would talk about the break-up later on.

All the papers respected the request, except for the *News of the World*. When the story appeared, it was given a massive six pages of coverage.

Doreen was knocked for six. It was all very well agreeing to go on *The Late, Late Show*, but that was for the good of the family. This latest bout of publicity rocked her world.

The producers of *The Late, Late Show*, however, deemed the break-up to be of interest to their viewers, who would want to know the reason for the end of the seemingly happy marriage.

'Gay said he wanted me to come on the show, and he wanted to talk about the split "for a few minutes". Now, I had never disagreed with anything Gay had suggested before, but I couldn't go along with this. So I said, "Look, Gay, I'll talk about the split, but I won't do it in three minutes. If you want to talk about it, then that's what the interview will be about. I'm not going to go onto a serious subject and start to play the clown. It won't sit right." And he protested, saying, "No, we have to mention the split. It's been in the papers." And I said, "Yes, but a subject like that has to be done properly. I'm not going to gloss over it."

'In the end, I went on the show and Gay never mentioned the split. The interview was the usual, funny exchange.'

What would he have said to Gay Byrne?

'Well, I would have said I was on my own for six months in the apartment trying to sort myself out.

'The fact that I met Jenny was a happy coincidence, but also a complication I didn't need. I couldn't even straighten out the life I had. I would have left Doreen anyway.

'And, meantime, the kids were blaming Jenny, which added to the tension. The kids had no time for her. Fiona came to the apartment once and I hid Jenny in the car park! So I had to sit down the children and say, "There is no law that says you have to like Jenny. But one thing I demand is good manners. That's not a lot to ask." From that moment, they did me proud.

'But the children had also seen their mother abandoned and this made them think, "Feck you, Dad, for breaking mum's heart." And they got very angry – for months, in Fiona's case. She felt I'd really betrayed her mother by leaving.'

The kids would come to be very close to Jenny, seeing her as a friend and confidante. Which was just as well because, by the beginning of the new millennium, Brendan and Jenny were utterly inseparable. They formed a new production company. There was even talk about whether or not they would have kids together.

'When I talked to Fiona and Danny about this, they said, "We draw the line at that, Dad." But I knew their characters enough to know that if a baby came along, they'd welcome it with open arms.'

Brendan says Jenny had no problem with his being a father-of-three.

'I would have said to whoever is with me, "If you have a problem with this, we have no future. It'd break my heart, but these children are going to be my children when they are fifty." I would be saying, in the middle of dinner, "I got a call from Fiona, she's not happy, I gotta go see her." And I'd go. But Jenny was never going to have a problem with this. Her attitude was, "One of the reasons I was attracted to you is because, after my own father, you're the finest father I've known. And if you change in that way, I wouldn't like you."

'Some women, and men, think, "If you're giving that level of devotion to your children, you're taking it from me." If you feel that, you don't understand life. Jenny does. And that's why I love her.'

He believes the relationship will last forever.

'God, Jaysus, I hope so. But I'm not an expert on any of this. What I do know is I thank God for sending her to me, this woman who does *The Times* crossword and smokes Consulate. She's incredible.'

Gay Byrne once asked Brendan if Jenny helped take the place of his mammy.

'Could be,' he replied, smiling. Why did Brendan agree? Because Jenny has some similar traits to Maureen O'Carroll. Jenny is a fighter, she'll tackle anyone and anything she feels will threaten her world. She's a passionate, well-read and incisive woman. She can read a script and know instinctively what will work. What she also has in common with Maureen is she believes implicitly in Brendan. Almost from the moment she met him (after she'd cast aside the thought that he was a Mafia member), she recognised his talent, his imagination and sense of humour. The pair were on the same wavelength. Every night at teatime, the world stops while they watch the BBC's *Eggheads* together, trying to answer as many questions as possible. They like the same things. They love the same celery and apple health drink they take each afternoon. And they love their life together, at home and on the road. Jenny isn't a mother substitute. But like Brendan's mammy she's a big personality in her own right, with a strong voice. Perhaps Brendan even still thinks of Jenny as a gobshite at times. And they do love a good argument on occasion. But there's no doubt they were born to become the perfect double act.

His comic mammy, Brendan knew, offered the solution to his financial problems. The success of *Last Wedding* made the follow-up inevitable and he spent the early months of 2000 writing *Good Mourning Mrs Brown*. The action returns to Larkin Court in Dublin City, which follows the events surrounding the funeral of Grandad. Except he isn't actually dead.

Along the way we get involved in Dermot's efforts to go 'straight', Father Quinn's doubting his vocation, the final days of Maria's pregnancy, the changing of water to wine, the battle for a £50,000 insurance cheque and even a divine resurrection. What more could you ask for?

There are also a few typical Agnes lines: 'You've heard of Dr Dolittle – this is Dr Do Fuckall.' And where would Mrs Brown be without a malapropism or two? 'It says, "You should splash cold water on your scrotum." What if you drive a Volkswagen?'

What Brendan seems to have developed cleverly is Agnes's fractured personality. While she is able to ape motherly love, there's a part of her that's judgemental. She loves her gay son Rory to bits, but still wonders 'if they'll find a cure'. She encourages daughter Cathy to find love. But then points out Cathy's best years are behind her and she'd better not be too fussy. She looks after Grandad, who's not even a blood relation. But reminds him every single day he's 'one step closer to the coffin'. Agnes welcomes Buster Brady into her home as if he were one of her sons. But then reminds the rest of the family to check their handbags and wallets when he's gone.

'Buster,' she says, hugging the baseball-capped rascal, almost teary-eyed.

'Yes, Mrs Brown?'

'Buster, you're the son I never wanted.'

She's consistently funny. And thought-provoking. When a couple of Mormons come to the door, their unrelenting oversell of the Bible is halted immediately by one Agnes line.

'If Noah had two of every breed of animal on a small boat, how could two hamsters have caused such chaos in my one house?'

Brendan left his cast behind to travel to the States in the autumn. To Harvard, no less, America's principal seat of learning. Brendan was asked to go to promote his Mrs Brown books at the Harvard Book Fair as part of a major book tour.

But he wasn't overly impressed by the offer.

'Jenny and I fell out briefly over this. My publishers were hugely excited about the offer. They couldn't believe that Mrs Brown had made it to the book fair because the criteria were pretty stiff.

'I said, "Yes, okay, let's do it, but it didn't strike me as a big deal." But Jenny kept saying, "This is Harvard, Brendan. You haven't been to school since you were twelve and now you're being asked to read your book at Harvard."

'But I couldn't be bothered. "Well, it's great, Jenny. But it's just another reading."

'And we had this big row. She just didn't think I took it seriously enough. In fact she didn't think I took my writing seriously enough.'

Perhaps it's because it seemed to come easily to him – writing plays in days or just a few weeks, writing a book in a couple of months.

However, the American trip did turn out to be incredibly special.

Just before Brendan, Jenny, Danny and Rory set off, Brendan had received a letter sent via Penguin USA, asking if he would give a reading in a town called Bethlehem in Pennsylvania.

'We've heard Brendan O'Carroll is doing readings in the States. He has simply *got* to give a reading at the Morovian Hotel,' it read.

Penguin replied saying thanks, but that Brendan only had 32 dates available. And perhaps on the next trip . . .

But the Bethlehem bookstore people were having none of it. They wrote back saying, 'Every Halloween we celebrate with all the bookstore workers dressing up as characters from the Mrs Brown books and the windows are done up like Moore Street.'

What? Shop assistants dressed up like Agnes and her fruit-market pals? Someone made up to look like Cathy Brown?

Again, Penguin wrote back to the Bethlehem bookstore and said they were delighted that Brendan had such fantastic fans, but unfortunately he had no dates left to do a reading.

The next letter said, 'Look, you don't understand. The Morovian Book Shop is the oldest bookstore in the United States. And it is considered an honour to be invited to speak at the bookstore. And this is an honour we are determined to bestow on Mr O'Carroll.'

Finally the big guns rolled out. The fourth letter came from the mayor. It mentioned, with a tug at the heart strings, that many of the local people were from steel families, and they'd struggled in the same way Mrs Brown had. They could readily identify with her . . . so if anything could be done at all?

'So Penguin came back to me, and said, "Look, you've two days off in your schedule. And if you want to we can book one of those days to go to Bethlehem."'

Well, God loves a trier. Particularly a trier from Bethlehem. How could Brendan refuse that heartbreaking appeal? He did the book tour, including the signing at Harvard University, and declared it, 'Amazing'.

Brendan was stunned to see hundreds of people turn up and buy his book.

'If I'm being honest, I think I had an inferiority complex about being there. I had written a few books, but they were only fun books. I was in a world of serious books, and serious writers. I couldn't believe so many people believed in me as a writer. It was incredible. And the amazing thing is, in the States I am known as a writer. Most people have never seen the stage show or know I'm an actor. To them, I'm Brendan the writer. And I love that. My mother would have been so proud.'

It was 5 August when Brendan flew into Baltimore and made his way to Bethlehem, 'A gorgeous little city.

'I flew into Baltimore at five in the morning, then into Bethlehem at seven, went to the hotel, had a couple of hours' kip because usually it's signings all day and then a reading at night.

'But there were no bookstores to sign at, so I had a good rest, and got a phone call from Penguin to tell me I'd be picked up at whatever time.

'Then the car arrived for Jenny, Danny and Rory and me. And the car had an escort. And there was a carnival going on in the street. And there was a huge banner up. BETHLEHEM WELCOMES BRENDAN O'CARROLL. And there were Irish dancers in the street! I could hardly speak.

'And so we arrived at the bookstore. But what I didn't know was that the Morovian Book Shop is in fact an entire street. All the stores, even if they say "Pharmacy" or "Grocer" on the front are in fact a bookstore.

'So they walked me up through the whole store to a hundred hellos. And by this point I was stunned.

'We were taken outside into the crowds where dragonfly cookies were being handed around and I can't tell you how overwhelmed I was. I said to Rory, "What is all this?"

'And he said, bemused, "I don't know." I tried to work it out. Agnes Brown is basically about a woman who brought her kids up in poverty, but she never thought she was poor because everyone else was. They probably identified with her a lot.

'Then one of the managers of the store said, "Welcome, Mr O'Carroll." And I said, "Thanks, but this is all incredible." And she said, "You ain't seen nothing yet."'

And he hadn't. Just at that point, City Mayor Donald Cunningham took to the podium in the street, the microphone was switched on and he made a polite speech. Then he boomed out to the hundreds of people: 'I declare the fifth of August to be . . . Brendan O'Carroll Day!'

Brendan O'Carroll, the boy who had never made it to secondary school, was now a celebration day. The Lord Mayor of the American town had written to the Mayor of Dublin to ask for permission to honour one of its citizens, which of course was granted.

'I cried,' says Brendan. 'I couldn't help myself. I broke down. It was one of those moments when I said to myself, "Look at me, Ma, I'm flying."'

Danny beamed with pride. Jenny was ecstatic. A couple of tears also welled up in Rory's eyes. It was a magical day for the boy from Finglas. And the remarkable thing was no one in the entire country was aware Brendan was a performer. The honour was all about his writing.

The income from writing didn't keep up with Brendan's spending, however. And now that his gigging days with Gerry Browne were over, Brendan had to look for a new source of earnings.

Thankfully, it came in the form of a panto offer. Such was Brendan's popularity in Glasgow, Pavilion Theatre boss Iain Gordon reckoned the Irishman would be perfect for panto. That's how he came to appear in *Treasure Island* as Dame Bird's Eye, a character not a million miles away from Agnes Brown, but without the swearing.

It was the first time he had ever been in panto and, he says, probably the last.

'Oh God, it was hard work. It takes up your entire life. Even when I got half an hour to do Christmas shopping, I'd find myself asking store assistants if they had something, and if they said no, I'd say, "Oh yes you do!" It was crazy.

'The only way to get through it is to have fun – and it was a great crowd.'

He's accentuating the positive. Brendan was there for the wages. He didn't want to be performing someone else's lines for 11 weeks and over 70 performances. But the money was good – so good, in fact, that he was able to think about buying a home in Florida, near Disneyland. It was appropriate Brendan would make his second home near the kids' fun capital of the world.

Brendan didn't spend all his time in Glasgow, however. On Sundays he travelled back to Dublin to see eight-year-old Eric, and he'd make the odd TV appearance or attend a civic function, such as unveiling an art exhibition with the Irish Prime Minister. On Tuesday mornings, it was back to Glasgow and wearing a dress.

Brendan was always accompanied by daughter Fiona, who also appeared in the panto as the Principal Girl, and by her fiancé Marty, and son Danny now working behind the scenes.

During the panto run, Brendan became close to a young actor who would become a fixture in the Mrs Brown circus.

(The 'e' in Browne had since been dropped, perhaps to remove any association with Gerry Browne.)

Former *Take the High Road* soap star Gary Hollywood had split up with his wife, and met his future wife, Sharon, who was the panto choreographer. His life was in turmoil and Brendan once again took on the role of godfather, talking Gary through the depressing times and dispensing advice. Then, at the end of the panto, Brendan offered Gary a job appearing in the Mrs Brown touring show.

Brendan even insisted Gary bring Sharon on tour as well.

'Brendan O'Carroll is like no other employer; you don't just join the cast, you become a member of the extended family,' says Gary. 'He and Jenny look after you. And when we go our separate ways for the holiday breaks, everyone keeps in touch. We go to each other's celebrations, to weddings, to birthdays. And, after shows, we go out and party together. It's rare when Brendan hasn't hired a bar with a karaoke machine and we all sing. You should hear Brendan sing Elton's "Don't Let the Sun Go Down On Me", or Danny sing Robbie Williams's "Angels". Then the whole group will sing "The Fields of Athenry" and it brings tears to your eyes. Working with Brendan is like being part of an ongoing party because he has created this closeness, this sense of everyone belonging, that's really unique.'

After the panto run, Brendan flew to Florida with the family, and stayed until St Patrick's Day in March. Then it was time to return home to stage his second Mrs Brown adventure. And hope the love for Agnes Brown was growing.

Moving On

BRENDAN'S second Agnes Brown play, *Good Mourning*, was a huge hit in the spring of 2001. It sold out in Dublin's Gaiety Theatre, playing to more than 85,000 people over three weeks, and did fantastic business in Glasgow, Newcastle, Manchester and Liverpool. In fact, a shoehorn couldn't have squeezed any more punters into the halls.

Brendan and the cast were flying. But the boss wouldn't allow anyone to take success for granted. Every performance had to be special.

'Years ago, with my very first play, I noticed that after the second or third week, the actors had become really complacent. They knew their lines, they knew when they were supposed to speak, but I noticed they had kind of glazed over.

'To me comedy is like classical music. It has to be done with passion and, if it's not, the audience will spot it. It's got to look like you're up there giving it socks, or the audience will go, "They're not really enjoying themselves, so we shouldn't really be laughing."

'So on one of the nights, to try to get them out of their glaze, I asked one of them a question that wasn't in the script.

'Well, it was like looking at six passport photographs. They just stood there in shock. But it worked. They didn't relax on stage again. And that's why I suddenly ad-lib in the middle of a Mrs Brown play. You need to keep everybody on their toes.

'But as I've developed the idea I realise it's only funny if the audience are in on it as well – because they are paying. So what I try to do is keep the play fresh by introducing little bits every night that nobody has seen before.

'And the cast just goes with it and enjoys it. We have as much fun on stage as the audience has watching it.'

One of the 'bits' he will introduce is a Mrs Brown song. As she makes her way around the living room, or shuffles down the stairs, she'll often break into a little song. It's often something so unexpected as a line from 'Bohemian Rhapsody', or 'Don't Cha Wish Your Girlfriend Was Hot Like Me?' and neither the cast, nor the audience, know it's coming.

'Marty (now the company production manager, who also plays Mrs Brown's son Trevor) is great for coming up with the song ideas. I'll be standing in the wings and he'll whisper a line in my ear. I'll just go on and do it and it gets a great reaction.'

In 2001, however, the Mrs Brown stage production was still developing. Brendan's son Danny, now 18, became an assistant stage manager, desperate to learn the business. And he was to be followed soon after by his girlfriend, Amanda Woods, who would go on to play Betty in the Mrs Brown stage shows and on television.

Danny and Amanda met in Donegal the night before Brendan and his troupe were due to perform there.

'It was love at first sight. Danny was working as crew and he had gone up the night before me. He rang me the next day asking where I was. I said, "Danny, I'm only in Cavan." Half an hour later, he rang again saying, "Are you here yet?" I said, "I'm only in Monaghan, will you relax?" He was clearly bursting to tell me something. And when I arrived in Letterkenny in Donegal he announced, "I think I've met my Jenny. Her name is Amanda Woods and she's the one for me."

'I think she has been a fantastic influence on my son. But when they started dating, I said to him, "She's a lovely girl, but let me warn you in advance, Donegal girls don't leave Donegal." He said, confidently, "I'll put that right."

'He's now happily living in Donegal.'

Danny and Amanda married in 2006 and have two sons. Amanda boarded Brendan's bus, in the first instance working in merchandising. But Brendan reckoned Amanda fancied acting. So what if she'd never acted before? It had never been a requirement in the past.

'I knew she was terrified of going on stage, so one day I announced she'd be playing the part of Betty. And she was fantastic.'

Meantime, 20-year-old daughter Fiona, who'd studied film production, also joined the team.

'The most important thing is to show your children that you have confidence in them so that they, in turn, have confidence in their own abilities – something which my own mother taught me. She also taught me the value of making other people happy. And she told me that whatever you do in life, you should do it to the best of your ability.'

Danny would later play the role of hapless young criminal Buster Brady, while Fiona would play Agnes's daughter-in-law, Maria, who is married to Dermot.

Dermot would be played by Paddy Houlihan, also a virgin stage actor, but Danny's best friend. Brendan had liked Paddy since he was a little boy and believed he had the comedy bones to make it on stage.

And he wasn't wrong.

The Mrs Brown troupe was now entirely made up of close friends, partners and family. Brendan had created a world within a world in which he'd become the godfather, but without the pinstriped suit and the propensity to have family members whacked.

The mix worked. Audiences could see a troupe on stage having the time of their lives and it all helped create atmosphere. In fact, the success of *Good Mourning Mrs Brown* resulted in talks with a film distribution company about landing *Sparrow's Trap* a cinema release.

'During the whole time when people were owed money, the thing that was forgotten about was the movie. But I always knew it was a damn good movie and believed if I stood by it, everything would work out.'

Brendan again pledged the original investors would get their money back.

'Before I started the *Sparrow's Trap* project, I had a choice of whether to do the film or write the play. And if I had the choice again, I would do things the other way round. It has all worked out in the end. But, to tell you the truth, if you'd asked me then if there was light at the end of the tunnel, I'd have told you that I couldn't even see the tunnel, never mind the light.'

The film never did make it into the cinemas. Brendan did, however, launch a new project. The production company he set up with Jenny (the pair had now moved to a new home in Blanchardstown) began taping the Mrs Brown plays to sell as videos. It proved to be a lucrative sideline.

Most of 2002, meanwhile, was spent touring *Mrs Brown's Last Wedding*.

'I know a bandwagon when I see it,' said Brendan playfully at the end of each performance in the likes of Dublin, Glasgow, Manchester, Birmingham, Newcastle and Liverpool.

He was getting big audiences in all the big cities, apart from London. (London West End theatres demanded six-month runs, and even Brendan's optimism, or patience to cope with being in one town for that length of time, wouldn't run to that.)

'But who would have thought when I left school at just twelve years of age, that today, thirty-seven years later, an audience would be sitting in theatres all across Ireland and the UK waiting to see something I wrote?'

Who indeed? But the theatres were full. And the audiences knew they were guaranteed well over three hours (way beyond the traditional length of a theatre show) of laugh-till-you-cry comedy.

The O'Carroll circus spent months on the road, broken up by the now customary trips to Florida, where Brendan could relax by his swimming pool and write.

And now that he had created two hit comedy plays, it was time to see if he could do it again. Brendan didn't take long to come up with the third play in the trilogy, *Mrs Brown Rides Again*, to tour in the spring of 2003.

The play begins with perhaps the best of the Mrs Brown openers. Agnes is in her kitchen and we hear her dog bark outside in the garden.

'Feck! I've forgotten to feed Spartacus.' And she takes a tin of dog meat from the cupboard, opens the kitchen door and throws it outside. Big laughs emerge from the audience. Then she pauses dramatically and says, 'Feck. I've forgotten the tin opener!' She goes to the kitchen drawer, takes out a tin opener, opens the door and throws it outside. Massive laughs ensue. Why? It's impossible to analyse, but Agnes is a mix of dotty, unpredictable – and slightly scary.

The main plot hinges on Agnes becoming increasingly unhinged. Her kids are planning a surprise party, so they stop speaking when Agnes enters the room. All she overhears them whispering is, 'She's smelly and wees all over the place', and thinks they are planning to put her into a home. But she doesn't know they're talking about the sick Spartacus.

Meanwhile Dino, the boyfriend of gay son Rory, announces he wants them to have a baby together; Cathy brings home her condescending academic boyfriend; and another son, Dermot, cooks up a raffle-ticket scam with his moronic mate Buster.

There are gags galore, involving bikini waxes ('It's only for the craic'), condoms, childbirth and heart attacks.

Agnes, as always, does distressed like no one else.

'In the crazy world of female impersonation comedy, there's cross dressing, very cross dressing and then there's Mrs Brown,' wrote one critic.

And indeed one of the best tributes paid to the Brendan/ Agnes creation was the award for 'Best Actress' at the Liverpool Theatre Awards show. (One presumes the theatre critics in Liverpool were entirely aware that Mrs Brown was in fact a fully functioning male.) Brendan was delighted to receive the award. All in all, he was in a much happier place. His personal life certainly seemed on an even keel.

Doreen spoke to an Irish newspaper about the break-up with Brendan, but it was far from critical. The pair, she said, remained 'good friends', which was what the kids wanted to hear. And Brendan, meanwhile, spoke about the new love in his life, Jenny, in glowing terms. The pair had now bought a home in Holystown, on the edge of a beautiful golf course and close to Finglas.

'The apple never falls far from the tree,' he says, smiling. (Although the apple would spend a fair amount of time planted in Florida.)

But this wasn't Brendan settling down. He still had the need for adventure. He talked about setting up his own airline to operate domestic flights in Ireland. He went as far as developing business plans and looking for funding. It didn't come off, but he held onto the aviation notion for some years to come. And the plans are still in a drawer, given he's had more pressing commitments in recent times, such as world domination.

Brendan was also talking about going into politics again. He said he would put himself forward in the Finglas area for election to the Dáil within five years. Back in 1995, he had contemplated nailing his colours to the Democratic Left ticket. At this point, he was adamant that he would become an independent socialist candidate.

If elected today, the first thing Brendan O'Carroll TD would do would be to 'tackle real drugs issues, real crime issues'.

'The problem is not getting the kids off the drugs, the problem is filling their day. The beauty of being a drug addict is you wake up in the morning and your whole day is filled, snaring the money to get your fix. Every day that you shoot up is an achievement.

'You've achieved. You've got something that you can see and hold in your hand. That is not a dishonourable quest. It's dreadful that it involves drugs, but it's not dishonourable. Every one of us gets up in the morning and hopes that, by the end of the day, we achieve. What we need to do is give them *something* to achieve. There is an army of people out there willing to put this country right. There's nobody who doesn't want to make a contribution, even the guy shooting up.

'I would use my vote to force the government to set up a civil maintenance brigade, numbering fifty thousand people off the unemployment register. Their job would be to keep the country looking good from top to bottom, even down to having stormtroopers. Potholes in Cavan? The stormtroopers are in; bang, bang, bang, potholes filled!'

It's not hard to see why Brendan would win the populist vote.

'All these people want is a week's wages and to achieve every day. That can be provided and I'd love to start such a brigade.'

There haven't been too many entertainers in Ireland and the UK who've revealed not only political ambitions but thought-out plans. But then few entertainers think like Brendan O'Carroll. He is a natural problem solver, whether it's a friend's domestic crises or a Dáil Éireann social policy.

'I will go into politics one day. If they can have a poxy actor as President of America, I don't think it's at all implausible.'

Brendan's ambitions have always been to work to get enough money to not have to work.

'At the stage I go into politics, I will probably not have to work. John F. Kennedy, for example, didn't need the presidency. I spoke to Courtney Kennedy (daughter of Bobby Kennedy) once, and she told me that the Kennedy family, to this day, get a dollar on every bottle of spirits imported into the United States of America. It goes back to something they organised in the 1920s. John F. Kennedy didn't need the bread. He just took a dollar a year for the presidency.

'He wanted to make a contribution, plus he wanted to get his leg over. Several times a day. But he wanted to make a contribution and, fuck me, he did.

'He didn't need the money, so why should we only vote for TDs who need the money in Ireland? In fact, some of the TDs who are in there for the money are dangerous.'

With that sort of rhetoric, why wouldn't the public vote for the man who was already the People's Champion?

Meantime, Brendan had to carry on working. He was feeding the dream. He liked to live well. Extremely well. He wasn't going to buy a coffee in a cheap café when he could afford a cappuccino in Bewley's. With that thought in mind, he bought Danny and Fiona homes next door to his in Florida.

The circus had to keep touring.

BIGGER BROWN

BRENDAN wasn't just generous with his cash, he was generous with his time. Over the periods when we'd meet, he'd reveal almost every detail of his professional and private life. No question went unanswered. But that's not to say the conversations were all based around him. Our meetings came to be called *Tuesdays With Morrie*, in reference to the bestselling book in which a young man spends quality time with his sage and mentor.

Brendan did indeed become a mentor and, on occasion, a counsellor. He talked me through the death of a friend and he spent the longest time offering advice on a play I was writing at the time.

I was struggling to work out what it was really about, this story of a soap actor whose character drives a taxi, but can't come to terms with losing his acting job and is forced to become a taxi driver in real life.

'I know what you've written, Brian. You've come up with *It's A Wonderful Life* in a Glasgow taxi.'

And he was right. And from that moment, the play picked up speed, eventually appearing at the same theatre as the

Mrs Brown plays (thankfully with enough months separating them and not affecting *Hacked Off*'s box office).

We became closer. He came to my house. He got to know all the family, my sisters, and my mother and Auntie Ethel (who'd read all the Mrs Brown books before she'd heard of the stage play), and all thought the Irishman a comedy magician.

We talked of everything from VAT bills to baldness.

'I remember going to the barbers at fifteen, and him saying, "You're not going to have this too long, Brendan." But it's never bothered me. I've been offered a hair transplant but I'm used to being bald.

'And can you imagine me with hair? I'd look like Bobby Ball.'

We talked about a publication date for this book. But he pushed the subject aside.

'Let's wait until I'm famous.'

'But you are famous, Brendan. In Ireland certainly, and in half a dozen major cities in the UK. And in North America.'

We talked about his mammy, of course. Maureen O'Carroll was rarely far away from his thoughts.

'This will sound completely mad. I loved my mother dearly – but the best thing she could have done for me was die.'

'Why, Brendan? That's an astonishing thing to say . . .'

'I'll tell you why. I could never express myself as an individual because I was always worried about whether she would approve.

'I have taken some incredible risks in my career, like becoming a stand-up comedian when my pub business went bust, but if my mother had been alive she would never have let the business go under – and I would never have become a comedian.

'I have learned and lived more since my mother died because I have had failures – lots of them. But despite that I loved her so much and it makes me really sad that she can't be here to see all of this.'

His eyes filled up at the thought. 'I suppose she's up there somewhere looking down on me.

'But I will always regret the fact that she has never seen me performing on stage or read one of my books.'

It was perhaps not surprising that Brendan would tell me constantly to enjoy every single moment I could with my mother, wishing he'd had a little more time with his own. And even when he was out of town, he'd text. We'd speak on the phone. Sometimes when we'd arrange to meet either in Manchester or Glasgow, he'd be later than a broken alarm clock. But he'd always smile and apologise, and it was hard not to forgive a man who was always travelling at the speed of a runaway train, either writing, or setting up the next deal, whether it was to buy an airline or a flat in Shanghai.

And the gang, the troupe, would always be around. And the hugs would be so constant that sometimes it was almost possible to forget you were Scottish. Then he would be off again on tour. And it was great to see the success story continue.

Brendan's *Mrs Brown Rides Again* went down a storm at the Olympia in Dublin in January 2003, playing an incredible 31 shows. The accolades came thick and fast with the *Irish People,* for example, describing the Agnes Brown creator as 'Ireland's most successful comic writer'.

The O'Carroll roadshow then took off to New York in time for the St Patrick's Day celebrations as part of an 11-city, 70-bookstore tour of America to promote his books, in particular *The Young Wan.*

His right hand was aching from the constant signing of autographs, and no doubt his face muscles had been stretched into a smile too many times to count, but Brendan was feeling exhausted, sitting in the dining room of the Fitzpatrick Manhattan Hotel, for a different reason.

'I had sidestepped the hotel's raucous party the night before, but stayed up late. I stayed up watching the news on Iraq, watching war begin. And I was worried. I thought, "Bush has no foreign policy knowledge."'

Brendan agreed to a series of interviews on his trip. During one chat in New York with the *Irish Voice*, Brendan revealed the generous side of his nature when the interviewer referred to him as 'Mr Brown' and he offered no correction. He doesn't often suffer fools gladly.

But he certainly didn't hold back from putting fellow Irish writer Bill Cullen in his place during the same chat. Bill is a businessman and author of *It's A Long Way From Penny Apples*, his own story of growing up poor in North Dublin, and working in the markets of Moore Street. Bill Cullen butted in as Brendan was just about to talk about *The Young Wan* and how the prequel to *The Mammy* emerged.

'Five thousand copies of my book sold out last night on the QVC shopping channel in two minutes,' boasted Cullen to Brendan. And he added, 'That's a hundred thousand dollars in two minutes.'

'Really? I have five books of my own,' countered Brendan. 'And can't you see I am being interviewed?'

Brendan says he enjoyed Cullen's opus. But he couldn't imagine Agnes Brown having anything to do with that ever-so-serious Dublin world.

'She would have had feck-all to do with all those negative Nellies in his book. They would have been too heavy for her.

'I knew a few Nellies in my day. But they're not for me

either. That's why I select memories. My memories are all very happy. The other ones I can't remember.'

The book tour had gone well, although it was not without incident. Brendan wasn't even wearing his Agnes skirt and cardie when he was propositioned by a man.

'I was having a drink before a reading in Sonoma, California, and this old guy comes up to me.' Brendan takes on a hillbilly accent. '"You got nice teeth, boy, like a woman."'

The terrified comedian and staunchly heterosexual father-of-three ran away from his potential suitor.

'It was like a scene from *Deliverance*,' he says, of the Burt Reynolds hillbilly horror movie. 'All that was missing was the banjo.'

Brendan knew these book promotions were important, not just to the publisher who'd given him such a nice advance, but to his production company.

'By this time I was supporting forty people – everyone: the cast, the crew, the production team back in the office.'

He was determined none of his 'family' would struggle as he had as a youngster.

'We did okay back then. We thought we were rich. We just didn't have any money.'

But then again, he wasn't slow in inviting as many people along on the circus ride as he could afford. Or even, at times, not afford. Fiona, Danny and Eric, now ten, were all part of the travelling O'Carroll book tour.

'My publisher Viking wanted to know why I needed eleven hotel rooms in New York. I said they were for my family and friends.'

Back in the UK, it was time to tour again with *Mrs Brown Rides Again*. Again, the audiences were more than prepared to saddle up.

'She remains a classic comic invention,' said the *Liverpool Post*. 'A sixtyish woman with a well-rounded figure, she strides through her family home like a tiger, sometimes protecting her young from would-be suitors, sometimes attacking them.'

Brendan took the moment to appreciate how far he'd come, from rags to riches in the form of the movie deals, to losing the lot, and now to building a Mrs Brown empire.

'You know, I'd love to be able to say that I had a grand plan, but it's not true. There have been things that have happened to me and I've thought it was the end of the world, but then I've discovered it was meant to be. Everything happens for a reason. I guess my writing comes from these sorts of experiences.'

Brendan had developed his own philosophy on life, part Buddhist, part Zen. He had come to believe life was pretty much mapped out, but if you get a signpost you should follow it. And if you have a negative experience, try your hardest to see the positive in it.

If he has some regrets, it was having spent so many years trying to be a great waiter or a great cleaner. What he should have done is follow in the footsteps of Brendan Grace and try sooner to become a great comedian. That's why he encourages his kids and friends to follow the path they feel they are pulled to. Therein, happiness lies.

In 2004, he loved the experience of working on the Channel 4 comedy *Max and Paddy's Road To Nowhere*, starring Peter Kay and Paddy McGuinness. Brendan played Gipsy Joe, an Irish crook who sells Max and Paddy a dodgy TV set.

Brendan and Peter Kay in particular would go on to become good friends.

Yet, while Brendan was now moving in established comedy circles (TV writer Caroline Aherne became a big fan, and she'd later write comedy drama *The Security Men* for her Irish pal, in which he'd star alongside Bobby Ball and Paddy McGuinness), he still had pitfalls to face.

Yes, he could do no wrong in places such as Glasgow, Birmingham and Liverpool, reprising *Good Mourning* to loud acclaim. But in Manchester, the response was now more muted.

And reviews from the likes of the *Manchester Evening News* weren't entirely favourable.

'Smash hits they might well be, but there is little attempt to disguise the fact that his trilogy of Agnes Brown plays are merely a platform to transport Brendan O'Carroll's anarchic surreal sense of humour. Whenever he leaves the stage, the whole shebang falls a little flat.'

It's hard to argue the plays aren't a platform for Brendan's sense of humour; he writes them. He created a window into a world of farce and fun. But implied in the critique was a danger Mrs Brown fans would become a little bored looking at the same scenery.

In 2005, it was back to the beginning of the trilogy with *Last Wedding* doing the rounds. But in August that year, Brendan's thoughts were on a real wedding. His. He and Jenny married in Florida, with a huge cast of family and friends in attendance, including BoyZone star Keith Duffy.

'It was a magical day. I couldn't have been happier. I knew Jenny was the woman I wanted to be with for the rest of my life.'

Brendan also decided to take a break from wearing the wig and women's tights. He went back to the relative simplicity of stand-up, touring his show *How's Your Wibbly Wobbly Wonder?*

'Being a stand-up is like playing poker, you look the audience in the eye and ask them to suspend disbelief because you're about to tell them stories that are not true. It's like "two elephants walking down a street". Two elephants don't walk down a street, they don't talk to each other, and one of them does not wear sunglasses. But, unless I get them to picture that, and for that moment believe it, the joke is not going to work.'

That's not to say Agnes didn't make an appearance, vocally at least, and the show sent audiences home happy. Interestingly, Brendan's material had altered immeasurably from the stints in the early Nineties. This was a much more family-friendly Dubliner in evidence. Albeit, with more than a few fecks thrown in.

In the summer of 2006, Brendan was back in Florida but this time he had invited a couple of guests along: myself and my partner, Fiona. It was a chance to spend time with Brendan away from the pressures of performing, relaxing with his family. That's not to say he ever relaxed totally at his gorgeous villa in Kissimmee. During the stint, he was working on a deal for a syndicated cartoon series of *Mrs Brown's Boys*, which he eventually concluded. And he did come up with ideas.

What was particularly fascinating to watch was his closeness with Jenny, with his grandchildren, and how he simply loved having his family around.

'They mean everything to me. All this, it's for them. I work thirty weeks a year and the rest of the time I'm here. I'm not going to give up on the time I have with the kids.'

What did the week reveal to the biographer? Many things. What he once said about loving cleaning products since his time as a cleaner in Jeyes in Finglas is true. Walk down the domestic product supermarket aisle with him and the blue eyes light up.

In a more serious moment, however, Brendan revealed how Agnes Brown was both a blessing and weight on his shoulders.

'I don't want to be playing her forever. I'm fifty-one years of age and I don't want to be putting on the false tits for too much longer. What I want to be able to do is make enough money to be able to retire and do something else. Politics. TV. Whatever.'

Brendan certainly wasn't in that sort of financial league. But he believed the dream could still happen.

Meanwhile, the holiday over, it was back to being Agnes Brown, performing all three plays consecutively across the UK with three weeks of Mrs Brown festivals. The strategy certainly didn't do the O'Carroll bank balance any harm. But he knew he'd have to come up with a new show, such was the demand for a fresher Brown family. And so the 'fourth in the trilogy' emerged, *For the Love of Mrs Brown*. It was a play that took Agnes in a whole new direction. In fact, right out of the window.

The central storyline involves Agnes realising (to paraphrase Benny Hill's comedy milkman Ernie) 'a woman's needs are many-fold'. After friend Winnie McGooghan reveals she once had 'an organism', Agnes too reckons it's time to have some fun in life.

Meantime, Rory leaves behind some recreational pharmaceuticals in Agnes's kitchen, which she takes, thinking they're for heartburn. The result is Mrs Brown on LSD. In one of the best sight gags ever to have played out in a theatre, a drug-fuelled Agnes appears in a Wonder Woman costume and proceeds to fly right through the back-door window.

It's a scene that brings the roof off every theatre it plays in.

Brendan had come back with a bang. Subplots? Yes, lots as usual, such as Cathy announcing to her mammy she wants a boob job. A puzzled Agnes replies, 'But Cathy, you've got a job!'

And sex, the main subject matter of *For the Love of*, was right up Brendan's personal back alley. It took him back to his *Outrageous Comedy* times, and he couldn't wait to write up naughty gags.

Such as? It's coming up to Valentine's Day, and Agnes is thinking about looking for a man on the Internet. Cathy informs her mammy that, 'If you are going on a first date nowadays, a man will expect you to perform fellatio.'

Agnes looks shocked and says, 'Me? Sing opera? He'd have a better chance of getting a blow job.'

The show opened in Glasgow in February 2007 to rapturous reaction.

'I was shitting myself before the opening. You write something you think is funny. But you never know until you start to perform and hear the audience reaction. But it's been wonderful. Even better than I'd hoped.'

The following year, Brendan and the troupe toured Britain, Ireland and Canada with *For the Love of Mrs Brown*. Critics enjoyed it, and they acknowledged that Agnes Brown fans loved it. But the critical voice in the likes of the *Liverpool Post* was noticeably a little stronger.

'Admittedly, this series was never intended to be Ibsen, but you still feel that it would make a better sitcom than it does a piece of theatre. The signs are all there: the atrocious theme music, the stereotypes on show, the slapstick comedy and the quick-fire jokes. But the play is overlong and the concept is as stretched as Agnes's tights. If you are new to the franchise, the show is well worth seeing. But if you have been before, you might feel a sense of déjà vu throughout.'

Were Agnes's tights becoming a little saggy at the knees? Was the Mrs Brown show starting to wear a little thin? Surely not? Agnes on drugs is hardly a dull concept.

Was the journalist right, however, about the TV notion? Could Mrs Brown work in a TV sitcom format? It had been a radio sitcom back in 1992, but Brendan's stage show had been running in theatres for over eight years. He had also been filming, making Agnes Brown DVDs for three years and selling them in vast numbers. If it had the potential to be a TV show, wouldn't someone in the business have recognised it by now?

'Not a chance. It was right under their noses and nobody saw the opportunity.'

Would the seemingly myopic TV producers ever see the potential in putting Agnes and co. on the telly?

THE DYING COW

BRENDAN knew that his comedy act was like a shark; it had to keep moving or it would die. The show was still well received, but audiences had dwindled down to the die-hard core.

He couldn't take it to London because the the play couldn't sustain a six-month run. It was too risky. And Brendan would have been bored out of his head being in one place for that length of time. (The show hadn't sold well at the likes of Hammersmith.) And while it had played well in Canada, the size of the O'Carroll circus meant the box office had to be incredibly good in order to make any return.

In the spring of 2008, Brendan tried to expand the fan base, playing venues such as Edinburgh Playhouse, with its 3,000-seat capacity.

'We thought we could make it work in Edinburgh, playing one of the biggest theatres in Europe. But it was a tough sell.'

Edinburgh didn't have the same earthy, working-class audience as the likes of Glasgow, Manchester, Birmingham, Newcastle and Liverpool. Some cities simply didn't see Agnes as one of their own.

'Dublin women tend to marry young. They get married at

nineteen and become forty immediately, have kids and raise a family. Then, when they are forty, and the kids are doing their own thing, the mothers become sixteen. You get these women of forty, fifty and sixty talking like teenagers and, coupled with colloquial language, you are going to get something quite extraordinary – like Agnes Brown.'

The inability to spread the gospel according to Agnes, especially in the south of England and Wales, was worrying. So many prejudged the show (as I had), and decided the adventures of a big-mouthed matriarch in small heels weren't for them. Brendan knew there was only a finite number of times his character could keep flapping her tea towel in Rory's face, and making imaginary cups of tea.

What seemed a tragedy, though, was this was held to be one of the funniest comedy shows ever to grace the stage. What needed to happen was that someone important had to see the show; someone who had the ears of the powers-that-be and could take it on to the next level.

Brendan had always argued the need to remain positive. His mantra was, 'The world turns every twenty-four hours, so relax and let it happen. And if there's a problem you have to find a solution. But if you try, the solution will find you.' Yet, what he needed wasn't a solution, it was a miracle.

In October 2008, I took a close pal along to see the reprise of *For the Love of Mrs Brown* at the Pavilion Theatre in Glasgow. But he wasn't just any pal. Ian Pattison is the writer and creator of BBC sitcom *Rab C. Nesbitt* and several other shows. Ian had never seen a Mrs Brown show, but he'd listened hard when I told him how good they were.

But Ian likes clever, sophisticated comedy. He's a huge Woody Allen fan who loves plays by Oscar Wilde, Joe Orton and Alan Bennett. Would Agnes come anywhere close?

Would he like Mrs Brown? No, he didn't like the show. He loved it. More to the point, he loved it so much he was prepared to shout it from the rooftops. Or at least down a phone line to London.

In recent times, Ian had worked with the BBC's London-based producer Stephen McCrum on a sitcom, *The Crouches*. He called the producer that night and said he'd seen the future of British sitcom.

Ian suggested strongly that his chum should fly to Glasgow and find out why the city's collective cheeks were wet from tears of laughter.

Stephen McCrum reacted without hesitation and booked a flight for the next day. On hearing this, I called Brendan and asked if he'd have any problem if I brought in a 'special' guest to see the show.

'Great,' he said. 'Can't do any harm.'

It didn't. Stephen McCrum sat in the stalls and was taken aback by what he saw.

'The audience, to a man and woman, were laughing fit to burst, alongside ushers who were about sixteen or seventeen and also pissing themselves,' he said later.

More importantly, he believed it could transfer to television.

After the show, we took the TV producer to the Number One dressing room to meet the star, just as he was removing make-up and padded breasts.

'I'm Stephen McCrum from the BBC, Brendan. Great to meet you.'

'And you too, Stephen. Howareye?'

'Great. Would you like to make a sitcom for the BBC?'

'I would, Stephen!'

Of course, TV sitcoms aren't commissioned straight off.

A pilot episode has to be written and then given the green light. (TV produces more pilots than British Airways, but most don't make the airwaves.)

And Brendan had a massive problem to overcome: how can you reduce three hours and fifteen minutes of stage madness into 30 minutes of small-screen hilarity?

Brendan gave Stephen McCrum some problems of his own. The comedian insisted on using his regular cast, his family and friends. (He would later bring in his best man Mike Nolan to appear as the manager of Foley's Bar. Fiona Gibney, Jenny's sister, would join the circus as Winnie's daughter Sharon; Emily Regan, now Paddy Houlihan's wife, graduated from wardrobe to playing Barbara, and Jamie O'Carroll, Danny's son, would play Bono, Agnes's grandson.)

While the BBC hierarchy commended Brendan's loyalty, they wanted him to work alongside tried-and-tested television performers. Both sides argued the case. The BBC pushed, saying the series could only go ahead if he agreed to the new people. Brendan stood his ground with a determination his mammy would have loved. And the Beeb backed down.

Then Brendan insisted the pilot, featuring an Irish cast (except for Gary Hollywood), be filmed in Glasgow. Why? He believed the city's Pavilion Theatre had saved him, and it had been the venue where his theatre show was discovered for television. It had a magical connection for him. The BBC agreed.

But he still had to write the script. Weeks turned into months and he couldn't manage to get it right. He enlisted the help of Ian Pattison along the way – after all, Brendan had never written a sitcom before (the five-minute radio slots weren't in the same league), but the efforts didn't produce the necessary result.

While Stephen McCrum tried to keep the BBC bosses onside, Brendan took off to Florida to write, to try to find a format that worked. But it didn't look hopeful.

'It's really hard,' he said on the phone. 'I want to try and capture the atmosphere we have in the theatre, but I just don't know how.'

He wrote idea after idea – and then dumped them in the bin. Thoughts flew out of his head faster than the pigeons from the pop crate he'd kept as a boy.

Brendan wanted to somehow capture the spontaneity, the energy that made Mrs Brown work in theatre. But how?

Then he had his eureka moment.

He couldn't contain his excitement during a phone call.

'I've got it. I *know* how to make this sitcom, Brian. I'm going to film as if it were a live theatre play. That way, the audience at home will get the atmosphere of the gigs.

'We're not going to try and convince them they're in someone's living room, we're going to let them in on the joke, let them see that we're filming a show. We're going to film it live and we're going to let them see the mistakes, the cameras, the lot. It will be brilliant.'

'It will be a major disaster, Brendan. TV shows don't reveal all. Some TV shows such as *Shameless* have the central character speaking directly to camera, but never to remind the audience they are watching a piece of fiction. Stephen McCrum will have kittens when you tell him that.' But that's not what was actually said to Brendan. Only thought. What was said to Brendan was: 'Gosh, I don't know. You may be right . . .'

In the Mrs Brown stage shows, Brendan regularly breaks the fourth wall. When Dino, for example, utters a line, 'Mrs

Brown, you can't say that!' Brendan will quip, 'I feckin' can. It's in the script.'

Would that work on television? Would he be able to convince Stephen McCrum and script editor Paul Mayhew-Archer that this stage trick should appear in the pilot? Stephen McCrum compared Brendan to sitcom legend Leonard Rossiter, crediting him with 'incredible comedic intelligence'. But even he was nervous about Brendan's idea to let the audience in on the act.

The BBC bosses had another concern. Would British and Irish viewers accept the locker-room language?

Brendan dug his heels in. 'I said, "If Agnes Brown says twenty pounds or twenty fecking pounds, does it matter? There are much worse words than feck. Rape or murder are worse." I argued that it's colour. To take the feck out would be like taking every second word out of a Wordsworth poem. It wouldn't work. And here's the thing: she's the only person in the show who swears. Agnes Brown wouldn't allow anyone else to swear.'

With the pilot script completed, the producer fought hard to get clearance for a show that used the F-word (albeit the Irish version, 'feck') 34 times in this first 30-minute episode.

But, on top of all that, the TV politics of the time militated against success. In late 2008, the BBC had been caught up in the debacle surrounding presenters Jonathan Ross and Russell Brand, in which the pair had left rude messages on actor Andrew Sachs's answering machine.

Brendan believed this would seriously prejudice his own chances.

'I thought the whole sitcom idea was a bit pie-in-the-sky, to be quite honest. Especially since there had been false dawns in the past.

'Then when Jonathan Ross and Russell Brand got into trouble over Sachs-gate, I thought, "Well that's it, there'll be no series for us." I thought the BBC would look at the script and all they would see was swearing and nothing else.'

Thankfully, Stephen McCrum convinced the BBC that Brendan should have his shot at glory. The pilot would be filmed in Glasgow in October. But even Brendan's natural PMA was seriously contained at this point. And he was simply being realistic. Most TV ideas fail. That's the truth of it.

He had to hope that the stage-show audiences would pick up.

In April 2009, the clan were safely home in Dublin's Olympia Theatre, performing *For the Love of*. Again the audience clapped till their hands were sore, with critics comparing the on-stage madness to a mix of *Monty Python* and the *Carry On* movies, and Brendan hailed as a 'gifted comic'.

But, gifted or not, the writer knew he couldn't keep the bank manager happy with the returns from the likes of Dublin and Glasgow.

In the summer months, Brendan returned to stand-up, with the *How's Your Wobbly Bits?* tour. He wanted to feel what it was like to be on stage on his own again, to recharge the batteries. But, most importantly, it was a far cheaper show to take on the road than Mrs Brown.

Yet, at least he had another new Agnes Brown adventure to offer the world. While trying to develop his sitcom pilot in Florida, Brendan had also, rather remarkably, come up with the fifth play in the 'trilogy', *How Now Mrs Brown Cow*.

The backbone of the story sees Agnes expecting her priest son Trevor to come home from Boston for Christmas. Cathy's been in touch with her brother and knows he just can't make it, but no one wants to pass the bad news on to the mammy.

Meantime, Agnes is getting mysterious phone calls from a firm of solicitors who specialise in adoptions, and her brood are wondering which one of them is adopted.

But the third plot strand offered up the best comedy potential. Agnes is convinced she'll land the role of the Virgin Mary in the church Nativity Show, and shows the family how she'll perform the role. Brendan's scene of Mrs Brown on a pretend donkey ride searching for an inn for the baby Jesus is nothing less than hilarious. As always, the sight gags are a guarantee of laughter, with Dermot working as a penguin and Grandad being bashed on the head repeatedly with a tin tray to the loud backdrop of the theme from TV classic *Rawhide*.

The ending is entirely predictable – Trevor makes it home and the family sing in harmony next to the Christmas tree. But that doesn't mean it's any less effective. Steven Spielberg, eat your heart out.

Brendan opened the show in Glasgow in October, and filmed his pilot the following week.

'Peter Kay came up to the filming and said he thought it was amazing, a seminal moment in television. But I wasn't sure. What I knew was I'd done my very best. My feeling was, "If it works, fabulous. If not? It just wasn't to be."'

Brendan's voice was, unusually, downbeat. He said the audience had enjoyed the show, but then Glasgow audiences adored Agnes. What would decide her fate would be BBC bosses back in London.

Would the concept, the swearing, the crudeness, the fourth-wall-breaking idea work? Would Scotland be the place from which massive fame would appear?

Meantime, the Mrs Brown circus took off again. But the tour bookings weren't looking good at all. Brendan and Jenny had to work harder and harder to get bums on seats. Some dates' box offices were almost as small as Buster Brady's IQ.

Each gig demanded more publicity, but that in turn was difficult because journalists were running out of ways to describe the stage show: *The madcap Mammy and her dysfunctional family*; *an urban terrorist in big knickers*.

Audiences who'd gone to see a Mrs Brown show three or four times a year were cutting back, clearly feeling the pinch.

Brendan and Jenny had serious talks. They had brought in several millions in ticket prices since they'd formed their company nine years ago, but their outgoings were horrendous – and rising – while ticket sales were ever-decreasing. Brendan didn't pay Equity minimum, he paid top dollar, and he had more than 20 cast and crew working on the show.

For a year or so, he'd had to cut back on costs, paying the actors for their working stints as opposed to guaranteeing their wages all year round. But this couldn't continue. The bank account revealed the bottom line: Brendan and Jenny were skint.

The train Brendan and his company had ridden for so long was slowing down. Added to which, he and Jenny couldn't count on the sitcom amounting to anything; the odds were stacked high against them. And by the time the troupe arrived in Hull, at the New Theatre, in November 2009, it was about to go off the rails.

The show went well enough; the cast enjoyed themselves on stage, but they were more subdued than they would normally have been. They sensed the reality. They sensed that the fat lady had sung for the very last time.

At the end of the show, Brendan confirmed the cast's worst fears. It was over. He and Jenny couldn't afford to keep the show on the road.

His family, his friends, who were – to all intents and purposes – as close to him as family; the people he'd brought together to form this amazingly successful band of brothers and sisters, had to be disbanded. They'd have to find new jobs. They'd have to go it alone. For most, the prospect was terrifying.

The tears flowed. The sadness was palpable. The dream was over. This was certainly not an ending Spielberg would have written for *Mrs Brown's Boys*. And they all went back to their hotel disconsolate. And for the next two weeks they grieved, and wondered what to do with their lives.

But then the Hollywood moment did come about. Brendan called one afternoon to announce the news.

'Brian, we've got the green light for the sitcom series! We've done it! It's actually going to happen. I told you I'd be famous.

'And I told Jenny something really good would come out of meeting you. And it has. You're not a friend. You're family. And we love you.'

The fortune teller had called it right. Brendan was set to be a star.

AGNES BROWN'S WORLD

WHEN Brendan was a little boy growing up in Finglas, watching television was a delight – but also the cause of constant frustration. No sooner had he settled down to watch *Coronation Street*, which he still loves, or American imports such as *I Love Lucy* or *The Fugitive*, than the coin meter on the back of the television would run out.

Maureen O'Carroll was all too often so strapped for the two-shilling piece required to bounce Lucille Ball's face back onto the screen. She'd hunt around the house, looking for a button that would fit the slot, and pay the price later when the electricity man came to collect.

In the New Year of 2010, Brendan allowed himself a smile when he thought back to those times. Not only could he afford to power as many TVs as he chose, he was set to become not just a TV star, but a co-producer of his own series, in partnership with BBC1 in the UK and RTÉ One in Ireland.

This meant he would be paid a dividend on every show sold abroad and every DVD released. And he was set to earn serious money. All the Can-Do Kid had to do was deliver six cleverly crafted episodes.

That in itself wasn't a major task, now that he'd cracked the magic formula. After all, he had 18 years of Agnes, from the radio scripts to the stage shows, to 'borrow' from.

'I have absolutely no problem recycling old gags. The old is new if it hasn't been seen for a long time. And, you know, every time we have a new child, we tell them the same fairy tales we were told when we were kids. And they still sound great.'

What a great argument for reworking theatre plots as TV scripts. But would it attract a modern audience? And while Mrs Brown was a working-class favourite, would he widen the demographic and appeal to polite society? Would suburban England, for example, accept his feckin' language?

The series wouldn't be filmed until the end of the year.

Meantime, *Mrs Brown's Boys* continued to tour. The show that had died in Hull had been brought right back to life, thanks to the defibrillator that was television. And a special highlight of the summer tour was a return to Toronto, and a chance for Brendan and co. to meet up with his sister, Fiona.

The cast and crew were living in hotels in the city and Fiona invited them, en masse, to her home out in Buckhorn for a barbecue.

The team travelled by bus, but Brendan, who's not a country boy at all, drove. After two hours, he arrived in the nearest large town, Peterborough, and figured the journey had been pleasant enough. But then he had to make his way through dirt roads, over rivers and hills for another hour, all the time surrounded by dense forests. When he arrived at Fiona's house, it seemed like the middle of nowhere.

He pulled into the driveway, got out of the car and hugged his sister with a pitying smile. 'Fiona, why didn't you tell me you were in the Witness Protection Programme?'

During the Toronto stint, Brendan revealed his steely side. The godfather loved his extended family, but he wouldn't see them step out of line. And it was obvious some of the cast were not up to speed with their lines. Brendan read them the riot act.

'We're in Canada to work. This is not a vacation! So tomorrow when you show up, you'd better know your lines. And think on this: where else would you make so much money for working three hours a night?'

Brendan's hairdryer treatment worked. But, back across the pond, would his sitcom create as much heat? The series was filmed in Glasgow at the end of the year, and audiences queued up for tickets. He was playing to the converted, of course. What really mattered would be the viewing figures on transmission. Thankfully, when the first show was broadcast on 21 February 2011, the audience reaction was positive, with almost three million tuning in; a good figure for a post-watershed slot. Some newspaper writers loved it, such as *The Times* and *The Guardian*, describing it as 'postmodern' and 'hilarious'.

However, there were critics who would cheerfully have drowned Agnes Brown in a bath of Foley's cider.

'The whole thing is entirely predicated on viewers finding a man dressed as a foul-mouthed elderly woman intrinsically funny,' noted the TV reviewer with the *Irish Times*. 'If you do, you're away in a hack, and the viewing figures are astronomical, but if you don't, and you think that died out with Les Dawson and Dick Emery, then it's a long half-hour.'

The *Irish Independent*'s comment not only gave Agnes and her entourage a kicking, the writer then stepped on her glasses and smashed them.

'*Mrs Brown's Boys* is the type of TV programme that makes you vaguely embarrassed to be Irish.'

It wasn't just the Irish reviewers who didn't like the show. Nor was it the broadsheets. Some of the tabloids such as Scotland's *Daily Record* described the show as 'dire'. Did Brendan care?

'I don't give a toss about the critics. We do it for the audience. I don't want to write something that somebody in such-and-such newspaper would like. I can only write what makes me laugh, and as a writer you hope the audience will agree.'

The audience did agree. The numbers swelled and the first 2011 Christmas Special achieved 6.61 million viewers. The Christmas Eve and Boxing Day shows were the most watched programmes on TV, achieving a total of 15 million views per episode, including repeats.

The bandwagon rolled on. *Mrs Brown's Boys* had been nominated for a BAFTA award in 2011, stunning (almost) the critics into silence, and in 2012 the show was nominated again. Would it win this time around?

Jenny reckoned it would, and cleared a space on the windowsill. Brendan wasn't happy, though. He was afraid she would jinx the big night. But he didn't have to worry. *Mrs Brown's Boys* won the BAFTA, the most prestigious prize in British television, for Best Situation Comedy.

Brendan and the team celebrated like there was no tomorrow.

'It's mad.'

The award gave the show a new impetus. Foreign sales grew, with the show expanding worldwide to Australia, New Zealand, Iceland, South Africa, Turkey, Slovakia and Romania. It wasn't hard to see why. As Brendan says, 'Mrs Brown is everybody's mammy. She's the Jewish mama, she's the black mammy. She's a universal creature. Most societies have such a creature, this woman who would lay down in front of a train for her kids.

'I had the idea at one point of taking Mrs Brown to Broadway, with an Italian, Jewish or black actress playing Agnes. It may still happen.'

What had also happened by this time was that the Mrs Brown stage shows had become a huge box-office success. The troupe were no longer playing to a couple of hundred people in Hull, they were now playing in arenas up and down the country, to five and six thousand fans at the likes of the Manchester and Nottingham arenas. And the audiences knew exactly what to expect.

'The last thing I wanted to do was a sanitised version of Mrs Brown on TV and have a nice audience coming to the theatre and saying, "Holy Shit, what is this?" But thankfully, the BBC supported us all the way.'

The halls are so big, giant screens have to be installed.

Yet, it's not all about the money. Brendan was offered a $40 million deal with American broadcasters HBO, makers of the likes of *The Sopranos*, which he turned down.

'It meant going to sit in an office for two years writing sitcoms and never seeing my family. And how much money do you need?

'We don't take anything for granted, though. None of us. Bugsy was a window-cleaner, Pepsi was a mechanic, Rory worked in EMI, Jenny worked in the bank, Eilish worked for Guinness and I was a waiter.

'You're always terrified that one day they will find out you are a waiter and want their money back.

'But here's the thing. And this is the most important thing. I work when I want, I can take off to Florida and be with my wife, my kids and my grandchildren. What money can do for you is buy you time, and that's the time off to spend with people you want to spend it with. And when I do work, I'm with the people I love. In that respect we're all really lucky. We're like the feckin' Partridge Family.'

Playing sell-out shows to giant crowds every night has certainly made pulling on the Agnes wig and cheap skirt far less of a task.

'When that first laugh comes from those five thousand people, it's actually so loud it moves your clothes. You can actually feel your clothes vibrating. I just love being on stage. I love the power it gives you. I love to see the faces of the women in the front row. I love to be able to talk to the audiences at the end of the night, to read their requests, because that extends the connection I have with them. And while performers often don't want to meet the fans, I'll stand outside and sign autographs until my wrist aches. I know how much they love to meet the performers. And I get as much of a buzz from meeting them, hearing them say how much they've loved the show, as they get from me. Being up there on that stage and watching an audience laugh is one of the greatest feelings in the world.'

Does it beat sex?

'No, although at the end of the show I do get a round of applause.'

Yet, despite the astonishing global success of the show, Brendan, in a quiet moment of detachment, now admits that sometimes the critics can get to him.

'I can learn from some of them but, truthfully, they also hurt. God, they are just like somebody taking a hot rod and sticking it in the middle of your back. It's a terrible, horrible feeling.

'Anyone would tell you, it doesn't matter how big the ratings are, it doesn't matter if you get two hundred magnificent critiques. When you get one bad one, that's the one that puts a knot in your stomach – and just twists it. It's the one bad one that always sticks in your mind.

'I haven't read them in ages but that doesn't make a difference, because there is always someone willing to tell you about it.

'Yet, at the end of the day, I don't do this for them. They're the only ones who don't pay for a ticket. They get in for free.'

And, as always, he makes sure he gives value for money, especially now that show prices have been hiked for the big venues.

'I know for those buying tickets, it's not just about spending twenty-five euros or whatever. It's about getting your suit dry-cleaned, your hair done, the babysitter in, a few drinks beforehand. And I don't want my bit to be the bit that lets that night down.'

Television had fuelled the live shows' success, which in turn shot the TV audiences to the eight million-plus mark. And, in January 2013, now on the third series of the show, *Mrs Brown's Boys* won the National Television Award for Best Situation Comedy.

Accepting his award, Brendan thanked fans of the show and his cast. And in a nod to the fact he was employing almost everyone he knew, added a dedication to Maureen O'Carroll.

'The only person that's not in the show is my mother. And that's because she is dead.'

The success story hasn't stopped. Brendan signed a deal to syndicate the *Mrs Brown's Boys* cartoon series around the world, and was also offered the chance to write the Mrs

Brown movie he'd always wanted, with a £3.6 million budget, backed by the BBC and Universal Pictures. The working title is *Mrs Brown's Boys – D'fillum*.

'I've got a great idea for it,' he said, speaking from Florida. 'I've got no time to write it, but I'll get it done.'

He'll write it himself this time. He'll star in it, alongside the usual cast and perhaps a few famous names.

'I'd like to have U2 make an appearance as the wedding band.'

The fillum won't be a remake of Anjelica Huston's *Agnes Browne*. It will be an out-and-out comedy, along the lines of the classic sitcom movies such as *On The Buses* and *Up Pompeii*. Will it work? The storyline will see Agnes Brown battle against developers, politicians and bankers who team up to close a Dublin fruit market. Agnes enlists the help of Cathy's new boyfriend, who's a solicitor (Brendan hopes *Downton Abbey* star Hugh Bonneville will play the role), and rolls up her cardie sleeves in preparation for war.

Brendan's idea is solid. And he didn't have to look too far for inspiration. His mother Maureen O'Carroll once fought against injustice on a national scale. And if she were alive today, Brendan believes it's the sort of cause his mother would be fighting.

He will also bring back *Mrs Brown's Boys* for a 2013 TV Christmas special. But can he cope with the pressure of writing while continuing to perform?

'I have convinced myself that I always write better when I am under pressure, which is just a cover-up for leaving everything to the last minute. I have always written alone but I have no discipline whatsoever. Jenny is the one that drives me. As well as being an exceptional muse, without her I would sit and read all day.'

So he says, but it seems unlikely, given his fear of becoming lazy, and the fact he hasn't stopped racing forward from the moment he could crawl. And he loves to create stories.

'Sometimes it comes really easily, just flows. But then there are those horrible, horrible times when it is just word-by-word, and you wonder why you ever told anybody you were a writer, because you just write shite.'

The 'shite' is set to make Brendan O'Carroll more than £50 million over the next five years. In 2014, he'll tour Australia and Canada with the show. When the tickets were announced in Australia, where the TV series is a smash hit, eight millon dollars' worth were sold in 24 hours, before the hotlines overloaded. And that was just for two of the venues of a nine-city tour.

To add to the growing O'Carroll legend, the US Comedy Channel have bought the rights to screen his sitcom. And several European broadcasters have bought the format rights, which means a Slovenian or Turkish Agnes is about to appear on television anytime soon.

Yet, the boy from Finglas, who'd once had to rely upon his uncles Vincent and Paul to eat, hasn't turned his back on the world he grew up in. There aren't many Irish charities he doesn't support, such as providing 1,500 poverty-stricken families with Christmas turkey dinners, via the St Vincent de Paul organisation.

And he's been working with autism agencies, giving over money to buy iPads for kids, which is reckoned to improve their cognitive awareness.

'For some reason, autistic kids like the show. Experts don't know why, perhaps it's the swearing, who knows? One woman wrote to me to express her gratitude that her son had said his first word when watching the show. I laughed when I read what it was. "Bastard".'

As for *Mrs Brown's Boys*, it has now entered the league of classic television, one of the shows that will be talked about for decades to come. Why does it work? Agnes Brown, of course. Every family has one: the busybody, the scathing commentator, the women with bile on her breath who can still hug her kids like they are babies.

There's a wonderful innocence, a naivety, which harks back to Maureen O'Carroll not realising the fridge wasn't in fact a shiny cupboard. Mrs Brown is also an enigma. She's a much-loved housewife, except that she's a man.

Brendan has long argued Agnes is his mammy, or she's part Dolly Dowdall, or she's Gerry Browne's mammy, or she's the women from Moore Street. But she's aggressive. Sometimes wicked. There must be something of Brendan O'Carroll in there too? He laughs mischievously as he answers.

'There is a bit of her in me, all right. I have five sisters and lost my dad very young, so life for me has always been from a female perspective.'

What's clear is the major influence for Agnes Brown is Maureen O'Carroll. And Agnes is Maureen is Brendan. Maureen O'Carroll lives on in the form of her youngest son, the special one. He has her mindset, her intelligence and quick-wittedness, and, just as importantly, her voice. Not only in a physical sense, with his rasping pitch, but in his ability to cremate an offender at three paces. Brendan, like Maureen, can make a passing remark that can practically hospitalise – and get laughs in the process. What's evident is that his early life spent adoring and absorbing – and often battling – with this force of nature has helped form his own personality. And the result of this amazing alchemy, which the world can wallow in, is the wonderfully irascible Agnes Brown.

Mrs Brown's Boys is one of the biggest sitcoms of the twenty-first century, yet its comic roots are in variety theatre and Sixties sitcoms. And while modern media demands slick and sophisticated, Mrs Brown is rude, crude and lewd. Why do you laugh when you shouldn't?

And while many modern hit comedies emerge from big writing teams, Mrs Brown is the invention of one very clever man. Is it magic? Perhaps it's just feckin' funny.

Brendan himself isn't sure why it all works.

'The funny thing about it is that basically I'm doing what I've been doing for many years, but I think it's just a question of timing.

'We're in a recession and people are scared, people are a bit down. So they need a laugh first of all and, traditionally, no matter who you are, comedy always does well in a recession. But in dark times people also get nostalgic. They want to look back at the times when summers were longer, the Christmases were brighter and family life was better. And we remind them of that.

'But all this is guesswork. I can only think what my mammy used to say about disco music. You don't analyse it, you just dance to it. And it is what it is. There are people who will love it, and people who won't. But I think the people who love it are the audience that comedy forgot.'

Brendan argues that alternative comedy in the 1980s killed off mainstream humour for a time.

'I think somebody at the BBC read in a magazine that comedy is the new rock'n'roll. And they actually believed that, and started pitching it only to the 18- to 25-year-old market. And left the rest behind. But we're redressing the balance. We're going for the audience that loves to laugh out loud.'

And they do. And the success is down to Brendan O'Carroll's drive, his self-belief, his ability to almost walk out of a meeting for his sitcom pilot and bluff his way to a 12-episode deal.

Brendan is still a gambler, he still has the cheek of the devil and, as Agnes Brown would most likely say, testicles the size of turnips.

'Way back, when I'd only been doing stand-up for a year or so, I got a call from a guy who wanted me to do a date. I'd already booked a caravan holiday, so I said, "Sorry, I can't." He said, "OK, I'll give you £500." I said, "No, I'm actually not working that weekend." He rang me back later: "OK, then it's £750. And that's me last offer." I said, "Look, I'm not working," and he said, "You've some cheek . . . Right then, £1,500 – and that's it!" I said, "What date did you want me to do?"

'I learnt a lesson then. The scarcer you are, the more valuable you are.'

What Brendan also has is innate belief in his own ability.

'Funny lines just come naturally to me. Of course, it's a bit like playing snooker, you can pot the black a thousand times in practice, but you still have to go out and do it on the night. But no matter what other problems I've had in my life, making people laugh has never been one of them.'

Where does Brendan go from here? He filmed a pilot show for the BBC, *Mrs Brown's Celebrity Quiz Show*, but decided not to progress the idea for now, for fear of overexposing the Agnes Brown brand.

However, he will continue to tour for the foreseeable future, making vast fortunes in the process (a week in Dublin alone at Christmas 2013 will produce ticket sales of £1.6 million) and making sure every one of his troupe has the mortgage paid off and is set for life.

He's now talking again about going into politics some day soon. He'll certainly be able to afford to.

But has success changed him? He's been well known in Ireland since the early Nineties, but now he's a global celebrity.

'I believe in being nice to people. I believe in trying to make someone's day, as I did when I was a waiter at the Gresham in Dublin. I also believe in karma, what goes around comes around. And not just in heaven. You get the payback on earth. For example, I was in a restaurant in LA during the *Agnes Browne* film development process, and we were having a meal in a restaurant when suddenly the diners stopped eating, everyone got up and left. O. J. Simpson had walked in.'

But it's hard to keep your feet on the ground when you're in constant demand, from promoters, film and TV executives. And from a writer trying to pull together his biography. The *Tuesdays With Morrie* sessions in Glasgow have been on hold for a little while.

'We will get back to them soon, I promise you. I loved our chats. But it's different now. To not be able to get from the check-in to the aeroplane without stopping for forty photographs is really weird.

'I don't even think my mother, if she were alive, would want a photograph of me.'

Twenty years ago, however, Brendan was asked what he'd do if he ever became famous.

'I'd get someone to take a photo of me standing next to my 747 jet while sipping a cocktail, and I'd send it to one of the teachers who said I'd never amount to anything.'

And now that he's an overnight success story at the age of 58?

'I know at some stage I'm not going to be here and I'd like to leave something to my children and to my grandchildren. Hopefully the royalties coming in off the books, the TV series, the animation series and the rights we sell worldwide . . . well, no matter what happens to me, my grandchildren will be all right.'

His face breaks into a grin.

'And I'm old enough to know that me going out and getting a Maserati or a Ferrari is just not on. I'd look like a wart on a frog's arse.'

Brendan doesn't need the flash car. It's enough for him to know he's made millions of people laugh the world over. He's a one-man recession tonic. And his own smile has never been wider.

'I'm just enjoying it all, Brian. My life, so far, has been magical.'

He's written his own Spielberg ending. But Agnes Brown would play it all down. She'd probably sum up Brendan's phenomenal success with her catchphrase.

'That's nice.'

ACKNOWLEDGEMENTS

I'd like to thank Ian Pattison, Robert C. Kelly, Lorne Jackson, Davey Coburn and Mick McHugh for their ability to rub liniment on bruised knees and ego as I knocked over hurdles during the writing process.

Brenda Paterson was, as always, there to keep me going in the right direction.

And I'd also like to thank Fiona Robertson, without whom I'd never have left the starting blocks.

Picture Acknowledgements

Every effort has been made to contact all copyright holders. The publishers will be happy to make good in future editions any errors or omissions brought to their attention.

AKG Images/Hell's Kitchen Productions: 18; Alamy/AF Archive: 14; © BBC Photo Library: 24, 25, 26, 27, 28, 29, 30, 34; Brian Beacom: 4, 5, 35; Andy Buchanan: 20; Courtesy of Dublin City Library & Archive: 6; Getty Images: 23; © Irish Photo Archive: 3, 8, 9; The Irish Times/Joe St Leger: 13; Kobal Collection/Universal: 17; PA Photos: 21, 31, 33; Rex Features: 22, 32; © RTÉ Stills Library: 7, 11, 12, 15. All other photographs from the collections of the O'Carroll Family and Gerry Browne.

An invitation from the publisher

Join us at www.hodder.co.uk, or follow us
on Twitter @hodderbooks to be a part of
our community of people who love the very
best in books and reading.

Whether you want to discover more about a book
or an author, watch trailers and interviews, have the
chance to win early limited editions, or simply browse
our expert readers' selection of the very best books,
we think you'll find what you're looking for.

And if you don't, that's the place to tell us what's missing.

We love what we do, and we'd love you to be a part of it.

www.hodder.co.uk

@hodderbooks

HodderBooks

HodderBooks